Security, Identity and Interests

A Sociology of International Relations

Bill McSweeney addresses the central problem of international relations – security – and constructs a novel framework for its analysis.
He argues for the unity of the interpersonal, societal and international levels of human behaviour and outlines a concept of security
which more adequately reflects the complexity and ambiguity of the
topic. This book introduces a new way of theorizing the international
order, within which the idea of security takes on a broader range of
meaning, inviting a more critical and interpretative approach to
understanding the concept and formulating security policy. The
recent shift to sociology in international relations theory has not as
yet realized its critical potential for the study of security. Drawing on
contemporary trends in social theory, Dr McSweeney argues that
human agency and moral choice are inherent features of the construction of the social and thus international order, and hence of our
conception of security and security policy.

BILL McSWEENEY lectured in sociology at the U   and currently heads the International Peace Studi
the Irish School of Ecumenics.

Security, Identity and Interests

Series list continues at the end of the book

Security, Identity and Interests

A Sociology of International Relations

Bill McSweeney

CAMBRIDGE
UNIVERSITY PRESS

PUBLISHED BY THE PRESS SYNDICATE OF THE UNIVERSITY OF CAMBRIDGE
The Pitt Building, Trumpington Street, Cambridge, United Kingdom

CAMBRIDGE UNIVERSITY PRESS
The Edinburgh Building, Cambridge CB2 2RU, UK
http://www.cup.cam.ac.uk
40 West 20th Street, New York, NY 10011–4211, USA   http://www.cup.org
10 Stamford Road, Oakleigh, Melbourne 3166, Australia

First published 1999

Printed in the United Kingdom at the University Press, Cambridge

Typeset in 11/12.5 Palatino   [CE]

A catalogue record for this book is available from the British Library

Library of Congress cataloguing in publication data
McSweeney, Bill, Dr.
Security, identity and interests : a sociology of international relations
/ Bill McSweeney.
     p.   cm.
Includes bibliographical references and index.
ISBN 0 521 66177 3 (hardback). – ISBN 0 521 66630 9 (paperback)
1. International relations – Sociological aspects.
II. Series.   II Title: Security, identity, and interests.
JZ1251.M37   1999
327.1'01 – dc21   99–11332   CIP

ISBN 0 521 66177 3 hardback
ISBN 0 521 66630 9 paperback

For Mary, Catherine, Anna, Ella, and Sammy

Contents

Acknowledgements

An earlier version of chapter 4 was published in the *Review of International Studies*, volume 22, number 1, 1996, and some of the material pertaining to Northern Ireland appeared in *Security Dialogue*, volume 29, number 3, 1998. Permission of the editors to republish is acknowledged.

Several friends and colleagues have generously read and criticized parts, or all, of the book. I am grateful to the anonymous referees of the publisher, to Ken Booth, David Coombes, Mark Haugaard, Patrick Keatinge, John D'Arcy May, Mary McSweeney, Jim Skelly, Dan Smith, Gillian Wylie. I am happy to acknowledge, also, the support of the Irish School of Ecumenics, whose executive Board and director, Geraldine Smyth, were generous in their forbearance and active encouragement.

Introduction

Security is a slippery term. It is employed in a bewildering range of contexts and to multiple purposes by individuals, corporations, governments and academic specialists. It is enlisted to refer to things and people, to means and ends, to external events and innermost feelings.

Its recruitment by professional theorists and policy-makers to their particular interest in modelling and practicing international relations has given it a narrow, tangible objectivity which has slipped easily into popular understanding. But this technical usage should not stop us raising questions about how a term which evokes so much of the complexity and richness of routine, human, relations can be fixed in a definition which excludes reference to the normal, the commonplace, the everyday. In the past decade, moreover, the need for a radical rethinking of security has materialized in the emergence of particular events which have not been amenable to satisfactory explanation in traditional terms.

This book can be viewed as a general response to such events and to the fundamental problem of security which they signal. More specifically, it arises out of a sense of puzzlement in regard to particular international security issues and the explanations available in the academic literature. The puzzle sprang from events which followed the ending of the Cold War, which were clearly matters of security, but the facts of which could not be accounted for satisfactorily within the conventional framework. The attempt to do so pushed the analysis progressively back to the need to rethink the concept of security.

Such rethinking had begun a decade before the collapse of communism and was stimulating a vigorous debate in policy-making and research centres by the end of the 1980s. The inadequacy of our way of thinking about security was apparent to some theorists and political leaders even when the Cold War itself was at its most intensive, and the division between East and West looked set to endure for many decades to come. This initial demand for a deepening and broadening of the concept – which will be discussed in chapters 3 and 4 – sprang as much from a perception of the dysfunctional impact of particular Cold War policies as from the critique of the confrontation itself. The effect on developing countries of low-intensity proxy wars between the superpowers and the heightened tension consequent on the decision to deploy Intermediate Nuclear Forces in Europe in the early 1980s both placed in question the adequacy of the definition of the goal which such policies purported to serve.

But it was the fall of the Berlin Wall, and the rapid disintegration of the Warsaw Treaty Organization and the Soviet Union which followed it, which provided the shock to the theoretical systems from which international security had been born as a concept and 'security studies' as its appropriate academic discipline. Foremost among the factors which stimulated the need for radical reappraisal of our idea of security and the policies which can best achieve it was the very novelty of peace. The fact of not having an enemy was, for Europeans at least, an odd and singular experience, sending some in search of an underlying threat which would resurrect the security problem which had knitted together the fabric of international relations for centuries, and without which it was difficult to imagine a viable international system. For more than security was at stake. The world of anarchy and state sovereignty which governed interstate relations required insecurity as its condition. If the tangible enemy had walked away, an intangible replacement had to be found if governments, diplomats and international theorists were to sustain a coherent image of the world of international politics. If there was no identifiable enemy in a world defined as a jungle, either the real world must be different to what it was hitherto thought to be or the threats which are believed to constitute its insecurity must be rediscovered, lurking in some elusive form in the volatile relations between states.

For theorists who balked at the wholesale re-examination of the international system, the latter was the prudent option and the answer lay in defining the condition of post-Cold War Europe as a 'security vacuum'. The absence of the enemy was as dangerous as its presence; the void in terms of military threat needed to be filled by a military response. This was the strategy adopted by the North Atlantic Treaty Organization in its decision to expand the NATO alliance eastwards to embrace three of the newly independent states, rather than risk the erosion of its credibility and support among its member-states.

Other theorists saw in the end of the Cold War the challenge and opportunity to reassess the concept of security in the context of a sweeping examination of traditional ways of seeing the world in which security and insecurity arise. Drawing insights from social theory and philosophy, a variety of schools of thought united in the critique of the scientific pretensions of mainstream international theorizing and of its central concept of security. The incapacity of this mainstream to account for the dramatic turn of events at the beginning of the 1990s led its critics to question the basic assumptions which had directed scholarly inquiry for a generation. A narrow, state-centred and military-focused definition of security served the needs of a discipline confident in its ability to map the international order objectively and to apply the methods of natural science to the relations between states. The critique of this positivistic approach to the social introduced an instability-of-the-object into the study of international affairs: how actors construct their relations and theorizing is chronically implicated in creating and recreating the world which theorists observe. Security and insecurity are a relational quality, not a material distribution of capabilities, threats and vulnerabilities independent of such relations.

The end of the Cold War encouraged particular developments in international politics which also directed critical attention to international security questions. The emergence of nationalism as a force in Eastern Europe raised the problem of the relevance of domestic factors in the relations between states and the relevance to security of the internal structure of states against the traditional emphasis on the international. One important feature of this newly visible domestic dimension coincided with broader intellectual trends to elevate the concept of identity and to shift the weight of analysis from the materialist focus of positivism to the cultural and the social. Collective identity in its nationalist and ethnic form emerged to prominence in the debate and rhetoric on the new European order, both as a potential threat to the state and as a value threatened by it. The new emphasis on identity in postmodernist cultural theory reinforced its significance for international scholars, who began to explore its analytical potential for understanding the nature of the international system and the capacity of states within it to learn to manage their security.

If the priority accorded to the state and the international over the domestic was rudely questioned by the events accompanying the end of the Cold War, the collapse of communism also stimulated movement in the opposite direction. The retreat into the domestic microprocesses of identity formation was matched by the related extending across national borders of the forces which govern personal and institutional relations. Globalization, the term which expresses this dual process of fragmentation and expansion of social relations, was not a creature of the Cold War or of its ending. But it was accelerated and dramatically exposed by the end of the superpower confrontation which, until then, had relatively isolated one half of the world from the economic, political and cultural spillover of the other.

The central position of the state in the literature of security studies, and the dominance of the idea that 'national security' represents an attainable and indispensable goal for the achievement of security, could not be sustained in the face of such global interdependence on the one hand and the fragmentation of the state into competing ethnic and other institutional allegiances on the other. From both developments – fragmentation into new political entities and the expansion of global links of interdependence – the orthodox concentration on state security could not be upheld. From the beginning of the 1980s, ideas about 'common' security and the regional interdependence of security had challenged the myth of the unitary nation-state and its need and capacity to secure itself. The end of the Cold War exposed the fragility of the state in the face of complex forces within it and of trans-state limitations on its practical sovereignty outside it. In terms of military, economic, environmental and cultural factors impinging directly or indirectly on society and state institutions alike, the threats to security after the Cold War are not conceptually very different from those which endangered state and people before it, though our knowledge of them undoubtedly raises our sense of vulnerability. It is in the inadequacy of the range of responses to such threats that the poverty of our traditional conception of security is mostly revealed.

The traditional emphasis on military response to counter threats to the state – whether military or non-military – still counts its ardent supporters within the ranks of academic and military strategists. At the end of a century of many hundreds of wars which failed to demonstrate their utility in terms of the goals of the main participants

4

and the human cost of pursuing them, militarist rhetoric has lost credibility. As a principle based on an assumption about human nature and international anarchy, it failed spectacularly to accommodate the ending of the Cold War. The grain of wisdom in its guiding adage – *si vis pacem, para bellum* – serves to deflect attention from the question of identity, which is central to our conception of security and to any attempt to match security policy to the threats to which it is a response. If the identity of states is eternally fixed in egoism, the preparation for war must indeed be the indispensable basis of security policy. If the structure which determines the relations between states is objectively and inescapably anarchic, then insecurity is an environmental constant and the condition of peace must be the eternal vigilance of military autarky. But then how did the Cold War end?

Several current problems of security policy raise similar doubts about the traditional framework and analysis of security, in each of which the question of identity emerges as a fact prominent in discourse and as a tool of understanding. What conception of security underlies the continued integration of the European Union? The Northern Ireland peace process was made possible by transforming the security policy of the principal actor which had manifestly failed to achieve its objectives. The narrow, militaristic definition of security is hardly an adequate basis for understanding the dynamics of this process. By contrast with these two, a third phenomenon presents itself as a direct consequence of the demise of communism and the ending of the Cold War. How do we assess the security implications of NATO expansion? Some comments about each will help to explain why they are viewed as anomalies ill-adapted to the explanatory framework of orthodox security studies.

In 1990, the European Community initiated the process of political union against the background of German unification, the end of the Soviet threat, and the historical opportunity and need which these events created to develop a more fully integrated foreign and security policy for the EC.[1] In the optimistic climate of the time, with the internal market on the verge of completion and the Cold War on the verge of extinction, the process of integration was moved dramatically

---

[1] The expression 'European Community', or EC, or 'Community' will be used throughout to denote the organization of European states up to the adoption of 'European Union' by the Maastricht Treaty in 1992, unless greater precision is required by the context.

towards the 'high politics' of common defence and integrated political structures. The vision of a Europe bound by constitutional and political ties in a community structured to withstand the inevitable disintegrative pressures of economic association alone, seemed to be within grasp. Within two years, however, the people of Denmark led a popular movement of resistance to the fulfilment of that dream – at least in the form in which it was offered by member-states and the Community in the Maastricht Treaty on European Union.

European integration has always been a response to a security problem. There is little dispute about this. The disagreement touches on the nature of the security problem which stimulated integration in the 1950s and the interpretation of the security policy which was the founding members' response to it.

On one side of the argument, the policy embodied in the Community is an integral part of a complex alliance of Western European states under the hegemony of the United States to balance against the perceived threat of the Soviet Union. There is nothing in such a policy to indicate a major departure from the traditional practices of states from the end of the nineteenth century to shore up their territorial vulnerability by banding together in a military alliance. As long as the threat of one superpower persists, it is in the material and immediate self-interest of the threatened states to ally themselves with the enemies of that power. When the threat recedes, the alliance weakens, to be replaced by other configurations of military power. The simple logic of alliance theory corresponds with commonsense observation of everyday behaviour in the schoolyard.

The sudden jolt which Maastricht delivered to the complacency of state leaderships and Community bureaucracy seemed to validate this jungle theory of alliance formation and cooperation between states. If the close cooperation which developed from the European Coal and Steel Community and intensified over the period of the Cold War was a function of the common threat from Eastern Europe, the removal of that threat in 1991 should see the unravelling of the Community. In this view, the establishment of the European Community was 'an epiphenomenon of the Cold War', as one theorist expresses it; it was driven primarily by 'political reasons that had more to do with security than standards of living'.[2]

It seems equally plausible, however, that the Cold War inhibited,

---

[2] Review by Anthony Hartley, *The World Today*, January 1994, pp. 19–20.

rather than caused, European integration. Undoubtedly the emergence of a common enemy and the allocation of the defence role to NATO played some part in the cohesion of the Community, but its most visible effect over the period of the Cold War was to *prevent* the integration of a military dimension with the economic and political. It does not explain the degree of legal, political and economic integration achieved over that period to point to the fear of a common enemy as its primary cause. The upgrading of common interest in the progressive development of interstate and trans-state integration, with the inescapable pooling of state sovereignty which this entailed, represents a security policy which cannot be reduced to the military balancing of alliance theory.

The concept of security itself, furthermore, is problematic in its usage in relation to integration. What the school of thought represented in the citation above shares is a conception of security reduced to its narrowest military dimension. In this light, it is obviously correct to judge that the 'security' function was undertaken by NATO, while the Community embarked on the non-security dimensions of cooperation. Indeed it was only with the Single European Act in 1987 that we find explicit reference to 'security' in the legal instruments binding the member-states in a Community, and then only in respect of what was termed its 'economic and political aspects'.

Yet it is clear that whatever the personal motives of the individuals who founded it, the EU was a security policy from its inception. Even with the calculated exclusion of military defence, the process of integration itself bound the member-states in a network of interdependence which made the recourse to military means of resolving disputes progressively more difficult. It is not necessary to impute idealistic motives to the individuals who founded the Community to see that the product of their endeavours had the consequence of creating a 'security community' – whether they intended it or not. The addition of the military sector under the rubric of 'political union' was inhibited by the Cold War, but never abandoned as an aspiration. At the end of the Cold War, when the newly liberated states of Eastern Europe looked for international instruments to institutionalize their new freedom, membership of the European Union presented itself as the obvious means to that end. Even without an army, the EU was seen by candidate countries in Eastern Europe as a community capable of embodying the reality of security against the range of threats to their new independence. Survey research in six Eastern

European countries over the period 1990–1996 showed that public support for joining NATO was consistently lower than represented by their governments, and substantially lower than support for EU membership.[3]

The traditional understanding of security and security policy represents European integration as a non-security policy in response to a specific security problem. The evidence points as plausibly to the need to conceptualize European integration as a security policy in response to a non-specific and non-military security problem. While NATO membership offers maximum military security with minimal cost to formal sovereignty, the EU offers a broader spectrum of security, no military guarantee and makes substantial demands on formal sovereignty. Which offers the better chance of securing Europe depends on how we understand security and security policy.

A second puzzle concerns the shift in the policy adopted by Britain in respect of security in Northern Ireland. Here the ending of the Cold War also provides a signal for reassessing the evidence, though its impact is not so clear for our understanding of the change of policy.[4] British security policy in Northern Ireland was directed towards the military defeat of the enemy, the IRA, and the defence of the union of Northern Ireland with mainland Britain. How did it happen that a ceasefire on the part of the IRA in August 1994 was welcomed with enthusiasm by its nationalist supporters and viewed with despondency and suspicion on the part of the unionist community which had been the target of so much IRA violence? Why should the IRA, in an act of apparent surrender, now abandon the instrument of violence by which, for three decades and more, they have single-mindedly pursued their goal of British withdrawal? Almost four years after the ceasefire, the Belfast Agreement of May 1998 was the culmination of protracted negotiations on fundamental changes in the constitutional status of Northern Ireland.

The facts are susceptible of a range of interpretations: British security policy, traditionally focused on the goal of military victory, has finally succeeded in weakening the IRA – materially in its capacity for violence, politically in terms of its legitimacy with the nationalist

---

[3] Georgeta V. Pourchot, 'NATO enlargement and democracy in Eastern Europe', *European Security,* 6/4, 1997, pp. 157–174.

[4] On the impact of the end of the Cold War on conflict in Northern Ireland see Michael Cox, 'Bringing in the "international": the IRA ceasefire and the end of the Cold War', *International Affairs,* 73/4, 1996, pp. 671–693.

population, and organizationally in respect of its internal coherence. In effect, this explanation points to an IRA surrender. It is the final vindication of the verge-of-collapse theory, rehearsed at regular intervals since 1969 by British security spokespersons, only to be repeatedly rebutted by an IRA very much alive and active. An alternative version of this theory points to the United States rather than Britain as the source of the collapse. Without continued US support, directly and through political pressure on Britain, the IRA could not sustain its military activity. Given the evidence of increasing American concern to find a solution to the conflict in Northern Ireland since the mid 1980s, it is inferred that US pressure was exercised in favour of a solution coinciding with the demands of the British government for a military victory.

Both accounts are weakened by lack of supporting evidence and by their failure to make sense of the known facts – most obviously, the dissonant reactions of republican and unionist supporters to the alleged capitulation of the IRA. I shall argue that a more persuasive case can be made to support the view that the ceasefire was announced in the context of the continuing strength and capacity of the IRA, of increasing US pressure on the British government for a radical shift of security policy away from the goal of military victory, and of a weakening of British resolve arising from a new awareness of British interests in the province. Of central importance in this new policy were the changing identities of the main actors and the role of the sovereign governments in London and Dublin in managing them.

If European integration presents itself as a security policy in response to unspecified threats, a third puzzle in the security geography of the post-Cold War period provides a contrast, a foil for the first. In response to intangible threats from Eastern Europe, NATO expansion is proposed as a very tangible and traditional security policy. It, too, presents a challenge to the traditional analysis of international security.

After the defeat of Germany in World War II, the Western European states dismantled the alliance which had accomplished the victory and began the process of integrating the defeated state into a peacetime community and a separate military alliance. How should we understand the expansion of that military alliance after the collapse of the enemy to which it owes its origin and from which exclusively it drew its solidarity and acquired its prestige and military efficiency? Here again the ending of the Cold War provides the sharp focus for evaluating the divergent views on security and security policy. With the American announcement, on behalf of NATO, that its enlargement to selected new democracies of the former Warsaw Treaty Organization was scheduled for the fiftieth anniversary of NATO's founding in 1949, significant contours in the map of European security for the future have been made visible. After some years of speculation, lobbying, and bargaining between likely new entrants, the security question raised by the demise of communism has been answered by the only remaining superpower.

Precisely what the significance of the new development is may still be a matter of contention, but there is little dispute about the victory of NATO in the battle for survival between the security agencies competing for the hegemonic role in post-Cold War Europe. The United Nations (UN), the Organization for Security and Cooperation in Europe (OSCE), and the Western European Union (WEU) as an integral part of the EU remain marginalized. They will have a role in the future management of military security, but the executive function goes to the agency with the military experience and firepower. The security question posed by the collapse of bipolarity was defined as a 'security vacuum', a demand on the West to 'export stability' to Central and East European states, and the answer which emerged from the years of debate, of lobbying, of bargaining with likely winners and losers, was NATO. At least in its capacity to survive what seemed to be a terminal condition, the Atlantic Alliance has demonstrated the proud boast to have been 'the most successful defensive alliance in history'.[5] For the medium term, at least, it is game, set and match to NATO.

NATO expansion challenges the views of theorists of alliance behaviour and presents a problem of interpretation for analysts of every persuasion. If NATO expansion is the solution, what is the problem? What do military alliances do when the threat which gave rise to them, and persisted throughout their existence, disappears? What is the question to which a military alliance without an identifiable enemy is the answer? In particular, NATO expansion is accompanied by the widespread acknowledgment that Russia poses a security problem of some dimensions for Europe, and its relationship with the United States is critical to clarifying it. Additionally, it is held

---

[5] North Atlantic Council, 'London Declaration on a transformed Alliance', July 1990, para. 2.

that the enlargement of the Alliance redresses the fateful division of Europe at Yalta. If Russia is no longer an enemy, and the overriding security problem in Europe is US–Russian relations, how do we interpret the decision announced at Madrid in July 1997 and judge its likely consequences for the people whose security depends on it?

These are some of the concrete issues which raise the general conceptual and explanatory problem brought into sharper relief by the ending of the Cold War, and they will be drawn upon again to illustrate various aspects of the argument which follows. Many others might equally be addressed in terms of the efficacy of traditional military conceptions of security and the need to reassess the complex dynamic involved in threat-perception and the appropriate security response. Both the Middle East and former Yugoslavia are subjects of a security policy which is styled a 'peace process', while the Basque problem in Northern Spain has yet to acquire one. All three raise problems of analysis which draw into relief the adequacy of conventional ideas about security and its appropriate instruments.

In the chapters which follow, a case will be presented to show that the world in which we live is not one – and never was one – which presents itself to us for independent response to its objective stability or uncertainty, like a volcanic region which will punish its inhabitants who do not understand its structure and respect its sovereignty. Our response is a condition of the social world we inhabit; our security policy is a choice we make among options – limited by history, by the 'accomplishments of our ancestors', in Nietzsche's phrase, but always entailing human agency and choice.

Following analysis of the usage and etymology of the term 'security' in the next chapter, part I of the study addresses what is loosely called objectivist approaches to international security, characterized broadly by their common subscription to the application of scientific methodology to the social order. These approaches are surveyed in chapter 2, and their advocates criticized for their objectivist and narrow focus on perceived threats and military vulnerabilities in respect of the state. By their own criteria of assessment, the methods and assumptions they employ are judged inadequate to address the inherent ambiguities of the central concern of their work.

Attempts to broaden the concept of security are examined in chapters 3 and 4, with particular attention to the seminal work of Barry Buzan. Chapter 3 offers an extended critique of his work, widely deemed to have transformed the study of international security. It is argued that Buzan, while providing a more useful analytical framework, fails to account for the fundamental idea which links the security of the state to the human perception of insecurity on which state policies rest for their legitimacy. His extension of the concept of security to include what is termed 'societal identity' is discussed in chapter 4. While this work is seen to compromise the basic framework of the earlier Buzan, the linking of 'security' with 'identity' points to more promising possibilities.

Part II of the study is an attempt to develop an analytical and theoretical framework for realizing these possibilities. Following an extended conceptual analysis in chapter 5, an alternative sociological approach to international security is presented in the next three chapters of part II. Security is seen as inextricably related to identity, and security policy to the reconstruction of collective identity. In the process of reproducing collective identity lies the key to the production and reproduction of security and security policy. It is argued, however, that a current trend in the literature on identity is deficient in its capacity to explain the facts on the ground in particular concrete instances. Even when understood as a socially constructed reality, it is argued, the rise and transformation of collective identity – and the security questions entailed – cannot be explained without equal emphasis on the role of material interests. Finally, in the last two chapters, the discussion of the practice of security draws together the concrete issues which provide an empirical grounding of the book with the conceptual and philosophical analysis of part II.

We choose our security problems as we choose the interests and identity which accompany them. This terse compression of the overall argument will be qualified, of course. It serves here to highlight the general thrust of the discussion and to measure the distance to be travelled between the idea of security criticized in part I and the alternative approach of part III.

1   The meaning of security

Security, it was noted, is an elusive term. Like peace, honour, justice, it denotes a quality of relationship which resists definition. It has an active verbal form which seems to take it out of the realm of the abstruse, and a hard tangibility in its nominal form which promises something solid and measurable. But it eludes the attempt to capture it, to enclose it. It is a ubiquitous term, pressed into servicing young and old, rich and poor, the experience of the mundane and analysis of the affairs of state. Where to begin to look for its meaning, and whether it makes sense to expect a unitary meaning basic to all usages, are a challenge which calls for the joint labours of history and philosophy.

There are two images which come to mind when we think of the word. The noun 'security' evokes the picture of a solid object, like a lock, alarm, or weapon used to protect or defend against intrusion or attack. Or it denotes an investment in property, shares, pension – in some cultures, children. When such instruments or investments are in place, we imagine, 'security' as inner experience is the consequence. When the house is guarded, the street is policed, the shares are purchased, then we feel safe, defended against the indeterminate actions of others.

On the other hand, this activity may have a quite different consequence: our display of 'security' also displays vulnerability and makes us feel unsafe. Furthermore, it serves to condition attitudes in those undefined 'others' who may perceive our defence as a threat, as an incitement, even though some may read it also as a deterrent. In other words, it may limit the actions of others, but it leaves their assumed attitudes and intentions unreconstructed. Our efforts have yielded insecurity. One solution to this is to escalate.

A security industry helps individuals and families, as well as shops and corporations, to escalate. In Hollywood, armed professionals form part of a hierarchic set of security instruments, each independently subject to the logic of escalation, with the Los Angeles Police Department supervising the security guards who invigilate the systems which protect the valuables of the wealthy – each instrument a response to a classical dilemma: *Quis custodiat ipsos custodes?*

This predicament arises from the same mistrust which underlies the so-called 'security dilemma' in the literature of international affairs. The states' perception of the intentions of its regional rivals causes it to escalate 'security' in one instrument, or in a chain of instruments, and this results in a sequential interaction of misperception, with the consequence of greater insecurity which no one intended.

This evokes a vision of security as a negative freedom – the absence of threat – and it conjures an image of tough realism familiar in the world of international politics. Even a soft realist like Arnold Wolfers saw it thus: 'security after all is nothing but the absence of the evil of insecurity, a negative value so to speak'.[1]

There is another image from which to begin an inquiry into the idea of security, and it is one which, it will be argued, equally makes sense of the concept and as plausibly merits inclusion in any attempt to define it as the restrictive definition current in international affairs.

This is a positive image, evoked typically in the adjectival, rather than the nominative, form of the term. When we speak of 'security' in the nominative, we associate the word with objects, commodities, which have a specific function in relation to other commodities. There is a certain security, or confidence, in the fact that they are objects, tangible, visible, capable of being weighed, measured or counted. They protect things and prevent something happening. When we speak of 'secure', on the other hand, it suggests enabling, making something possible. (The familiar distinction between 'freedom from' and 'freedom to' illustrates the difference, and it is closely related.)

This positive connotation of the adjectival form contrasts with the negative freedom from material threats. The mythical image is that of Mother and Child – hardly an icon to grace the walls of the Rand Corporation or the Pentagon. The condition of security which it represents is commonly thought of as that which the mother provides

---

[1] Arnold Wolfers, *Discord and Collaboration: Essays on International Politics*, Johns Hopkins Press, Baltimore, 1962, p. 153.

for the child, but it is really a property of the relationship, a quality making each secure in the other.

It is this human sense of security, embodied in the primal relationship, which, it will be argued, carries a profound message for our understanding of international security and security policy.

The temptation to dismiss such imagery as sentimental, feminine, utopian, and therefore incapable of transfer to the international arena for rigorous analysis, is powerful in the world of policy and scholarship which specializes in these matters. No doubt one reason for this is the exclusion of women from the policy-making and theory-building community which sets the conceptual terms on which security is pursued and the topic is studied.[2]

Another reason why security, as a commodity rather than a relationship, seems more attractive is the considerable advantage it offers to the student schooled in the conviction that the social order can be expressed in the form of scientific generalizations. Trained to see the sciences as superior to the humanities, the student raised in the security studies tradition and faced with a choice between two commanding images of the subject matter will naturally opt for the more tangible, operational, the one which makes more sense in scientific terms. In these terms, rigour is equated with measurement of objective facts. The world of sentiment is a subject of reasoning and philosophy, poetry and sociology, but the 'real world' of material threats and vulnerabilities is one where knowledge can be translated into numbers, accumulated into a progressive science, and sold on the promise that it 'works'.

Perhaps the most common objection to human security as the foundation of policy and research is the difficulty of translating it to the collective level of the state. It makes sense to speak of states as actors, but it is hardly meaningful to attribute moral sentiment to them as well. We cannot aggregate the human feelings of being secure or insecure and arrive at a sensible measure for the state, from which to construct a security policy. This is a theoretical problem which will be addressed later in part II. What can be noted here is the way the problem is posed in the orthodox tradition of security studies. The centrality of the state-as-actor is assumed, and with it the need to measure, or quantify, the conditions in which its security or insecurity is achieved. The meaning of security is thus determined by a prior theoretical assumption of the primacy of the state, the irrelevance of

---

[2] See chapter 5 for further discussion of this point.

sub-units within it, and the choice of a quantitative method of inquiry appropriate to the state as the irreducible and material unit.

Of course the bifurcation of security into the material world 'out there' and the inner world of human relationship, reflected in the nominative and adjectival forms of the word, exaggerates the gap between the two images. They are not mutually exclusive: the subject who wants to be secure also needs to be defended; the Rambo warrior may have something to say to the Mother and Child. The point is that one view of security dominates the academic discipline and is presented, not as an option, a choice, but as the only one which is valid and relevant.

I want to show that there is a choice; that the alternative image is indispensable to making sense of the concept; and that it demands more subtle analysis, not less, to incorporate it into an adequate definition; that the assumption of security studies which ignores the human dimension is contradicted by the practical dependence of policy-makers and theorists alike on the human individual as the ultimate referent, or subject, of security. Thus the individual is ignored in conceptualizing the idea of security at the state level, only to be reinstated as its basic rationale – as it must be – in order to make sense of, and legitimize, the policy derived.

Contrary to the orthodox view of security studies, security must make sense at the basic level of the individual human being for it to make sense at the international level. The nominative form, and its commanding image of security as a commodity, needs to be complemented by the adjectival usage as a relationship. We shall return to these rival images later in this chapter.

Usage and meaning

Etymologically, the noun 'security' has evolved from a positive, comforting term to a negative one. From being a psychological condition of the care-free into which we are easily lulled – 'mortals chiefest enemy' as the witches describe it in Macbeth – it is a material condition which we worry about, tighten, fear. 'Secure' once meant 'careless' (se + cura), or 'freedom from concern' – almost the reverse of current usage implying 'careful'. Thus, warning of domestic discontent and its threat to the state, Bacon wrote 'Neither let any Prince, or State, be secure concerning Discontentments.' Although this 'careless' sense of the term dropped out of usage at the end of the eighteenth century, the 'Saturday Review' could still capture it in the middle of the nineteenth: 'Every government knew exactly when there was reason for alarm, and when there was excuse for security.'[3]

This old sense of the word derives from the same root, and overlaps in meaning, with the English 'sure', French 'sûr'. Larousse Modern Dictionary notes the French usage: 'Do not confuse sécurité, the feeling of having nothing to fear, and sûreté, the state of having nothing to fear.' The connotation of 'careless' is thus related to the sense of 'certitude' carried by the term 'sure'. The Oxford English Dictionary expresses it as 'having or affording ground for confidence; safe; (objectively) certain'.[4] Etymologically, therefore, the freedom of security is related to the possession of knowledge, confidence in the predictability of things, in knowing the objective order. Nietzsche reflects this usage when he asks rhetorically if our need for knowledge is not:

> precisely this need for the familiar, the will to uncover everything strange, unusual, and questionable, something that no longer disturbs us? Is it not the *instinct of fear* that bids us to know? And is the jubilation of those who obtain knowledge not the jubilation over the restoration of a sense of security?[5]

The verb 'to secure' was first predicated of people. It became attached to states, metonymically, allowing England to be described in 1889 as 'rich because she has for so many years been secure'. A secure object, such as a fixing, bridge, or possession, is probably a late development in the usage of the term.[6] Eighteenth-century examples of usage illustrate the emergence of a new sense of establishing a person in a position of comfort, an office, or privilege, rather than protecting from perceived threats. This may indicate the impact of capitalist social and economic change.[7]

It appears that the meaning of the noun 'security' has narrowed over the centuries, by contrast with the adjective and verb. Though we

---

[3] *Saturday Review*, 17 July 1858, cited in OED.

[4] *Oxford English Dictionary*, vol. ix, p. 370.

[5] F. Nietzsche, *The Gay Science*, p. 355, cited in James Der Derian, 'The value of security: Hobbes, Marx, Nietzsche, and Baudrillard', in David Campbell and Michael Dillon (eds.), *The Political Subject of Violence*, Manchester University Press, Manchester, 1993, p. 102. This link between security and knowledge will be further discussed in chapter 9.

[6] *The Spectator*, 21 December 1889, cited in OED.

[7] Paul Chilton, 'Security and semantic change', unpublished ms, n.d.

commonly speak of a secure person, we do not routinely use the nominal form, without specifying one's 'sense', or 'feeling' of security.[8] The noun became attached to, and interchangeable with, property, land, money, fortifications – these things are said to have, or to be, 'security' – and to the means by which such things are made secure: armies, weapons. To speak of military weapons as 'security' can be unpacked etymologically as 'the means by which the thing (property, money, institution) is protected to secure the person'.

Montesquieu understood 'security' in relation to political freedom: 'political freedom consists in security, or at least in the opinion which one has of one's security'.[9] Adam Smith, likewise, referred to the 'liberty and security of individuals', the freedom from the prospect of violent attack on the person or the person's property;[10] the sovereign, as individual, shared in this liberty; but what the state must do in order to ensure such freedom for the individual is not 'security', but defence: 'the first duty of the sovereign, that of protecting the society from the violence and invasion of other independent societies'.[11]

Emma Rothschild locates the meaning of 'security' as a concept relating to individuals and groups, as well as states, in the period from the mid-seventeenth century to the French Revolution. 'Its most consistent sense – and the sense that is most suggestive for modern international politics', she writes, 'was indeed a condition, or an objective, that constituted a *relationship* between individuals and states or societies.'[12] This followed the earlier usage of Leibnitz, defining the state as 'a great society of which the object is common security'.[13]

'Security', thus, is a human value overlapping with the values of freedom, order, solidarity. In this semantic complex, the state is understood as an agent of, or instrument for, the protection of values proper to human nature, and deriving their meaning and priority from the human individuals in whom they resided. The state was an instrument for the achievement of these values – and the sovereign as an individual shared in them – but the state was not their subject, the

---

[8] *Ibid.*

[9] *De l'Esprit des Lois*, cited in Emma Rothschild, 'What is security?', *Daedalus*, 124/3, 1995, p. 61.

[10] Adam Smith, *The Theory of Moral Sentiments*, and *An Inquiry into the Nature and Causes of the Wealth of Nations*, cited in Rothschild, 'What is security?', pp. 61/62.

[11] *Ibid.*, p. 62.

[12] Rothschild, 'What is security?', p. 61.

[13] Onno Klopp (ed.), *Die Werke von Leibnitz*, Klindworth, Hannover, 1864–1873, cited in Rothschild, 'What is security?', p. 61.

grounding of their meaning and the site of their relevance, or the calculus by which they were to be understood and measured.

The common modern sense of 'security' as an attribute of the state, ensured by military and diplomatic means, came into political usage at the end of the eighteenth century, aided by reasoning about the nature of the social contract, which likened the state to the individual. The theory of the social contract was understood by Rousseau, as it was also by Locke and Montesquieu, as the product of individual desire for security and liberty: 'this is the fundamental problem to which the institution of the state provides the solution'. Rothschild concludes:

> It was in the military period of the French Revolution, above all, that the security of individuals was subsumed, as a political epigram, in the security of the nation.[14]

From 'defence' to 'security'

Most countries have a Department of 'Defence', yet describe the function of this state institution as 'security', not 'defence'. The change from 'War Department' to 'Defence' was a function of the changed conditions of peacetime, making the existing label obviously anomalous. No such obvious change of conditions accompanied the shift of terminology from 'defence' to 'security'. What is conveyed by this choice of label can be inferred from its origins in the United States, where it first occurred.

The shift to 'security' was linked to the concept of 'national interest' and to the perception of its content in relation to the new idea and doctrine of 'national security'. We get some idea of the political background which stimulated the change, in the concerns expressed before and during World War II. A growing preoccupation with the organization of defence/security arose out of the need to unify the administration of the armed services and a concomitant concern to link the functions of the State Department and the 'defence' sector.

Daniel Yergin cites a seminar prior to American entry into the war, in which the concept of national security was invoked to understand the relationship between military and foreign policy matters. Two years earlier, Walter Lippmann had warned that the American desire for peace and the security of her geographic location had 'diverted

---

[14] Rothschild, 'What is security?', p. 64; citation from Rousseau, *Oeuvres Completes*, Gallimard, Paris, 1964, vol. III.

our attention from the idea of national security'. But the term 'national security' was not common in political discourse until the mid 1940s.[15] The concern with the unification of the armed services, during and after the war, added force to the need expressed for closer relationships between all the institutions seen as relevant to the novel and complex interests and vulnerabilities which presented themselves to the victorious power after 1945. 'National security' was an idea, a doctrine, and an institution, designed to bridge the traditional division between the interests of the state abroad and those of the state at home, and to merge the culture of everyday life with that of the defence of the national interest.[16]

The National Security Act of 1947 established the National Security Council and the Central Intelligence Agency to implement this design, and to promote the doctrine of total security. The law made the military a partner in the economy, and set the task for the National Security Council 'to advise the President with respect to the integration of domestic, foreign and military policies relating to the national security . . .'.[17] The idea of harnessing domestic culture to the service of foreign policy in the name of security was taken up enthusiastically and imitated by most Latin American countries, with less foreign than domestic threats in mind – Brazil in 1964, Argentina in 1966, soon followed by Uruguay, Bolivia, Chile and others, each with their integrated intelligence function on the pattern of the American CIA.[18]

One can speculate that the change from 'defence' to 'security' was required to escape the material and territorial limits set by the semantic legacy of 'defence', with its narrow military meaning clearly inadequate to the comprehensive scope now required. 'Our national security can only be assured on a very broad and comprehensive front', Navy Secretary James Forrestal told the Senate Committee on

---

[15] Walter Lippmann, *US Foreign policy: Shield of the Republic*, Pocket Books, New York, 1943, cited in Daniel Yergin, *Shattered Peace: The Origins of the Cold War and the National Security State*, Pelican, London, 1977, p. 194.

[16] The state need to saturate everyday life with the resonance of state security is ironic, given the resistance of orthodox security specialists to view the routine of mundane social relations as analytically relevant to the study of security and security policy. The theoretical significance of everyday life is a central part of the discussion in part II.

[17] Cited in Marcus G. Raskin, *The Politics of National Security*, Transaction, New Brunswick, 1979, p. 32.

[18] José Comblin, *The Church and the National Security State*, Orbis, Marknoll, 1979, pp. 64ff.

Military Affairs, and he explained: 'I am using the word "security" here consistently and continuously rather than defence.'[19]

A once-isolationist power now identified new global interests, at variance with its historic identity as a nation set apart from others, and new alien identities abroad which would facilitate a transformation of its own identity, in line with its new interests. As American James Der Derian puts it:

> Did not our collective identity . . . become transfigured into a new god, that was born and fearful of a nuclear, internationalist, interventionist power? The evidence is in the reconceptualization; as distance, oceans, and borders become less of a protective barrier to alien identities, and a new international economy required penetration into other worlds, *national interest* became too weak a semantic guide. We found a stronger one in *national security*, as embodied and institutionalized by the National Security Act of 1947 . . . [20]

'Security' in the Cold War had come a long way from its carefree origins and from its primary usage in reference to the person. Now it belonged primarily to the state; people, like the armed forces, were its instruments, and also, potentially, its enemies. The metonymy of language had moved the referent from the person to the thing, and to the instrument; the politics of national interest, in the conditions of the time, attached it literally to the state.

The content of 'national interest' had changed, from one of welfare in the early years of the New Deal, to one 'practically synonymous with the formula of national security' a decade later.[21] The state had become an organism, appropriating to itself the capacity for *cura* and its derivatives.

Yet the paradox remains, that the doctrine of the primacy of state in matters of security is parasitic on the belief of individual persons in their own primacy in the same respect. A nation can only be mobilized for national security in peacetime if the majority of the people identify the state and its enemies as the highest expression of their own personal security and fear. But what drives the security project, and defines its content and appropriate instruments, is the internal logic of the state. In the name of the people, and of a philosophical conception of human nature rooted in a human ideal of liberty, solidarity and

---

[19] Cited in Yergin, *Shattered Peace*, p. 194.
[20] Der Derian, 'The value of security', p. 109.
[21] Wolfers, *Discord and Collaboration*, p. 148.

order, security was appropriated by the state and operationalized by its theorists and specialist agencies.[22]

If the real world appears to confirm the policy-maker's beliefs in the primacy of the state and the essential insecurity of the environment in which it lives, this does not make it an objective world independent of policy and its implementation. The paradox of national security is reproduced through the practices of state and people, who define the term, objectify the reality, and implement the policies which it prescribes. The world of the Cold War really did look like the hostile arena to which a foreign policy, premised on the fundamental fear of physical survival, seemed the only rational option. That the security of individuals should be – in Rothschild's words above – 'subsumed in the security of the nation', under such conditions, was a heavy price to pay, but there was no alternative, it appeared.

The reproduction of the paradox of 'national security' is procured through state practices, which draw in the members of a society to an imagined community, whose fragile bonds were created by ancestors and must be recreated eternally by their debtors. Nietzsche expresses it in his sociological interpretation of religion:

> The conviction reigns that it is only through the sacrifices and accomplishments of their ancestors that the tribe *exists* – and that one has to *pay them back* with sacrifices and accomplishments: one thus recognizes a *debt* that constantly grows greater, since these forebears never cease, in their continued existence as powerful spirits, to accord the tribe new advantages and new strength.[23]

We learn to know the meaning of security through the practices which embody a particular interpretation of it. The state ritual of remembering the sacrifices of the dead remembers also the danger of others and the centrality of the state in confronting it, and, in the process, *re*-members the individuals in the community. 'We live in an age of instability and uncertainty' is the message intoned throughout the ages. Adam might have made the same observation to Eve on their exit from Paradise, but in that mythical moment, unlike now, it was a message devoid of an institutional agenda.

---

[22] The role of competition among the armed services and of their think-tanks in accomplishing this transition is well described in Fred Kaplan, *The Wizards of Armageddon*, Simon and Schuster, New York, 1983; see also Yergin, *Shattered Peace*, pp. 193ff.

[23] Friedrich Nietzsche, *On the Genealogy of Morals*, Vintage Books, New York, 1969, pp. 88/89.

Part I

Objectivist approaches to international security

2 Early stages of development

Measured in terms of growth since 1945, the study of security is probably the most prestigious sub-field of international relations. As many have noted, its growth and status were enhanced by the injection of money into the expansion of academic posts and publishing opportunities to sustain them. The main pressure behind this lever of opportunity was undoubtedly the relevance to US foreign policy of the realist approach to the subject during what Stephen Walt calls its 'golden age', until the mid 1960s, and its 'renaissance' from the mid 1970s.[1]

But to describe the most productive era of strategic studies, focused narrowly on military power and nuclear deterrence, as the golden age of security studies in the manner of Walt is to equate the study of security in the international arena with a particular agenda for its achievement. Its focus, philosophy, theory and method were set by the demands of the American policy-making establishment and the interlocking needs of academics. Until the mid 1980s, an apparently closed community of scholars found enough support in Cold War fears and policy incentives, and in the near-monopoly of realism in the wider arena of international relations, to ignore the fundamental problems raised by other disciplines in relation to security. Even more than other siblings of the international relations field, security studies was, until recently, a peculiarly American enterprise, fuelled by policy needs of the Western superpower after World War II.[2] It had become a

---

[1] Stephen M. Walt, 'The renaissance of security studies', *International Studies Quarterly*, 35, 1991, pp. 211–239. The variety of trusts and journals attracting scholars to the field are noted in Walt and in Barry Buzan, *People, States and Fear: An Agenda for International Security Studies*, 2nd edition, Harvester Wheatsheaf, London, 1991, p. 12.

[2] Ken Booth, *Strategy and Ethnocentrism*, Croom Helm, London, 1978; Steve Smith, 'The

discipline in its own right, closed to the conceptual and analytical developments in other areas of the social sciences.[3]

In the immediate post-war period, prior to the Soviet Union's acquisition of nuclear weapons, there was little to show by way of a body of literature dealing systematically with questions of military strategy in the nuclear age.[4] The subject had first made its entry into the general curricula of international relations in the years following World War I, but it was not until the mid 1950s that it emerged as an academic topic in its own right, under the heading of 'strategic studies'. Within a decade, its narrow focus broadened to include non-military considerations, and the label 'security' was increasingly being employed as an alternative to 'defence' or 'strategy'.

The term 'security studies', denoting a wider branch of teaching and scholarship than the military tradition of strategic studies, is of relatively recent coinage. American usage tends to conflate the two terms, by contrast with the European.[5] A distinction between strategic studies and security studies has evolved in the practice of scholars moving from the concern with military forces and weapons to the wider consideration of economy and politics. Buzan defines the focus of strategic studies as 'the effects of the instruments of force on international relations'.[6] This is not remote from the common, standard – if questionable – definition of 'security studies' as 'the study of the threat, use, and control of military force'.[7]

It appears that a progressive broadening of the issues impinging on

self-images of a discipline: a genealogy of international relations theory' in Ken Booth and Steve Smith (eds.), *International Relations Theory Today*, Polity Press, Cambridge, 1995; Stanley Hoffman, 'An American social science: international relations', *Daedalus*, 106/3, 1977, pp. 41–60; E. Krippendorf, 'The dominance of American approaches in international relations', *Millenium*, 16/2, 1987, pp. 207–214.

[3] Edward A. Kolodziej, 'What is security and security studies', *Arms Control*, 13, 1992, pp. 1–32; Edward A. Kolodziej, 'Renaissance in security studies? Caveat lector!' *International Studies Quarterly*, 36, 1992, pp. 421–438.

[4] Lawrence Freedman, *The Evolution of Nuclear Strategy*, Macmillan, London, 1981, p. 27.

[5] Ken Booth and Eric Herring, *Keyguide to Information Sources in Strategic Studies*, Mansell, London, 1994, pp. 131/132. The growth of interest in the broadening of the concept of security since the mid 1980s roughly dates the origin of the label 'security studies' to cover the wider political, economic and cultural concerns, within which the term 'strategic studies' has its traditional military orientation.

[6] Barry Buzan, *An Introduction to Strategic Studies: Military Technology and Internal Relations*, Macmillan, London, 1987, p. 13. Booth and Herring add an epistemological caveat to their similar definition: 'understanding and explaining the military dimension of international relations' – in their *Keyguide to Information*, p. 21.

[7] Walt, 'The renaissance', p. 212.

the narrower tradition of strategy in the context of deterrence, together with the opportunistic interest in widening the scope of the discipline, have contributed to the cross labelling. Joseph Nye would have both disciplinary interests converge under the heading of 'international security studies', in order to serve what he sees as the need to broaden the agenda of 'strategic studies'.[8] Buzan's view – that the latter should remain a distinct, specialized sub-concern of the former[9] – probably reflects the compartmentalized practice of scholars for the first decades of the Cold War. It is probably less confusing to borrow the label, if not its content, from Walt and others and to adopt 'security studies' to cover developments in both fields.

Most overviews of the study of international security treat the subject chronologically, from its origin at the end of World War II, and chart its progress through a mix of periodic fluctuation and 'approach'.[10] These are valuable as records of the discipline's history, but their multiplication brings marginal returns and runs the risk of being self-referential. A more useful approach in the context of this

---

[8] Joseph S. Nye, 'The contribution of strategic studies: future challenges', *Adelphi Papers*, 235, International Institute of Strategic Studies, London, 1989, p. 25.

[9] Buzan, *People, States and Fear* (1991), pp. 23ff.

[10] Among overviews of the study of security, the following are prominent and relevant to the discussion of this chapter: Arnold Wolfers, 'National security as an ambiguous symbol', *Political Science Quarterly*, 67/4, 1952, republished in *Discord and Collaboration: Essays on International Politics*, Johns Hopkins Press, Baltimore, 1962, pp. 147–165; Richard Ullman, 'Redefining security', *International Security*, 8/1, 1983; Robert Jervis *et al.*, *The Field of National Security Studies: Report to the National Research Council*, National Research Council, Washington, 1986; Joseph S. Nye Jr and S. Lynn-Jones, 'International security studies', *International Security*, 12/4, 1988; Jessica Tuchman Mathews, 'Redefining security', *Foreign Affairs*, 68/2, 1989; Lawrence Freedman, *The Evolution of Nuclear Strategy*, Macmillan, London, 1981; Walt, 'The renaissance', pp. 211–239; Helga Haftendorn, 'The security puzzle: theory-building and discipline-building in international security', *International Security Quarterly*, 35/1, 1991; Graham Allison and Gregory F. Treverton (eds.), *Rethinking America's Security: Beyond Cold War to the New World Order*, Norton, New York, 1992; Michael J. Hogan (ed.), *The End of the Cold War: Its Meaning and Implications*, Cambridge University Press, Cambridge, 1992; Michael Clarke (ed.), *New Perspectives on Security*, Brasseys, London, 1993; Richard Shultz, Roy Godson and Ted Greenwood (eds.), *Security Studies for the 1990s*, Brasseys, New York, 1993; Booth and Herring, *Keyguide to Information*; David A. Baldwin, 'Security Studies and the end of the Cold War', *World Politics*, 48, October 1995, pp. 117–141; Ken Booth (ed.), *New Thinking About Strategy and International Security*, Harper Collins, London, 1991; Sean M. Lynn-Jones and Stephen E. Miller (eds.), *Global Dangers: Changing Dimensions of International Security*, MIT Press, London, 1995; Keith Krause and Michael C. Williams (eds.), *Critical Security Studies: Concepts and Cases*, UCL Press, London, 1997.

book is to identify the controlling assumptions within different periods of this history, and to argue the case that the adoption of these assumptions brought with it a package of philosophical and epistemological positions, the later challenging of which exposed the foundation on which the study of security had been built. This is one of the aims of the book as a whole. The preparatory work is set out in this chapter.

Principal ideas and periods of development

Two basic ideas run through the history of security studies and can be used to divide the community of scholarship which comprises it into four periods. We can better understand this history as a cyclical recurrence of ideas than as the linear and cumulative progression of knowledge on which most assessments of the field are based.

The first idea conceives of security as a condition of the international community of states, deriving from interstate cooperation and the essential interdependence of international relations. The term 'common security' is appropriate to distinguish the concept underlying this approach – though it should not be confused with specific policy proposals which bear this label. It will be argued that a later usage of 'common security', which challenged the orthodoxy of the academic discipline in the 1980s, marked a return to an idea more prevalent in the period before and immediately after World War II.

The second view of security is that which has had the most profound influence on the organization of scholarship, on the resources allocated to it, and on the policy impact which it has achieved and which has contributed to our perception of its validity. This is the view that security is a property of the state, deriving from the balance of power consequent upon state behaviour. The concept of 'national security' serves to focus on the autarky of the state which underlies this approach, as distinct from the first.

In contrast to what I have called the images or visions of security in chapter 1 – those of material security and human security – the controlling ideas here discussed can be understood as organizing principles of theory and practice. The idea of 'common security' is linked logically to the image of human security. However, it will be argued in chapter 3 that this link is inadequately theorized. The idea of national security, on the other hand, emerges from the material vision of the concept. It shares with some versions of 'common security' a preoccupation with the state as its primary focus.

Allowing for the messiness of the real world of those scholars who were ahead of their time, or who lingered untidily beyond their time, four periods in the history of security studies can be distinguished. The first may be called the 'political theory' period, from the beginnings of the academic organization of international relations after World War I until a decade after the end of World War II. In this period, it is a variant of the 'common security' idea which marks the contributions of scholars to the understanding of security.

The second period begins in the mid 1950s and can be termed the 'political science' phase. This is the golden age, in the sense that it was then that the subject matter became organized as a sub-discipline separate from the wider concerns of international relations, and began to attract the funds, the journals, the prestige, and the policy relevance, which elevated the authority and influence of security studies beyond any of its sub-disciplinary rivals.[11] The concept of 'national security' characterizes the basic idea of this approach, as it does the basic interest being developed at the same time at the political level, in response to perceived threats to American national interests from the Soviet Union.

It is easier to say when this political science phase begins than to judge the time of its decline. For, in truth, it is still probably the dominant perspective in regard to the quantity of literature, of academics working in the field, and of money allocated to research in the area of security. The early 1980s may be taken as a rough estimate of the start of sustained critique of this approach, accompanied by the attack on its theoretical and philosophical premises in the wider arena of international relations theory.[12] The least that can be said is that, from then until the present, the study of security is open to a plurality of rival approaches. This third period, then, which can be labelled 'political economy', to signal the development of theories of interdependence which preceded and accompanied it, is grounded in the common-security idea from which the political science era departed – though it is now formulated in respect of a number of interrelated

---

[11] Walt, 'The renaissance'; Nye and Lynn-Jones 'International security studies'.

[12] 1979 marks the publication of Waltz's theoretical basis of a science of security. From 1980 to 1986, the various Commission reports on Common Security, Buzan's *People, States and Fear* (1983) and the critiques of neorealism in Robert Keohane's edited volume *Neorealism and its Critics*, Columbia University Press, New York, 1986, were published. For discussion and details, see chapters 3 and 6.

theoretical propositions about the character and levels of economic and political integration, by contrast with its precursor.

The fourth period which divides the history of security studies has scarcely begun. The end of the Cold War heralded the arrival of a variety of anti-positivist theoretical positions which carry their own internal critique of the controlling ideas of the political science period and that which preceded and followed it.[13] It is the stage of the so-called 'third debate' in international relations theory,[14] during which the conceptual, normative and philosophical attack on positivism, or objectivism, is mounted across a wide enough spectrum to encompass not only the most obvious targets of behaviouralism and neorealism, but many of the assumptions underlying the political theory and political economy approaches also. In its international political theory which must inform our understanding of security, this stage borrows something of the common security approach of the first and third periods, but it is difficult to discern any dependence of substance on the national security approach of the second.[15]

As yet, a coherent and substantial body of literature, specifically addressing the problem of security, has not emerged from the diverse orientations which comprise anti-positivism – critical theory, feminist theory, postmodernism, constructivism and (the most clearly focused) critical security studies.[16] Despite their differences, and opposition on

[13] Some recent discussions of the contemporary positions within the anti-positivist camp may be found in Steve Smith, 'The self-images of a discipline'; Mark Neufeld, *The Restructuring of International Relations Theory*, Cambridge University Press, Cambridge, 1995; Claire Turenne Sjolander and Wayne S. Cox (eds.), *Beyond Positivism: Critical Reflections on International Relations*, Lynne Rienner, London, 1994; Fred Halliday, *Rethinking International Relations*, Macmillan, London, 1994; Alexander Wendt, 'Constructing international politics', *International Security*, 20/1, 1995, pp. 71–81.

[14] Yosef Lapid, 'The third debate: on the prospect of international theory in a post-positivist era', *International Security Quarterly*, 33/3, 1989, pp. 235–254.

[15] Exceptions should be noted in respect of some 'constructivist' writers who see their work as a radical modification, rather than rejection, of realism. For example, Wendt, 'Constructing international politics'; Jutta Weldes, 'Constructing national interests', *European Journal of International Relations*, 2/3, 1996, pp. 275–318; Martha Finnemore, *National Interests in International Society*, Cornell University Press, 1996; Thomas Risse-Kappen, 'Exploring the nature of the beast: IR theory and comparative analysis meets the EU', *Journal of Common Market Studies*, 34/1, 1996, pp. 53–80.

[16] Note, however, the contributions to this critical literature on security of David Campbell and Michael Dillon (eds.), *The Political Subject of Violence*, Manchester University Press, Manchester, 1993; David Campbell, *Writing Security: United States*

some central questions of epistemology, these approaches share a number of common assumptions and positions: they understand structural constraint in cognitive, rather than exclusively material, terms; they view the international order as the construction of actors, and the task of the analyst as that of deconstructing the forms and concepts which constitute it; they see the role of identity, and its malleability as a social form, as significant for international relations theory and substantive international relations. For these reasons, further discussed in chapter 6, it is appropriate to describe this fourth (and current) period of security studies as its 'sociology' era.

This book is intended primarily to offer a contribution to this inchoate body of security literature, still in the early stage of its sociology period. The rest of this chapter will address briefly the first two stages of security studies, leaving the third for more extensive discussion in chapters 3 and 4. The fourth period is the focus of part II of the book.

The period of political theory

The study of security was not ignored in the decade following World War II. On the contrary, the questions addressed by the concerns of the earlier generation of scholars were more widely pertinent to the security problem, but were addressed in too broad and ambiguous a manner to be accepted as the topic of scientific inquiry by their successors.

During the period from the establishment of international relations as an academic discipline in 1919 until the middle of the 1950s, security was understood more as a multi-disciplinary and multi-dimensional problem, requiring the application of international law, international organization and political theory to the promotion of democracy, international institutions and disarmament.[17] Wright,

Foreign Policy and the Politics of Identity, Manchester University Press, Manchester, 1992; Ronnie Lipschutz (ed.), *On Security*, Columbia University Press, New York, 1995; Ole Waever, 'What is security? The securityness of security', in Birthe Hansen (ed.), *European Security 2000*, Copenhagen Political Studies Press, Copenhagen, 1996; Cynthia Enloe, *Bananas Beaches and Bases: Making Feminist Sense of International Politics*, Pandora, London, 1989; Ken Booth, 'Security and self: reflections of a fallen realist', in Keith Krause and Michael C. Williams (eds.), *Critical Security Studies: Concepts and Cases*, UCC Press, London, 1997.

[17] William T. Fox, 'Interwar international relations research: The American experience', *World Politics*, 2, October 1949.

Herz, Brodie and Wolfers were some of the key scholars who explored the political, psychological and economic aspects of war and peace, and – particularly in Quincy Wright – their philosophical and moral ramifications.[18]

For Bernard Brodie, writing in 1949, security was seen as one value of the state among others, and not necessarily the primary one. It was 'a derivative value, being meaningful only in so far as it promotes and maintains other values'.[19]

John Herz in 1950 coined the term 'security dilemma' to refer to the 'self-help' condition of states in anarchy, which motivates a search for security which has the unintended consequence of insecurity.[20] The potential of this idea for developing a more nuanced philosophically sophisticated understanding of the structure and constraints of anarchy was not explored at the time.

This was the period before security studies became an academic specialism, separated from the wider concerns of international relations, and the label 'political theory' serves to distinguish its more comprehensive scope from the narrow application of scientific method which followed it. Baldwin notes:

> It is as if the field came to be so narrowly defined in later years that the questions addressed during these early years were no longer considered to belong to the field of security studies.
> Whereas earlier research questions considered what security is, how important it is relative to other goals, and the means by which it should be pursued, the new focus [after 1955] was on how to use a particular set of weapons.[21]

The 'golden age' of political science

The orthodoxy which dominated the field until the end of the Cold War, and which still influences the majority of its publications, can be characterized as the scientific approach to the threat, use and management of military force in the interests of state security, from which questions not amenable to quantitative analysis are expunged or

---

[18] Fox, 'Interwar international relations', pp. 237ff; Quincy Wright, *A Study of War*, 2nd edition, University of Chicago Press, Chicago, 1965.

[19] Bernard Brodie, 'Strategy as a science', *World Politics*, 1, July 1949, p. 477.

[20] John Herz, 'Idealist internationalism and the security dilemma', *World Politics*, 2, January 1950, pp. 157–180.

[21] Baldwin, 'Security studies' pp. 122, 123.

marginalized. For three decades until the mid 1980s, questions of international security and security policy were channelled in a singular conceptual and theoretical direction, within the boundaries of an objectivist political science[22] – though not without some exceptions and some movement at the centre, which influenced more recent critical approaches.

It was the arrival of civilian scholars in the field in place of the military and diplomatic professionals who had previously populated it, and their enthusiastic application of scientific method and modelling to the possible uses of nuclear weapons, which generated the think-tanks, research centres and university curricula which constituted the sub-discipline of security studies.[23]

It is implicit in most studies of national and international security, including those characteristic of the political science period, that the ultimate reference is to people.[24] It is not just a question of the *object* which needs to be secured in any particular context of conflict or threat – the state, military weapons, national identity, social groups or individuals – but of where we must site the ultimate ground and rationale for securing anything (the *subject*).[25] It would be absurd to postulate a subject of security other than people, even for the scientists of Walt's 'golden age'. It is from the human need to protect human values that the term 'security' derives its meaning, as we have seen, and that a security policy derives its legitimacy and power to mobilize resources. The primacy of the state in the political science tradition has permitted a gap to develop between the meaning of the term 'security' as applied to individuals and its meaning for the state. In effect, the means have become the end; the object has become the subject of security when the state is made its ultimate referent.[26] If the

[22] John Garnett in his edited *Theories of Peace and Security: A Reader in Contemporary Strategic Thought*, Macmillan, London, 1970, p. 20, distinguishes between 'hard' areas 'handled very rigorously' and the 'educated guesswork, hunches and the like' of 'soft' areas. See also Freedman, *The Evolution of Nuclear Strategy*, pp. 177ff; Clarke, *New Perspectives*, pp. 46/47.

[23] Fred Kaplan, *The Wizards of Armageddon*, Simon and Schuster, New York, 1983.

[24] E.H. Carr, *Nationalism and After*, Macmillan, London, 1945, p. 58, advocated the primacy of 'security for the individual' at the beginning of this period; Buzan is, on this point, representative of the continuity of this concession to the individual at the end of it: 'The individual represents the irreducible basic unit to which the concept of security can be applied.' Buzan, *People, States and Fear* (1991), p. 35.

[25] This distinction will be discussed in chapter 5.

[26] This is to take issue with the views of Buzan, who expresses the traditional view within the discipline: 'There is no necessary harmony between individual and

state is the primary actor within the political science perspective, what is the focus of concern about its security? The concept of the undifferentiated state, cleansed of human contact in the Waltzian model, which viewed all states as like units, transferred to the international order the material basis of regularity of behaviour which Waltz found in nature. If human beings were taken to be the acting units, the quantification of their behaviour for scientific analysis would be complicated by the obvious difference in their interests and preferences as the stimulus to action. By assuming that the material unit of the state is an actor of undifferentiated interests as well as identity, Waltz could eliminate the problem *a priori*. All states share the same 'national' interest in the pursuit of security, defined above all in terms of military power. 'To say that a country acts in its national interest means that, having examined its security requirements, it tries to meet them.'[27] This echoes the position of Morgenthau in the early 1950s, who defines national interest in terms of the power to protect the state's 'physical, political and cultural identity against encroachments by other nations'.[28]

For many decades, realist and neorealist writers have been characterized as uni-dimensional in their attention to military force as the central issue of security. Ignoring pre-1955 views to the contrary – in particular the view of Arnold Wolfers rejecting the essential link between security policy and coercive power[29] – Walt reflects this tradition somewhat exaggeratedly in his sweeping statement: 'military power is the central focus of the field . . .'; 'security studies may be defined as *the study of the threat, use, and control of military force*'.[30] In Walt's view of the discipline, the focus on the military dimension locates the security studies literature 'comfortably within the familiar

national security'. Buzan, *People, States and Fear* (1991), p. 50. See chapters 3 and 4 for further discussion.

[27] Kenneth Waltz, *Theory of International Politics*, Addison-Wesley, Reading MA, 1979, p. 134.

[28] Hans Morgenthau, 'Another "Great Debate": the national interest of the United States', *American Political Science Review*, 46/4, 1952, p. 972; *In Defense of the National Interest: A Critical Examination of American Foreign Policy*, Alfred Knopf, New York, 1951, *passim*.

[29] Wolfers, *Discord and Collaboration*, pp. 154ff.

[30] Walt, 'The renaissance', p. 212. (Surprisingly, he claims to derive this definition from Nye and Lynn-Jones who do not employ it and are at some pains to distance themselves from so narrow a focus. Nye and Lynn-Jones, 'International security studies'.)

realist paradigm'.[31] Similarly Richard Shultz, charting the future of security studies within the same perspective, sees the programme for the 1990s as primarily concerned with the 'threat, use and management of military force'.[32]

The idea that the political science tradition is univocally focused on military power is a familiar criticism, but it is only partly correct. It is common among mainstream scholars, themselves in the political science mould, to echo this charge, and this raises a question about what exactly is being contested and what is novel in their proposals for expanding the research agenda.[33] In most cases, the deficiency is to be remedied by the recognition that 'there are also other threats to the security of states' which constitute the 'economic, natural resource and ecological dimensions of security. . . [as well as the] challenges of terrorism and drug traffic'.[34]

It cannot be maintained, therefore, that realists ignore the non-military dimensions of the subject. The causes-of-war literature, furthermore, is replete with illustrations of 'other threats to the security of states' than those of military force. Contrary to the convention which has grown around the notion of a realist obsession with military force, there is indeed the recognition of non-military factors. However, this recognition of the broader dimension extends only to non-military *threats* to state security, not also to non-military *responses*, or instruments of security policy. This broader version of security is not a novel idea. Economic threats in particular, political threats and societal threats have been seen as giving rise to interstate and civil wars since the time of Thucydides. The military action consequent upon political change in Czechoslovakia in 1968, in Vietnam in the early 1960s, and upon the invasion of Kuwait in 1991 was a *military response* to a *non-military threat* from the point of view of the major powers who intervened.

To the primacy of the state and the military focus of its security policy, as defining elements of the political science period, must be added the context, or setting, in which security can be attained. Self-

---

[31] Walt, 'The renaissance', p. 212.

[32] Shultz, *et al.*, *Security Studies*, p. 2.

[33] See, for example, Haftendorn, 'The security puzzle', pp. 13/14; Nye, 'The contribution of strategic studies'; Ullman, 'Redefining security'; Mathews, 'Redefining security'; Nye and Lynn-Jones, 'International security studies', p. 6.

[34] Nye and Lynn-Jones, 'International security studies', p. 6; Haftendorn, 'The security puzzle', p. 16.

reliance and independence in matters of security were basic to the notion of 'national security' as it was understood in the immediate post-war period. What needed to be secured was one's own state against the threats and potential threats posed by the capabilities of others. In conditions of nuclear deterrence, such a sense of self-sufficiency was inevitably modified in practice by the reality of mutually assured destruction, imposing the recognition of a mutual interest in survival. Superficially, this can be read as an early version of later ideas about security interdependence, trading under the label of 'international security', or 'common security'. But this does not capture the novelty of a new framework of security studies. Neither the concept of a 'security regime' nor the mutuality of nuclear deterrence, which was developed to a fine art in the work of Thomas Schelling, escape from the state-centred frame of reference which limits the scope of security in the national security tradition.[35]

Haftendorn sees the concept of 'international security' as 'based on a mutual interest in survival under conditions of nuclear deterrence and on recognition that an adversary will be deterred from attacking out of its own self-interest'. In contrast to national security, international 'implies that the security of one state is closely linked to that of other states, at least of one other state'.[36] This hints at a more radical reassessment of the traditional autarkic view, but as it is expressed it is quite consistent with that understanding of security interdependence which informed Schelling's work. This is the interdependence of strictly limited and strategic cooperation on the part of self-help states, as Mearsheimer more recently represents it in his trenchant defence of realism.[37] Where the immediate threat posed by other states declines, the 'mutual interests in survival' default to the national level, exposing the understanding of security attainable and desirable as autarkic. Security in its 'golden age' of political science is a condition of the state, to be achieved by the state, through the instrumentality of state military power.

---

[35] Robert Jervis, 'Security regimes' in Stephen Krasner (ed.), *International Regimes*, Cornell University Press, Ithaca, 1983, pp. 173–194; Thomas Schelling, *The Strategy of Conflict*, Harvard University Press, Cambridge MA, 1960.

[36] Haftendorn, 'The security puzzle', p. 9.

[37] John Mearsheimer, 'The false promise of international institutions', *International Security*, 19/3, 1995, pp. 5–49.

Self-images of the 'golden age'

The purpose served by the identification of the state as key actor, its priority as security referent, and military capabilities as the primary variable relevant to its security, is to provide the theorist with the basic materials essential to the application of scientific method to the study of international relations. That security so conceived was within the scope of the individual state – national security – followed from the particular scientific model developed by Waltz.

The self-image cultivated by the 'political science' of national security views the discipline as an objective and cumulative body of knowledge, ethically relevant but free of the distortion of values, and open to the influence of cognate perspectives on the study of war and peace. Of these, the most robust claim and the one which best characterizes the period under review is that of scientific objectivity.

Perhaps the most striking aspect of security studies, from a contemporary European perspective of pluralistic approaches to the study of international relations in general, is the dominance of a positivistic method applied to the subject matter. The idea that international relations scholars are engaged in a process of quasi-laboratory techniques, yielding cumulative knowledge which forms a corpus for the training of younger entrants into the field, who in turn add their scholarly efforts to the cumulus, dies hardest in the field of security studies. With its roots in strategic studies, it lends itself easily to the uncritical acceptance of quantitative methods, at the cost of philosophical and conceptual sophistication. Until the beginning of the 1990s, there was nothing comparable within the traditional approach in this field to the turmoil which today afflicts the wider arena of international relations – still more the discipline of sociology to which the pluralism of international relations owes much of its discomforts.

A sample quotation which captures the self-confidence of the genre may be offered:

> Security studies seeks *cumulative knowledge* about the role of military force. To obtain it the field must follow the standard canons of scientific research: careful and consistent use of terms, unbiased measurement of critical concepts, and public documentation of theoretical and empirical claims. Although no research enterprise ever lives up to these standards completely, they are the principles that make cumulative research possible. The increased sophistication

of the security studies field and its growing prominence within the scholarly community is due in large part to the endorsement of these principles by most members of the field.[38]

What is most obviously lacking, as has often been pointed out, is an adequate theoretical basis for the study of security: the pressure for policy relevance leads too easily to the 'production of analyses of pressing problems at the expense of basic research . . .';[39] theoretical work on the function of armaments, the causes of war and military competition has taken second place to the analysis of weapons developments;[40] while Richard Smoke states flatly that 'national security affairs is a field relatively lacking in broad general theories or even pretheories'.[41]

Acknowledgment of the inadequacy of a theoretical foundation, however, begs the question of what kind of theorizing, related to what kind of conceptual framework and epistemological principles, might furnish an adequate one. The idea that the international order constitutes an objective, material reality, accessible to the theorist through a 'correspondence' theory of truth, pervades the different schools of thought which define the orthodoxy of this period. From the behaviouralists of the 1950s, through the rational-choice and game-theory approaches of the 1970s, to neorealism, the common conviction is that the behaviour of the acting units is explicable in terms of laws or causal generalizations as determinate, in principle, as the laws of nature.

It is this basic conviction which accounts for the discovery of the state as actor and security referent, and the priority given to military force in respect of state interests – these are the material, quantifiable factors which permit the control of variables within the natural science model. (In a similar development within sociology, discussed in chapter 6, one can see the discovery of role and its elaboration in role theory as the condition for a science of the social. Both 'discoveries' were motivated by the need to rid the theorist of the messy complexity of human agency.)

---

[38] Walt, 'The renaissance', p. 222 (original emphasis).
[39] Jervis *et al.*, *The Field of National Security*, p. 21.
[40] Laurence Martin, 'The future of strategic studies', *Journal of Strategic Studies*, 3/3, p. 94.
[41] Richard Smoke, 'National Security Affairs', in Fred Greenstein and Nelson W. Polsby (eds.), *Handbook of Political Science, Vol VIII, International Politics*, Addison-Wesley, Reading MA, 1975.

Given the poor record of a science of international politics in regard to formulating the laws which govern collective behaviour, the plethora of competing perspectives giving rival accounts of the same world itself requires explanation. The 'inter-paradigm debate' offered a way of interpreting this rivalry in terms of a theoretical pluralism which respects the 'multiple realities of a complex world'.[42] However, for Holsti, some 'paradigms' are better than others; the criterion of evaluation is their 'correspondence with the observed facts of international politics'. Together with the primacy which he accords to the security problem, it is clear that a scientific realism is viewed as the model against which other paradigms are assessed.[43]

Many discussions of the state of security studies note the manifest need for an interdisciplinary or multi-disciplinary approach to security. In their state-of-the-field report in 1988, Nye and Lynn-Jones support the view that 'international security is not a discipline but a problem', and acknowledge that 'the economic, cultural, and psychological aspects of security were initially given scant attention'. 'The field is necessarily interdisciplinary', they claim:

> As long as the fate of the earth could depend on how states address security issues, it will remain imperative not to overlook the potential contributions offered by other disciplines, such as economics, sociology, history, physical sciences, anthropology, psychology, and law.[44]

Haftendorn argues a case for overcoming the ethnocentrism of the past and, in the process, permitting a breeze of fresh, interdisciplinary air into the area of security studies. It is not at all clear how ethnocentrism is logically related to interdisciplinarity. The ethnocentrism which has long been noted as a limiting characteristic of security studies and international relations theory in general, arises from a set of historical and political circumstances which are only casually, not causally, related to the pressures which impelled studies

---

[42] Kal J. Holsti, *The Dividing Discipline: Hegemony and Diversity in International Theory*, Allen and Unwin, London, 1985. Citation from his 'Mirror, mirror on the wall, which are the fairest theories of all?', *International Studies Quarterly*, 33/3, 1989, p. 256. See also Michael Banks, 'The inter-paradigm debate', in M. Light and A.J.R. Groom (eds.), *International Relations: A Handbook of Current Theory*, Pinter, London, 1985 and Neufeld, *Restructuring of International Relations Theory*, chapter 3.

[43] Holsti, *The Dividing Discipline*, pp. vii and 7.

[44] Nye and Lynn-Jones, 'International security studies', p. 6.

along a monodisciplinary rail. Expanding the opportunities of European and Third World scholars for publishing in the field of security studies might, or might not, add a fresh perspective on the subject. But it cannot be asserted that security studies would thereby 'develop into a truly international discipline . . . [which] would be studied from an interdisciplinary and intercultural perspective committed to the goal of global security'.[45]

Walt reads the security studies literature as fitting 'comfortably within the familiar realist paradigm'.[46] His apparent agreement with this constraint is, at first glance, tempered by the view that an 'interdisciplinary approach . . . had characterized the field since its inception'. It is plain, however, that his ideal of interdisciplinarity is restricted, like Haftendorn's, to the goal of many disciplines addressing many security problems primarily in the terms set by security studies. In the interim, while natural scientists and other outsiders undertook the 'serious and time-consuming preparation' for work in the security field, progress came from 'scholars within the field' (realists, one must assume) 'who drew upon other disciplines rather than from experts from other fields who suddenly turned their attention to security studies'.[47]

It seems clear, however, that the reviewers of security studies see no necessary role for an interdisciplinary approach to the problem. They apparently share the view of Nye and Lynn-Jones that many disciplines are better than one, but:

> because political conflicts between sovereign states are the key to many critical issues in international security, political science will continue to occupy the central place among the disciplines concerned with questions of war and peace.[48]

Are *political* conflicts at the root of questions of war and peace? Are 'sovereign states' the key actors? The case for the monopoly of political science is not strengthened by reference to the practices within the discipline under question. It is a fact that political science dominates the study of security, but it is not justified to infer from this some kind of essential bond between it and the object of study. There is a need for an *inter*disciplinary approach which can examine the assumptions underlying any particular academic tradition. This re-

---

[45] Haftendorn, 'The security puzzle', p. 15.
[46] Walt, 'The renaissance', p. 212.   [47] *Ibid.*, p. 230.
[48] Nye and Lynn-Jones, 'International security studies', p. 6.

quirement cannot be met by throwing open the subject to a free-for-all between practitioners of diverse disciplines, as is implied in the literature. The study of security is already multi-disciplinary; that is to say, it has long been a topic of concern to psychology, strategic studies, economics, sociology, history, law and the rest. Many different approaches to the same topic are as likely to deepen confusion as enlightenment, partly because of the inbuilt resistance of academic disciplines to ideas which take their relevance and meaning from quite different perspectives, literatures and communities of scholars, and which cannot be neatly extracted from one to the other like bits of intellectual lego.

The approach to a topic as elusive as security needs to be inter-disciplinary in the sense that insights and approaches from different disciplines are integrated into a unified and coherent framework, which permits questions to be raised outside the confines of any particular academic tradition. It is the concepts, theories, methods, of the various disciplines which must be brought together, not the practitioners.

As regards its self-image as ethically relevant, this is largely a retro-spective view from within a community of scholars belatedly facing the challenge of the normative from within a tradition which had earlier seen its scientific pretensions in opposition to ethical considera-tion. Carr's legacy to international relations theorists, and that of Morgenthau, was to separate the realms of morality and international affairs, of utopia and reality, as 'belonging to two different planes which can never meet'.[49] Even at the superficial level, the security studies tradition had paid little attention, until recently, to this central question of ethics on which the domestic legitimacy and moral

---

[49] E.H. Carr, *The Twenty Years Crisis 1919–1949: An Introduction to the Study of International Relations*, Macmillan, London, 1966, p. 93; Hans Morgenthau, *Politics Among the Nations: The Struggle for Power and Peace*, Knopf, New York, 1972. Recent reappraisals of their views on morality reveal a more balanced and complex picture, however, highlighting the selective manner in which the interests of their time heard what they had to say. See, for example. A.J.H. Murray, 'The moral politics of Hans Morgenthau', *Review of Politics*, January 1996, pp. 81–107; Ken Booth, 'Security in anarchy: utopian realism in theory and practice', *International Affairs*, 67/3, 1991, pp. 527–545; Paul Howe, 'The utopian realism of EH Carr', *Review of International Studies*, 20/3, 1994, pp. 277–298; Jaap W. Nobel, 'Morgenthau's struggle with power: the theory of power politics and the Cold War', *Review of International Studies*, 21, 1995, pp. 61–85.

justification of security policy turns.[50] Under the rubric of Just War Theory, of course, the question of the justification of war has an ancient provenance in early christian writings and in the revival of debate on this question in the Middle Ages. Prior to the emergence of security studies as a sub-discipline, Quincy Wright's *Study of War* (published in 1942) showed his concerns with the moral, legal, sociological and philosophical aspects of war, while Arnold Wolfers and others cited showed similar concern with questions of ethics and values. Most of the attention given to this area prior to the beginning of the 1980s, however, came from scholars with no claim to the security label – from theologians, ethicists, peace activists[51] – rather than from within the security studies community itself, thus creating an unhelpful separation between the analysis of security and its ethical standing.

Nye and Lynn-Jones note the recovery of interest in the topic but appear to regard the early neglect of ethics as a problem solved by more books and articles from whatever source, rather than a responsibility shelved by the core community. Moreover, the solution which they affirm is one which is entirely focused on the military and strategic consequences of scientific research, not on the research process itself nor on the multiple points in that process where value judgments are used unwittingly to buttress conceptual formation and theoretical argument. The normative significance of international relations theory is only superficially explored when it is restricted to value judgments implicit in the selection of the topic of inquiry or in the policy implications consequent upon its conclusions.

Haftendorn recognizes the place of values in the curriculum for teaching security studies, but similarly restricts their significance to the outcome in policy.

---

[50] For a critique of the ethical indifference of security studies, see Philip Green, *Deadly Logic: The Theory of Nuclear Deterrence*, Ohio State University Press, Columbus, 1966 and Anatol Rapoport, *Strategy and Conscience*, Harper and Row, New York, 1964.

[51] Michael Walzer, *Just and Unjust Wars*, London, 1977 as ethicist makes it into this company. See Paul Ramsey, *War and the Christian Conscience: How Shall Modern War be Conducted Justly?*, Duke University Press, North Carolina, 1961; National Conference of Catholic Bishops, *The Challenge of Peace: God's Promise and Our Response*, US Catholic Conference, Washington, 1983. Within the security studies community, notable exceptions include Joseph S. Nye, *Nuclear Ethics*, Free Press, New York, 1986; James E. Dougherty *et al.*, *Ethics, Deterrence and National Security*, Pergamon Press, Washington, 1985.

The dichotomy between a normative and an empirical science can be overcome if researchers keep in mind their moral responsibility for the political implications of their research and their commitment to the promotion of international peace.[52]

In saying nothing explicitly on the question of ethics within the discipline of security studies, Walt exemplifies its deficiencies. Given the prominence accorded to his survey, and the fact that it purports to examine the broad sweep of security studies from the vantage point of the 1990s, his assessment and its reception speak volubly for the persistence of these deficiencies into the present era. In his concluding discussion of norms he briefly summarizes his 'golden age' and his 'renaissance' as having had 'more real-world impact, for good or ill, than most areas of social science'.[53] The questions which arise when violence is enlisted in the service of politics and where scholarly independence is threatened by the politicization consequent on government funding are narrowed to a focus on 'the integrity of security studies' aided by the existence of 'several ideologically varied foundations'.[54] In his frequent claims for, and advocacy of, scientific rigour in the field, together with an apparent obliviousness to the demands of philosophical analysis in this most ethically relevant area of inquiry, Walt displays the stubborn prejudice among political scientists that normative questions intrude upon political analysis at the peril of rigorous scholarship.

There is a world of difference between emotive advocacy and distorting value judgments, on the one hand, and the explicit consideration of ethical analysis in scholarly inquiry. The attempt to expunge ethics from international relations theory leads more assuredly to distortion than the explicit reflection on its place in the research process. Far from endangering scholarship, the ethical dimension forms an essential part of scholarly focus in the social sciences, particularly in the field of security studies. As Kolodziej remarks in his critique of Walt, it is not the application of methodological rigour to security problems which is on trial. It is *more* rigour,

---

[52] Haftendorn, 'The security puzzle', pp. 15/16. She cites in support C. Daase and Bernard Moltmann, 'Frieden und das Problem der erweiterten Sicherheit: Für ein integriertes Verständnis von Friedenspolitik und Sicherheitspolitik', *Sicherheit und Frieden*, 7/3, 1988, pp. 176–180.
[53] Walt, 'The renaissance', p. 231.
[54] *Ibid.*, p. 230.

not less, which is called for by the integration of the moral aspect into the study of security.[55]

The deficiencies of the national security idea in the period of 'political science' encouraged the search for an alternative concept and approach to the understanding of international security. E. H. Carr – writing in a 'political theory' mode prior to being appropriated by realism – argued for a broader concept: a 'shift in emphasis from the rights and well-being of the national group to the rights and well-being of the individual man and woman', with 'security for the individual' elevated within a system of 'pooled security'.[56]

A comprehensive, or broad, concept in place of the military, state-focused one, poses the problem for theorists and policy-makers alike: how can the needs of 'the individual man and woman' be related to a system of state security? Who will protect the insecure individual, if not the collectivity? In the following two chapters, I shall examine the content and analytical implications of the 'broad' concept of security through the writings of the major schools and theorists who sought to develop it.

[55] Edward A. Kolodziej, 'Renaissance in security studies?', pp. 429–430. The worldview of the realist school of security was nicely summed up by an eminent practitioner, former British Foreign Secretary Douglas Hurd in a BBC radio interview 15 October 1997, and amply illustrated in his *The Search for Peace*, Little Brown, 1997. Criticizing the campaign for an 'ethical foreign policy' on the part of his Labour Party successor, Robin Cooke, he allowed that idealism can change the international order by a degree – one degree in 360, but no more, as he put it. The point is not to dispute the precision – 20 degrees or 120 would leave the same problem: Hurd's 359 degrees represent a world that is neither touched by, nor vulnerable to, the influence of morality. It is the world that is and will continue to be, he wants us to believe, however many hearts bleed and hands wring on the part of those who would choose it to be otherwise. As we shall see in chapter 8, however, there is no such world.

[56] Carr, *Nationalism and After*, pp. 71, 58, 36.

3 Broadening the concept of security

A discipline 'born and raised in America', to cite Stanley Hoffman[1], and nourished by American foundations and policy-makers, was poorly equipped to build the theoretical and philosophical base which its subject matter requires. National security was a political decision in search of a theoretical foundation.

However, there were some scholars offering different answers to the security problem during the Cold War period of realist dominance of the subject. They saw the 'national security' solution as the problem and sought to widen the concept and shift the burden of security from the individual state to the international level. Five approaches may be distinguished, all contributing towards broadening the concept of security, and all owing their family resemblance to the idea of interdependence and the break with realist autarky which this implies. For this reason, they can be grouped under the general perspective of 'political economy' – though they fit uncomfortably within any precise definition of this term.

I shall discuss briefly here the ideas of 'security community', 'security regime', 'neofunctionalist integration', and 'common security', before addressing at greater length a fifth approach – the idea of 'international security' as developed in the work of Buzan. In some part, each represents a new look at an old aspiration: that states can modify the negative condition of anarchy and can in some measure integrate their interests even at the level of security.

The idea of interdependence in the sense in which it has come to pervade the literature of international relations is a modern one,

---

[1] Stanley Hoffman, 'An American social science: international relations', *Daedalus*, Summer, 106/3, p. 59.

reflecting attempts by theorists in the 1970s to capture a contemporary post-war phenomenon. It owes little to the eternal facts of mutuality which deny the capacity of any actors – states or individuals – to function as isolated entities. Actors in the human and state systems are inescapably interdependent, and the consequences of this for the international system may be reflected at different times in theories of the balance of power, a concert of powers, bipolarity, or mutual nuclear deterrence. The connection between such ideas and the contemporary theory of complex interdependence is fragile, at best, and owes more to a banal observation about human nature than to any specific link in the history of ideas.

Nonetheless, it cannot be said that Keohane and Nye, whose explication of complex interdependence has become the commanding text, are without precursors.[2] Ramsay Muir in the early 1930s and Charles Merriam a decade later, Richard Cooper and Kenneth Waltz all contributed to the effort to conceptualize the modern phenomenon, while earlier perceptions of the relevance of economic inter-dependence to military force go back to the beginning of the twentieth century.[3]

Keohane and Nye adopted the term 'complex interdependence' to denote an ideal type of mutuality which contrasts with the conditions asserted within the realist perspective. Among these conditions, the threat of force and the primacy of military security within a hierarchy of issues controlling the agenda of foreign policy were emphasized, thus helping to forge a perception of reality conducive to military preparedness and antagonistic to interstate and transnational coopera-tion. Under complex interdependence, the realist hierarchy of political issues disappears and the distinction between the arena of foreign and

---

[2] Robert O. Keohane and Joseph S. Nye, *Power and Interdependence*, 2nd edition, Little Brown, Glenview, 1989.

[3] Ramsey Muir, *The Interdependent World and its Problems*, London, 1933; Charles E. Merriam, *Systematic Politics*, University of Chicago, Chicago, 1945 (cited in Jaap Nobel, 'Realism versus interdependence: the paradigm debate in international relations', *Bulletin of Peace Proposals*, 19/2, 1988, pp. 167–173); Richard N. Cooper, *The Economics of Interdependence: Economic Policy in the Atlantic Community*, McGraw-Hill, New York, 1968; Kenneth Waltz, 'The myth of national interdependence', in Charles Kindleberger (ed.), *The International Corporation*, MIT Press, Cambridge MA, 1970; Richard Rosecrance and Arthur Stein, 'Interdependence: myth or reality', *World Politics*, 1973; Normann Angell, *The Great Illusion: A Study of the Relation of Military Power in Nations to their Economic and Social Advantage*, Heinemann, London, 1910.

domestic policy is obscured, while the role of military force in the prosecution of such policy is diminished.[4]

The American provenance of most of the early literature on complex interdependence suggests that it was not just the objective world which had changed, so much as the interests of the United States in the 1970s which forced the search for new policies to address a less controllable environment than that faced by Morgenthau and his followers.[5] 'Much of what is being seen as interdependence is not new', as Russett and Starr wrote, 'but is just being recognized for the first time'.[6]

Interdependence is both an observation and a political strategy, a condition of the world and an opportunity to fashion it. The interdependence of states and the commonality of their interests, including security, is the root idea in a variety of attempts to escape the narrow focus and conceptual constraints of 'national security' within the perspective of 'political science'.

The concept of 'security community' has its origins in the work of Karl Deutsch in the early 1950s.[7] A security community – or, more precisely, a pluralistic security community – is one in which different states, enjoying similar conditions, and a stable expectation of peaceable relations between them, are structurally linked in a manner which reproduces these conditions. They include the compatibility of values, predictability of the interests and policy aims of élites, and democratic institutions. Based on recognition of interdependence as a structural condition, Deutsch's concept tended towards the relegating of war as the necessary and final means of resolving disputes between sovereign states.

Deutsch's 'security community' has been mainly reproduced as a footnote to the history of security studies, a felicitous coinage which proved more attractive to later scholars for its label than its substance. It has not received the critical attention in the literature enjoyed by the other concepts discussed here, and it was overtaken as a theory of

---

[4] Keohane and Nye, *Power and Interdependence*, pp. 23ff.
[5] Barry Buzan, 'Interdependence and Britain's external relations', in Laurence Freedman and Michael Clarke (eds.), *Britain in the World*, Cambridge University Press, Cambridge 1990, pp. 10–41.
[6] Bruce Russett and Harvey Starr, *World Politics: The Menu for Choice*, Freeman, San Francisco, 1981, p. 405.
[7] Karl Deutsch *et al.*, *Political Community and the North Atlantic Area*, Greenwood Press, Westport, 1955.

integration by the advent of neofunctionalism. The derivation of 'security community' from a single instance, and the dependence of that instance – the North Atlantic Community – on an 'external pacifier'[8] and a common external threat add to the volume of criticism which has marginalized it from a central place in the literature.

The 'democratic peace' thesis emerged in the 1970s, causally linking democracy with the emergence of a zone of peace and making some of the same connections between domestic political and cultural conditions and their impact on foreign policy as the Deutschian thesis.[9] The view that democracies do not war against each other is hardly a theory; it is at best a promising empirical observation awaiting a theory, and needing considerable conceptual refinement if one is to be formulated. Raymond Cohen has drawn attention to its inadequacies and to the factors which militate against its generalized application, in effect reducing it to a particular version of Deutsch's 'security community'.[10]

Despite their limitations, the concept of security community and the democratic peace thesis have an intuitive appeal in emphasizing a range of domestic and international conditions which inhibit war and which locate security and insecurity firmly in the relations between states, not in the independent capacities of each. The persistence of cooperation between states is also captured by the notion of 'international regime', which Stephen Krasner sees as constituted by the 'principles, norms, rules and decision-making procedures around which actors' expectations converge in a given area of international

---

[8] Joseph Joffe, 'Europe's American pacifier', *Survival*, 26/4, 1984.

[9] A sample of the developing argument can be found in Melvin Small and J. David Singer, 'The war proneness of democratic regimes', *The Jerusalem Journal of International Relations*, 1, 1976, pp. 50–69; Georg Sorensen, 'Kant and processes of democratization: consequences for neorealist thought', *Journal of Peace Research*, 29/4, 1992, pp. 397–414; Nils Petter Gleditsch, 'Democracy and peace', *Journal of Peace Research*, 29/4 1992, pp. 369–376; Bruce Russett, *Grasping the Democratic Peace: Principles for a Post-Cold War World*, Princeton University Press, Princeton, 1993; Christopher Layne, 'Kant or Cant: the myth of the democratic peace', *International Security*, 19/2, 1994, pp. 5–49; Raymond Cohen, 'Pacific unions: a reappraisal of the theory that "democracies do not go to war with each other"', *Review of International Studies*, 20/3, 1994, pp. 207–223; Walter Carlsnaes, 'Democracy and peace', *European Journal of International Relations*, Special issue, 1995, pp. 1–427; Harvey Starr, 'Democracy and integration: Why democracies don't fight each other', *Journal of Peace Research*, 34/2, 1997, pp. 153–162.

[10] Cohen, 'Pacific unions'.

relations'.[11] Robert Jervis applies this idea to the problem of security, understanding a security regime to be 'those principles, rules, and norms that permit nations to be restrained in their behaviour in the belief that others will reciprocate'.[12] He emphasizes the persistence of self-interest as the motivation of the member-states; the distinguishing factor which lends stability to cooperation in a security regime lies in the fact that the pursuit of self-interest is projected into the longer term and the constraints generated by the regime structure serve to promote a convergence of these several interests with the interests of the whole.

While the state is still the key actor in both the security community and security regime, the agency of change is more explicit and emphatic in the concept of regime, through the role of the hegemon in creating and sustaining the system of cooperation. The strictures of Susan Strange in 1982, and her view that regime analysis constituted a peculiarly American academic fad, 'obfuscating and confusing instead of clarifying and illuminating, and distorting by concealing bias instead of revealing and removing it' appear to have been confirmed by the quiet decline of such analysis from the late 1980s.[13] Applied specifically to the problem of security, it is not clear how much further this concept takes us in understanding the dynamics of security relations than the early twentieth-century idea of collective security, or indeed the 'concert' system following the Congress of Vienna in 1815.[14]

While all point in the direction away from autarky towards a relational, community foundation for international security, none of them affords a satisfactory basis for understanding the critical question of how this is to be achieved or how it is to be sustained without the problematic presence of the common enemy.[15]

---

[11] Stephen Krasner (ed.), *International Regimes*, Cornell University Press, Ithaca, 1983, p. 2.

[12] Robert Jervis, 'Security regimes', in Stephen Krasner, *International Regimes*, Cornell University Press, Ithaca, 1983, p. 173.

[13] Susan Strange, 'Cave! hic dragones: a critique of regime analysis', in Stephen Krasner (ed.), *International Regimes*, pp. 337–354; See also Robert O. Keohane, *After Hegemony: Cooperation and Discord in the World Political Economy*, Princeton University Press, Princeton 1984; Isabelle Grunberg, 'Exploring the "myth" of hegemonic stability', *International Organization*, 44/4, 1990, pp. 431–477.

[14] Charles A. Kupchan and Clifford Kupchan, 'Concerts collective security and the security of Europe', *International Security*, 16/1, 1991.

[15] Nonetheless, they offer some pointers to Buzan's later framework in their emphasis

Integration theory as expounded by neofunctionalism furnishes the third example of early attempts to capture the problem of security. The idea that cooperation in technical, economic areas must eventually spill over into the higher-political areas of foreign and defence policy is the cornerstone of neofunctionalism and the basis of its theory of security. The so-called 'logic of spillover' is explained by Schmitter as the process whereby members of an integration scheme, cooperating on some collective goals for a variety of motives, but dissatisfied with the results, attempt to resolve their dissatisfaction by resorting to collaboration in another sector.[16]

The idea that the need to initiate and sustain cooperation can be managed and controlled by non-state actors, and that states are forced by the spillover mechanism to acquiesce in the pooling of sovereignty and the practice of cooperation, is the novel and contentious part of the neofunctionalist model. Neither the states nor their publics have shown themselves to be willing puppets in the roles assigned to them by the theorists. As with Deutsch, so with the neofunctionalists, the empirical basis was too narrow to support the general propositions, and too little attention was paid to the impact of the external factors on integration, including the solidifying influence of the common threat of the Soviet Union. The impression of an autonomous, efficient machinery of integration during the Cold War misled theorists into believing that its reliability was independent of such circumstance.[17] For all its deficiency, however, not least its unwarranted determinism and scientific pretensions, neofunctionalism contains the germ of a more satisfactory account of security cooperation than the other attempts at formal theorizing which have been reviewed.[18]

The idea that security must reflect a popular meaning of the term,

on the domestic conditions for security and the common relation to the concept of interdependence – close to Buzan's idea of the 'strong state' and 'mature anarchy'.

[16] Philippe Schmitter, 'Three neofunctionalist hypotheses about international integration', *International Organization*, 23, 1969, p. 162. See chapters 7 and 9 for further discussion of neofunctionalism.

[17] Disillusion with the theory and its rapid abandonment first set in during the early years of détente at the beginning of the 1970s as a consequence of internal malfunctions rather than external influences. Paradoxically the end of the Cold War coincided with a revival of elements of neofunctionalism. For one of the earliest critiques of neofunctionalism's inadequate attention to external factors see Stanley Hoffman, 'Obstinate or obsolete? The fate of the nation state and the case of Western Europe', *Daedalus*, 95, 1966, pp. 862–915.

[18] Neofunctionalism contains some sociological insights into cooperative behaviour which will be further explored in chapters 7 and 9.

and embody the concerns of ordinary individuals for human well being and freedom from fear, underlies the fourth attempt to go beyond the narrow constraint of 'national security' within the 'political science' period. This set of aspirations to broaden the concept focused attention on the security implications of North–South relations and the environment, and on the objective of sustainable development. The so-called Brandt Report of 1980, the Palme Report 1982, and the Brundtland Report 1987 all call for a reconceptualization of security in the light of interdependence between states in the international system and between the rich North and the developing countries.[19]

These reports carried a political weight and a media impact which helped to focus popular opinion on the idea of interdependence and its implications for security in a way not given to the individual writings of academics. The Brandt Commissioners addressed the disparities of wealth between the northern and southern hemispheres and the impact of the prevailing economic system upon this inequality. The Palme Report dealt with the escalating nuclear arms race between East and West and the ramifications of this competition in the poorer South. Finally, Brundtland was convened to assess the environmental issue and the impact of inappropriate models of development on its sustainability.

Thus, poverty, armaments, and the environment were made the interlocking sectors for a new conception and policy of international security: 'poverty, unemployment, inflation, the threat of world recession: the problems that make people insecure are economic as well as military'.[20] The Palme Report, written during the most tense period of the Second Cold War, draws attention to the security dilemma and the 'blind alley' of military competition.[21] It proposes enlightened self-interest in the creation of 'international political stability, expanding export markets, the preservation of the biological environment, the

---

[19] Report of the Independent Commission on International Development Issues (Brandt Report), *North-South: A Programme for Survival*, Pan Books, London, 1980; Report of the Independent Commission on Disarmament and Security Issues (Palme Report), *Common Security: A Programme for Disarmament*, Pan Books, London, 1982; World Commission on Environment and Development (Brundtland Report), *Our Common Future*, Oxford University Press, Oxford, 1987. A review of the Brandt Report was published in The Brandt Commission, *Common Crisis: North–South Co-operation for World Recovery*, MIT Press, Cambridge MA, 1985.

[20] Palme Report, p. 71. See also Brandt Report, p. 33 and Brundtland Report, p. 7.

[21] Palme Report, p. 100; Brandt Report, p. 117; Brundtland Report, p. 7.

limitation of population growth'.[22] The vision of security in all three Reports is outlined in Brandt:

> an important task of constructive international policy will have to consist in providing a new, more comprehensive understanding of security, which would be less restricted to the purely military aspects.[23]

However valuable these Reports were in drawing attention to the human and non-military dimension of security, there is in each a tone of moralism and a weakness of analysis of the central assumption about interdependence which reduced their impact. The assumption of the mutuality of North–South interests may be correct in a general moral sense, but it remains to be demonstrated empirically. For Andre Gundar Frank, 'the supposed mutual interest of North and South in global Keynesianism . . . seems not to be shared even in the short run, within the West'; the West is so caught up with its own internal economic competition that North–South mutual interest is not even a feature on these states' agendas.[24]

There is an ingenuousness in the combination of statist policy proposals and moral outrage in all three Reports which, in Galtung's comments in regard to Palme, 'show an almost unbelievable faith in negotiations and agreements'.[25] The case for 'common security' was based on a conceptual framework which contradicts it; its moral appeal rests on a dubious application of consequentialist ethics which made it vulnerable to a test of empirical evidence which it could never meet.[26]

Buzan's agenda for 'international security studies'

The publication of Barry Buzan's *People, States and Fear* in 1983 marked the beginning of a major shift in the academic debate on the

---

[22] Brandt Report, p. 64; Palme Report, p. 7; Brundtland Report, p. 295.

[23] Brandt Report, p. 124.

[24] Andre Gundar Frank, 'Keynesian paradoxes in the Brandt Report', *Third World Quarterly*, 11/4, 1980, p. 679. See also Mohammed Ayoob, 'Security in the third world; the worm about to turn?', *International Affairs*, 60/1, Winter, 1983/84, p. 46; also D. Seers, 'Muddling morality and mutuality', *Third World Quarterly*, 11/4, 1980, p. 689.

[25] Johan Galtung, *There are Alternatives: Four Roads to Peace and Security*, Spokesman, Nottingham, 1984, p. 142.

[26] Charles Taylor, *Sources of the Self: The Making of the Modern Identity*, Cambridge University Press, Cambridge, 1989, p. 6.

concept of security and merits extended treatment for its originality and its impact on security studies over the following decade.[27] Buzan sought to develop a broader concept, an analytical framework and a wider international context for the study of security than that offered in the 'national security' tradition.

In eight years following the first edition, Buzan's analysis of security met with respect verging on reverence from the academic community (at least in Europe, where the boundaries of normal discourse on the subject are more flexible than in the United States). Acknowledging the merits of a 'broad concept of security' and of Buzan's authority on the subject became a reflex of security scholars, and entered into the everyday lexicon of policy-makers.[28] If it warrants a special place in the history of security studies, it is also overdue for recovery from the deferential footnotes to where it has been largely consigned.[29]

The discussion will address his thesis in the second edition (hereafter referred to as Buzan 1991), noting only where necessary the points of departure from the first. A general outline and critique is followed by more detailed discussion of some key points.

An overview of the Buzan thesis

Buzan aims to establish the mutual dependence of national and international security.

> I seek to demonstrate that a simple-minded concept of security constitutes such a substantial barrier to progress that it might almost be counted as part of the problem.[30]

He sets the stage for his discussion in the context of two incommensurable traditions of thought which have monopolized debate on the central problems of security since World War II. Against idealist

---

[27] Barry Buzan, *People, States and Fear: The National Security Problem in International Relations*, Harvester Wheatsheaf, Hemel Hempstead, 1983. The second edition from the same publisher is entitled: *People, States and Fear: An Agenda for International Security Studies in the Post-Cold War Era*, 1991.

[28] See the discussion of NATO in chapter 10.

[29] For critical comments see Ken Booth, 'Security and Emancipation', *Review of International Studies*, 17, 1991, pp. 313–326; Steve Smith, 'Mature anarchy, strong states and security', *Arms Control*, 12/2, September 1991, pp. 325–339; Martin Shaw, 'There is no such thing as society: beyond individualism and statism in international security studies', *Review of International Studies*, 19, 1993, pp. 159–175.

[30] Buzan, *People, States and Fear* (1983), pp. 1/2.

proposals for the radical transformation of the international order and against the dogmatic insistence of realism on its immutable, anarchic character, he proposes a wider concept of security which weaves together elements of both traditions by welding international constraints with the realities of international cooperation, and provides a firm basis for a politics of security.

> The solid rooting of the concept in both anarchy and interdependence helps to sink a number of unhelpful illusions on both extremes that have clogged up policy debates. These include conceptions of national security based on reducing vulnerability by increasing power, pipe-dreams (and nightmares) of world government . . . and simplistic reductionist assumptions that all politics can be boiled down to the level of individual human beings.[31]

From this conviction Buzan begins his analysis, but within the general constraints of neorealism, and with a sharper nose for the limitations of change than for the opportunities.

To describe the task as the construction of a politics of security, with a policy agenda, may seem to misconstrue a work which, apart from a few pages at the end, avoids any discussion of security policy. The realist tradition of security studies was policy-*driven*, in the sense that a changed international environment generated a change in policy to serve particular national interests, and this in turn led to the elaboration of the power model of security to which Buzan aims to offer an alternative.

Although his work is not policy-driven, it is policy-oriented in an analytical sense – as any meaningful discussion of security must be – and prescriptive. He acknowledges that he may be accused of 'leaving the hard thinking about real policies to others' and pleads the necessity for a division of labour in response.[32] There is little question, however, that the enterprise as a whole must be judged in relation to its policy implications. Buzan has either provided us with the conceptual tools to frame policy or he has wasted his time. The abstract analysis of security makes sense only if it clarifies the mind in relation to the action appropriate to achieve it.

No formal definition of security is offered, and Buzan rests his case for this on Gallie's notion of the 'essentially contested concept'.[33]

---

[31] Buzan, *People, States and Fear* (1991), p. 370.
[32] *Ibid.*, p. 375.
[33] W.B. Gallie, 'Essentially contested concepts', in Max Black (ed.), *The Importance of Language*, Englewood Cliffs, New Jersey, 1962, pp. 121–146.

54

Since the nature of security 'defies pursuit of an agreed general definition', he argues, 'the formulation of such a definition is *not* one of the aims of this book'.[34] But Gallie's analysis on this point is vague and unsatisfactory, as I shall argue in chapter 5. Buzan's reliance on it merely passes to the reader the responsibility for inferring and making explicit the definition which directs his argument and without which neither we nor he would know what he is talking about.

One critical element of his definition of security is made clear at the outset. The referent object – the answer to the question 'Who or what is being secured?' – is the state. In references to the state on this issue, Buzan invariably qualifies it by the use of terms like 'primary', 'main focus', 'essentially'.[35] It is worth citing his own case against the exclusive focus on the state, which makes these qualifications necessary:

> Security as a concept clearly requires a referent object, for without an answer to the question 'The security of what?' the idea makes no sense. To answer simply 'The state', does not solve the problem . . . One soon discovers that security has many potential referent objects. These objects of security multiply not only as the membership of the society of states increases, but also as one moves down through the state to the level of individuals, and up beyond it to the level of the international system as a whole.[36]

Thus the primacy of the state is not intended to mean that individuals and the international system are excluded. (It will be argued, however, that Buzan does not fulfil this promise. Not only is the state the primary object of security; the conception of security which drives the argument allows no place for any other (sub-state) object. They are relegated to the status of 'conditions' for state security.[37])

Having argued that the primary object is the state – its security is prior to that of other candidates who depend on it for theirs – he draws the critical distinction between weak and strong states as the state-level condition for security. Here we come to the nub of Buzan's thesis. The fact that the domestic and international environments are

---

[34] Buzan, *People, States and Fear* (1991), p. 16.
[35] *Ibid.*, pp. 27, 51, 54.
[36] *Ibid.*, p. 26. Note the use of 'what' instead of 'whom' in the formulation of the question. As I shall show in chapter 5, the choice of the neutral pronoun invites the focus on instruments rather than subjects of security, thus shaping the implicit definition of security in terms of material means rather than ends, things rather than persons.
[37] *Ibid.*, p. 27.

inextricably interrelated complicates the problem of security analysis. Interdependence gives each government an interest in others' domestic affairs, making it difficult to see if a threat to government security comes from outside or inside the country concerned. In a significant departure from the Waltzian tradition, he distinguishes types of states in terms of their level of domestic institutional stability, their level of socio-political cohesion.[38] He shows that all states are not basically the same – that is an error which 'springs not only from their common possession of sovereignty, but also from the habit of looking at them from an external, system-level, perspective.' This 'distorts the view in relation to national security by covering over the domestic security dimension'.[39]

Strong states can do the job Buzan wishes to assign to them only if the environment – which conditions the behaviour of the state, in Waltzian structuralist terms – is not equated with the undifferentiated condition of anarchy. At the international level, he modifies Waltz's understanding of anarchy as a *uniform* condition of interstate relations, in favour of *a continuum of immature to mature anarchy*. This is exemplified at the regional level, where the coexistence of weak states in some areas is displayed in a regional 'security complex' – this refers to a conflictual situation – and in the condition of immature anarchy. Applying the idea of strong state to the international political system, he postulates a continuum of conditions (differing degrees of anarchy) which reflect the domestic conditions of the states involved.

In a chapter on the structure of regional patterns of security, Buzan develops the notion of security complex as a structural condition which constrains the member states within a pattern of competitive security relationships. The concept of the strong state functions to link the domestic arena to the international system, by showing how domestic socio-political strength, or cohesion, secures the state against fundamental internal conflict, while the linking of strong states in a regional configuration transforms the region into a 'mature anarchy'. Thus it secures the international system against the slide to the chaotic pole on the continuum of anarchy, which realism regards as the only position which states can occupy. Finally, he draws some conclusions about the implications of his analysis for security policy.

Thus, from the traditional, narrow focus on the uniform state within a uniformly hostile environment, Buzan claims to widen the focus of

[38] *Ibid.*, p. 90.   [39] *Ibid.*, pp. 102, 102/103.

security outwards from the state to the international system and inwards to the human collectivities which comprise the domestic arena. His concept of the strong state within a mature anarchy is the core of his analysis and of the policy implications and prescriptions which can be inferred from it. He wishes to show that, although it may not be sufficient, 'the creation of stronger states is a necessary condition for both individual and national security'.[40]

> strong states are no guarantee of peace. Building strong states may also have negative consequences for the security of many individuals and groups caught up in the process . . . All that can be said is that without strong states, there will be no security, national or otherwise.[41]

A correlative condition is the development of a mature anarchy.[42] Exactly how anarchy 'matures', if not through the agency of states, by virtue of their becoming 'strong', is not clear. How weak states become strong is not addressed. This is an agency problem which Buzan cannot resolve, because he has placed the state-actor in opposition to the regional structure. How are we to conceive the agency which moves the actor from weak to strong and the structure from immature to mature?

Individuals and the state

Buzan's aim is to help us understand what is meant by 'security' and to explore the conditions necessary for achieving it.[43] Like the national security theorists and practitioners of the 'political science' period, he must acknowledge the basic link between human individuals and security: 'The individual represents the irreducible basic unit to which the concept of security can be applied.'[44] But this is subsumed under his declared task: 'to demolish the reductionist illusion' that the security of the state can be reduced to that of the individual.[45] One is left wondering if this state security is something qualitatively different from that which, he claims, must be applied to the individual. Buzan implies that it is not so; that the grounds for the priority of the state are methodological, rather than substantive:

> To pursue individual security as a subject in its own right would take one deeply into the realms of politics, psychology and sociology.[46]

---

[40] *Ibid.*, p. 106, p. 323–324. [41] *Ibid.*, p. 106. [42] *Ibid.*, p. 324.
[43] *Ibid.*, p. 26. [44] *Ibid.*, p. 35. [45] *Ibid.* [46] *Ibid.*

It is surprising to find politics and sociology ranked as no-go areas for the study of security in the international context. This reinforces the conclusion that Buzan has not wholly detached himself from the Strategic Studies tradition which enshrines the state as the irreducible unit of analysis, and political science as the unique approach to understanding it. Between the state and individual human beings there are many collectivities of persons which, by his own argument, are fitting candidates for the study of security: 'Security is primarily about the fate of human collectivities . . .'. Having acknowledged this, however, he concludes in the sentence following: 'In the contemporary international system, the standard unit of security is . . . the sovereign territorial state.'[47]

The fact that the state is indisputably the most powerful *instrument* for the security, or insecurity, of the individual seems to be the deciding factor in Buzan's position. 'All that can be said is that without strong states, there will be no security, national or otherwise.'[48] This is a contentious claim, but even allowing it, it does not justify reserving to the state a primacy as the *referent* of security. Nuclear weapons are fairly powerful instruments of security also, and one might argue that without them, during the Cold War, there would have been no security for anyone in the West. We might also argue, therefore, that they need to be 'secured', as do their surveillance systems, perimeter fences and guard dogs further down the line. This raises a familiar ambiguity of common usage. But it would be nonsense to claim that weapons or guard dogs are the 'referent object' of security in the Buzan sense of sharing in the primacy attached to that term. Buzan has not adequately presented the case in favour of the state which would make the parallel with weapons invalid. Both the state and the weapons in its control are instruments for the security of individuals. In what sense, if at all, the state must be considered the primary referent of security remains to be clarified philosophically. Buzan's assertion of its primacy colours much of the argument which follows.

The question of values

Buzan's resistance to offering a definition of security leaves the reader with the task of identifying the defining elements. His appeal to Gallie

---

[47] *Ibid.*, p. 19.   [48] *Ibid.*, p. 106.

to support his case hints at a philosophical problem in relation to values. This concerns the value assumptions inherent in an idea which derives its meaning fundamentally from the subjective value judgments of individuals. Security is an 'essentially contested concept', Buzan writes, which contains 'an ideological element which renders empirical evidence irrelevant as a means of resolving the dispute'.[49] Such concepts 'delineate an area of concern rather than specifying a precise condition'.[50] He identifies 'peace', 'justice', 'equality' as similarly contested concepts in the social sciences. But whereas the question of values is inescapably linked to the analysis of justice and equality, the implication in Buzan is that this ineradicable value-orientation applies to security only at the level of individuals. Security at the state level is presumed to be value-free. Following his comment on the individual above, the question must be raised: why does state security also not 'delineate an area of concern rather than specifying a precise condition'?

What is essentially contested at the individual level is surely no less contested at the macro level of the state – unless, of course, we implicitly define states as like units, and their security in material, objective terms, cleansed of the complicating values which would inhibit its analysis by application of the canons of scientific method.

The domestic dimension and the role of sectors

'The security of human collectivities is affected by factors in five major sectors.'[51] This is how Buzan introduces the now-familiar distinction between the military, political, economic, societal and environmental areas which have come to signify the obvious face of his 'broad concept' thesis.

It is plain from the discussion that he sees the five sectors as different areas of vulnerability. Societal security, for example, concerns:

> the sustainability, within acceptable conditions for evolution, of traditional patterns of language, culture and religious and national identity and custom.[52]

---

[49] W.B. Gallie, 'Essentially contested concepts'; Richard Little, 'Ideology and change', in Barry Buzan and R.J. Barry Jones (eds.), *Change and the Study of International Relations*, Pinter, London, 1981, pp. 30–45; Buzan *People, States and Fear* (1991), p. 7, citing Little, 'Ideology and change', p. 35.
[50] Buzan, *People, States and Fear* (1991), p. 6.
[51] *Ibid.*, p. 19.   [52] *Ibid.*

> The sectors do not operate in isolation from each other. Attempts to
> treat security as if it was confined to any single level or any single
> sector invite serious distortions of understanding.[53]

Hitherto, we have been invited to consider three levels of analysis,
corresponding to three interrelated areas – individual (or sub-state),
state and international – each of which can be considered an object of
security.[54] In fact, the author ignores the sub-state level *as a distinctive
referent object* and employs it merely to illustrate the complexities of
state-level security. Moving to sectors, these are not objects of security
in their own right, for Buzan.[55] They are areas of vulnerability, and it
is the *vulnerability of the state* which is at issue.[56] The role of sectors,
then, is to demarcate the distinctive zones in which the state may be
threatened. The reader is left wondering what is the point of the
sectoral discussion in the first place.[57]

Where a sectoral division might give us leverage on the security
problem in its broader dimensions – in the area of security *policy*,
rather than *vulnerability* – Buzan fails to explain. For example, neither
his 1991 edition nor his earlier work offers any discussion of, or an
index reference to, sanctions – political, diplomatic or economic. He
seems to accept the decline of the utility of military force,[58] but there
is nothing new in recognizing multi-dimensional *threats* to security –
as argued in chapter 2. What promised to be new in Buzan is a
widening of the traditional conception of security *policy* to sectors
other than the military.

While insisting on the primacy of the state, Buzan writes that
security has many potential objects:

> These objects of security multiply . . . as one moves down through
> the state to the level of individuals, and up beyond it to the level of

---

[53] *Ibid.*, p. 363.   [54] *Ibid.*, pp. 26/27.   [55] *Ibid.*, p. 123.

[56] Buzan departs from this position in what he considers an exceptional case, namely,
the weak state existing 'in a condition of effective civil war . . .' where the idea and
the institutions of the state are internally contested to the point of violence: 'it can be
more appropriate to view security in very weak states in terms of the contending
groups, organizations and individuals, as the prime objects of security.' Buzan,
People, States and Fear (1991), p. 101.

[57] The apparent doubts or confusion in Buzan (1991) regarding the status of society was
addressed by him and others in the later development of his work in Ole Waever,
Barry Buzan, Morten Kelstrup and Pierre Lemaitre with David Carlton, *Identity
Migration and the New Security Agenda in Europe*, Pinter, London, 1993 – discussed in
detail in chapter 4.

[58] Buzan, *People, States and Fear* (1991), pp. 152/153, 171/172, 290/291.

the international system as a whole. Since the security of any one referent object or level cannot be achieved in isolation from the others, the security of each becomes, in part, a condition for the security of all.[59]

The new awareness of the complexity of security, and of the necessity of a broad framework for studying it, is particularly important in the relationship of the state to social cohesion at the domestic level – the arena in which states differ from each other in a security-relevant way. What does it mean to claim (as cited above) that 'the security of each [level] becomes, in part, a condition for the security of all'?

One might deduce, from several references to human individuals as irreducible objects of security, that it means that the security of the people is necessary for the security of the state, and that of the state is a condition for the security of the people. What Buzan is proposing, however, is that the state be secure unconditionally, and that a necessary prerequisite for that is not the security of the people, but the *absence of threat to the state* on the part of the people. This becomes clear when we examine his distinction between weak and strong states.[60] The indicators of strength and weakness are summed up in the concept of 'socio-political cohesion' which the author describes as the essence of statehood.[61] While it is clear that a high level of cohesion is an invaluable security asset for the state and, further, that it *may* indicate a high level of consensus among the population, Buzan dismisses the analysis of consensus as irrelevant to the security problem, although he acknowledges that such consensus may be contrived:

> An argument can be made that even strong states cultivate external threats as a means of maintaining their high levels of internal cohesion.[62]

Thus, it does not matter, for Buzan's purpose of security analysis, if the ideas which lend cohesion to the state 'stem from, and serve the interests of, particular groups or classes, so long as they command general support'.[63]

In a more telling passage, he underlines the irrelevance of analysis at the domestic level for the purpose of security at the level of the state:

---

[59] Buzan, *Ibid.*, p. 26.   [60] *Ibid.*, chapter 2, passim.
[61] *Ibid.*, pp. 96ff.   [62] *Ibid.*, p. 104.   [63] *Ibid.*, p. 82.

> It is one of the awful contradictions of national security logic that the suppression of sub-national identities might well contribute, in the long run, to the creation of stronger and more viable states.[64]

Despite the multi-level appearances, his concept of socio-political cohesion is a property of the state, not of the human beings who make it up. He makes this clear in his reference cited above to the irrelevance of how socio-political cohesion is achieved. This idea of socio-political cohesion in no way provides for human collectivities to be drawn in – even secondarily, as he claims – as objects of security. What matters in Buzan is that the state be strong, not that it be legitimate, in the sense of an authority believed to be valid and just. The majority may be insecure, but if they do not threaten the stability of the state, their condition is irrelevant to security.

It cannot be said that his acknowledgment of the broad significance of the domestic factor in international security constitutes a departure from the corpus, as distinct from the stereotype, of realist literature. Waltz, Kennan, Morgenthau and Henry Kissinger are representative realist commentators on the importance of variations in domestic political culture for state security.[65] As noted in the previous chapter, Thucydides takes us back even further. For them as for Buzan, the main concern is the impact of domestic instability on the capacities of the state. Essentially, the domestic sphere appears to be no more than a dimension of the state.

Despite his several comments to the contrary, therefore, there are not three levels of analysis under consideration, each of which is a security object in its own right, but two: the state and the international system.

The regional dimension

Grounded in the conceptual distinctions between strong and weak states and mature–immature anarchies, the analysis of security at the regional level is probably Buzan's most important contribution to the

---

[64] *Ibid.*, p. 123.
[65] Kenneth Waltz, *Foreign Policy and Democratic Politics: The American and British Experience*, Little Brown, Boston, 1967; George Kennan, *Memoirs 1925–1950*, Bantam, New York, 1969 ('Mr X' article, pp. 373–376); Hans Morgenthau, *Politics Among the Nations: The Struggle for Power and Peace*, Knopf, New York, 1972, part 3; Henry A. Kissinger, *A World Restored*, Gollancz, London, 1973.

debate. It merits a separate chapter in his second edition, where he extends and tightens the argument based on concepts introduced in his original work.[66] While the anarchy of the international system structures the international environment as a constant, it is at the regional level primarily that the second-level structures of enmity and amity are visible.

The term 'security complex' is offered as a label for 'patterns of *amity* and enmity that are substantially confined within some particular geographical area'.[67] There is some confusion of terminology here, which hints at a more substantial difficulty. A security complex is defined as:

> a group of states whose primary security concerns link together sufficiently closely that their national securities cannot realistically be considered apart from one another.[68]

In itself, this definition is neutral as to whether the pattern of relations is conflictual or cooperative. The choice of label makes the neutral intention all the more clear.[69] This is confirmed in several passing references to 'security interdependence' expressing the same neutral idea.[70] Moreover, Buzan underlines the neutral intent of the label following his definition: 'Security complexes emphasize the interdependence of rivalry as well as that of shared interests.'[71] He defines the complex in terms of a continuum, from 'chaos' at one pole to 'security community' at the other.

But almost the entire discussion of the concept refers to *conflictual* relations, not to the range of relations which the continuum offers.[72] He states:

> The principal factor defining a complex is usually a high level of threat/fear which is felt *mutually* among two or more major states.[73]

Thus the confusion arises from the fact that Buzan's term for the

---

[66] Buzan, *People, States and Fear* (1991), chapter 5, 'Regional security'. See also the 1st edition (1983), pp. 105ff.

[67] Buzan, *People, States and Fear* (1991), p. 190 (my emphasis).

[68] *Ibid.*, p. 190. The same definition can be found in the 1st edition (1983), p. 106.

[69] One assumes that the term 'complex' was chosen as a synonym for 'network' or 'configuration', not for its psychological connotation!

[70] See, for example, Buzan, *People, States and Fear* (1991), pp. 190, 191, 193.

[71] *Ibid.*, p. 190.

[72] As Buzan himself notes in passing, *ibid.*, p. 218.

[73] *Ibid.*, pp. 193/194.

continuum – 'security complex' – is the same as that applied by him to the conflictual end of it.[74]

Again, in the few slight references to the European Community, he refers to it as an example of a 'security community' and as the 'resolution of the Western European *security complex'*.[75] This follows what appears to be a similar confusion in the first edition, where he writes of a security community:

> As with security complexes, security communities imply physical propinquity among the members . . . Security communities might be seen in one sense as *resolved or matured security complexes.*[76]

What starts in both editions as a neutral definition of the 'security complex', covering the range of configurations from conflictual to cooperative, slips confusingly into a usage which implies that the only interesting 'complexes' for security theorists are the conflictual. It is difficult not to see here the realist preoccupation with structured conflictual relations, to the neglect of structured cooperative relations, the possibility of which is a condition of making sense of the concept of 'mature anarchy'.

A further indicator of his difficulty in this regard can be inferred from other comments on the European Community. While he regards it as a 'security community', he warns the theorist:

> if the European Community continues to integrate politically it will pass beyond the structure of an anarchic subsystem into the grey zone of semi-statehood. In other words, the pressure from outside on the Community as a single actor will begin to outweigh the internal anarchic dynamics of the subsystem.[77]

The realist in Buzan encounters problems with the idea that there could be any significant non-state actors in the system. If a regional configuration moves too far along the axis of anarchy in the cooperative direction, it must fall off and join the family of states as a superstate:

> Beyond security community lies regional integration, which ends

---

[74] If the continuum is a security complex, the polar opposites would be better termed 'security community' and 'conflictual association'.
[75] Buzan, *People, States and Fear* (1991), pp. 218, 340 (emphasis added).
[76] *Ibid.,* p. 115 (emphasis added).
[77] *Ibid.,* p. 194. See also the discussion of EC integration in Buzan *et al., The European Security Order Recast: Scenarios for the Post-Cold War Era,* Pinter, London, 1990, pp. 202ff.

anarchy and therefore moves the regional security issue from the national and international, to the domestic realm.[78]

Just as Buzan's preoccupation with the state prevents him from seeing a security role for the sub-state human collectivities at the domestic level, so neither can he allow the possibility of a non-state – or suprastate – actor at the international level. 'The European Community is *still sui generis* as an international actor. . .' he concedes,[79] but its days are numbered by the iron laws of the international system. This is confirmed in his final pages, where he again defends his state-centricity:

> The continuing primacy of the state as policy-maker seems a firm reality for the foreseeable future. Even in Europe, where a large group of states are steadily integrating their political economies, this will simply result in a larger entity forced to play a state-like role in the international system.[80]

Euro-sceptics and Euro-federalists may incline to the same view, for different reasons. This assertion that the state is sacrosanct and that the EU cannot survive in its *sui generis* form is supported by no argument, other than the implied lessons of history and the laws which govern the realist design.

The question of agency

Buzan clearly envisages change from less to more security in the international system and, it has been argued, prescribes and advocates a particular development at the regional level to achieve this. But it is not clear by what agency the system could evolve and could change, for good or ill. To clarify the point, it is necessary to draw a general and bold sketch of the conceptual framework which underlies Buzan's analysis. It is not one that the author himself provides, but is, rather, inferred from his more complex and diffuse picture.

Strong states alone cannot make for security for themselves or for others. If the international environment of anarchy imposes an equal

---

[78] Buzan, *People, States and Fear* (1991), pp. 218/219.
[79] *Ibid.*, p. 287 (emphasis added).
[80] *Ibid.*, pp. 371/372. See also the discussion of EC integration in Buzan *et al.*, *The European Security Order Recast*, pp. 202ff. In a later joint publication, there is passing reference to the idea of the EU as a unique, international actor: Barry Buzan and Ole Waever, 'Slippery, contradictory? sociologically untenable? The Copenhagen School replies', *Review of International Studies*, 23/2, 1997, p. 249.

and constant constraint on the state units, all that can be achieved by a weak state becoming strong is domestic stability, not international security. Anarchy as a general condition of international relations is fundamental to Buzan, but it is a condition 'within which many variations can be *arranged*. Some configurations of anarchy heighten the problem of national security, whereas others mitigate it.'[81] (The emphasis is added to his comment to draw attention to the problem of agency.) Thus, the state pivots around a variable domestic and international condition, its security determined by both.

In order to achieve security, it is necessary for the state to move from a weak to a strong position on the domestic axis, and for its regional reference group to move from an immature to a mature position on the international. The key question now is to understand how such a move is possible within Buzan's analytical framework. By whose agency and by what process is the change from weak to strong states, and from strong states in a hostile environment to strong states in a mature anarchy, achieved? A departure from neorealist thinking on the question of agency seems essential if Buzan's contention – that *variable* domestic and *variable* international conditions provide the basis for security – is to ground his implicit security policy in the realm of the feasible.[82]

Buzan evidently believes or trusts in the possibility that weak states can become strong and conflictual associations can become security communities, but his analytical schema inhibits the agency which might accomplish either, in effect making his policy wishful thinking.

The philosophical problems remain, and the fundamental one relates to the question: 'Security for whom?' While opening up new avenues of exploring the complexities and ambiguities inherent in security analysis, Buzan leaves the boundaries of the concept as he found them in the strategic studies tradition of his earlier training: security is an observable condition of the state arising from the balance of threat

---

[81] Buzan, *People, States and Fear* (1991), p. 174.
[82] This raises the agency-structure problem in international relations and social theory in general, aspects of which will be discussed in chapter 8. Buzan's analysis of it in a later work does little to clarify the philosophical problem or its resolution in the question at hand. If Schelling and Waltz can be seen as resolving it, it is hard to imagine who could be excluded. See Barry Buzan, Charles Jones and Richard Little, *The Logic of Anarchy: Neorealism to Structural Realism*, Columbia University Press, New York/Oxford, 1993, chapter 6.

and vulnerability in respect of material resources. If policy refers to what an agent can do to change itself and the structure in which it interacts with others, then Buzan's prescriptions are logically as fatalistic as those of Waltz. Some states are more fortunate than others; some anarchies are more mature. But Buzan cannot prescribe, any more than Waltz, how the immature is changed, how the weak become strong – or the reverse. We are stuck in our security configurations, for good or ill.

Buzan's political economy of 'international security' displays a richer, more complex, world than the national security of Waltz and the 'political scientists'. In asserting the variability of anarchy and state against the fixity of the neorealist model, he can be viewed as anticipating later arguments about the process of state learning. But he eschews the sociological perspective in which agent and structure can be interrelated in process, thus leaving the world of agents and structure no less static in his schema than they are in the world of realism.

Buzan's later collaborative studies introducing 'identity' into the national security equation of state, threat and material resources, promised to retrieve the human dimension of international security, and to modify the balance of state and non-state sectors in his analysis. This new development is discussed in the next chapter.

√

4   Identity versus the state

The revision of the concept and study of security, which Buzan's work announced in 1983, took a significant turn with the publication of his collaborative project on security in 1993. The introduction of the concepts of 'society' and 'identity' into the analysis of international security can be seen as a transitional phase in a shift within the mainstream tradition from material to cognitive structural resources and from state to human subjects of security.[1]

At first glance, their new emphasis on society and identity, conjoined in the concept of 'societal identity', answers some of the criticism levelled at Buzan. His failure, arising from his assumption of the primacy of the state, to accord significance or autonomy to human beings as the referent of security and to the sub-state groups to which they belong, was now apparently to be rectified.[2] Another factor which will contribute to its appeal and its influence is its focus on societal identity as the core value vulnerable to threats and in need of security. Identity has been a fashionable preoccupation of social

---

[1] Ole Waever, Barry Buzan, Morten Kelstrup and Pierre Lemaitre, with David Carlton, *Identity, Migration and the New Security Agenda in Europe*, London, Pinter, 1993 – hereafter referred to as Waever *et al.* See also their reply to a published version of this chapter ('Identity and security: Buzan and the Copenhagen School', *Review of International Studies*, 22/1, 1996) in Barry Buzan and Ole Waever, 'Slippery, contradictory? sociologically untenable? The Copenhagen School replies', *Review of International Studies*, 23/2, 1997, pp. 241–250, and Bill McSweeney, 'Durkheim and the Copenhagen School: a response to Buzan and Waever, *Review of International Studies*, 24/1, 1998, pp. 137–140.

[2] Ken Booth, 'Security and emancipation', *Review of International Studies*, 17, 1991, pp. 313–326; Steve Smith, 'Mature anarchy, strong states and security', *Arms Control*, 12, 1991, pp. 325–339; Martin Shaw, 'There is no such thing as society: beyond individualism and statism in international security studies', *Review of International Studies*, 19, 1993, pp. 159–175.

scientists for many decades prior to its emergence in the media as a major cause of upheaval in Central and Eastern Europe and a source of resistance to integration in the European Union. Identity is a good thing, with a human face and ephemeral character which make it at once appealing and difficult to grasp. From the pens of scholars who aim to situate their work in the neorealist tradition, it betokens a break with the image of that hard-bitten class which formerly consigned identity to the category of soft concepts suitable for novelists and sociologists.

The analysis of collective identity can be approached from the sociological angle of social constructionism, which focuses on the processes and practices by which people and groups construct their self-image. Or it can be approached from a more objectivist viewpoint, similar to that adopted in respect of the state in Buzan (1991). Waever *et al.* appear unsure and seem to want a foot in each camp. The argument setting out their basic approach is obscured by uneven and sometimes slippery language, suggesting some doubts among themselves as to the force of their argument and the degree of continuity of approach with Buzan (1991). There are passages which suggest the social constructionist agenda, but these are radically at odds with the bulk of the work which remains firmly objectivist, indeed realist.

In this chapter, I examine the authors' central concepts of society and societal security and offer an alternative understanding of identity which has implications for security. Finally, an assessment will be made of the continuity of the later studies with the seminal work of Buzan (1991).

Society and societal security

The societal dimension, which was subordinated to the state in *People, States and Fear*, is retained by Waever *et al.* as a sector of the state, but is also given a new status as an object of security in its own right. There is now 'a duality of state security and societal security, the former having sovereignty as its ultimate criterion, and the latter being held together by concerns about identity'.[3]

This elevation of society to the level of an independent object of security is the major shift in thinking which provides the core of the argument. It is the security of society, as distinct from that of the state,

---

[3] Waever *et al.*, *Identity, Migration*, p. 25.

and in interaction with it, which focuses attention throughout. What is meant by 'society' and 'societal security'?

It is clear that the term 'society' is not meant to connote a process of negotiation, affirmation and reproduction, or even to embrace the 'system of interrelationships which connects together the individuals who share a common culture', in a more traditional sociological formula.[4] Such a definition leaves as an open question the extent to which individuals *in fact* share a common culture. Waever *et al.* prefer a less fluid reality: 'a clustering of institutions combined with a feeling of common identity'.[5] It is an objectivist, Durkheimian conception, as they acknowledge. In fact, throughout the book, their concept of society loses all touch with fluidity and process, resulting in a near-positivist conception of identity.

> The key to society is that set of ideas and practices that identify individuals as members of a social group. *Society is about identity,* about the self conception of communities and of individuals identifying themselves as members of a community.[6]

In a more telling passage, we are left in no doubt that the value to be secured under the rubric of 'societal security' is societal identity:

> If it is societies that are the central focus of this new security problematique, then it is the issues of identity and migration that drive the underlying perceptions of threats and vulnerabilities. Societies are *fundamentally about identity.*[7]

The point is laboured: 'societal security concerns the ability of a society to persist *in its essential character* under changing conditions . . .'.[8] Both 'society' and 'identity' are here projected as objective realities, out there to be discovered and analysed. If, then, 'the purpose of this book is to examine the agenda of societal insecurity', we can take it that other components of society, and other values which that collectivity of individuals and social groups hold in esteem, are of little significance to the task at hand.

The authors are clear that the intention is not to humanize the concept of security in line with 'those theorists whose search for an alternative to state security leads them to individual security . . .'.[9] The reason why individuals and social groups are not the object of the

---

[4] Anthony Giddens, *Sociology,* Polity Press, Cambridge, 1989, p. 32.
[5] Waever *et al., Identity, Migration,* p. 21.
[6] *Ibid.,* p. 24 (emphasis added).   [7] *Ibid.,* p. 6 (emphasis added).
[8] *Ibid.,* p. 23.   [9] *Ibid.,* p. 24.

study are similar to those given in Buzan (1991): if we are to avoid methodological individualism, we must treat society as a 'reality of its own', in Durkheimian fashion, 'not to be reduced to the individual level'.[10]

Who speaks for the state? The question which poses itself in relation to the state-centric approach of Buzan's *People, States and Fear* arises with renewed force in the new formulation of the problem: Who speaks for society? 'Whose security?' now leads back to a prior question: 'Whose identity is to be secured?'. To their credit, the authors themselves raise the same question in presenting some counter-arguments to their approach in their final chapter. Referring to the legitimacy of societal security claims, they acknowledge:

> Anyone can speak on behalf of society, claiming that a security problem has appeared. When should this be taken seriously?[11]

It depends on what they mean by 'seriously'. In a puzzling retrospective comment, the authors reject the charge of reification on the grounds that their main interest is not in what increases or decreases security, but in the process of defining security threats.[12] But this and other similar reflections are far from clear, they are contradicted by several others, and they are impossible to match with the treatment of 'society' and 'identity' in the book which they have actually written. They would appear to undermine their entire work. If they were truly concerned with the process of social construction, they could not regard society as 'a social agent which has an independent reality'[13] (as they do) and they would have to conduct the analysis at the sub-societal level (which they emphatically reject). Despite the disclaimers, they do in fact view society as an 'independent variable,'[14] a social fact immune to process inquiry, whose values and vulnerabilities are as objective as those of the state.

Their response to their own question as to when security claims (and here this implies identity claims) should be taken seriously is – unhelpfully – 'Hindsight'. Only hindsight will reveal 'how much legitimacy an actor does have when trying to speak on behalf of society . . . [Actors] become consequential on a political scale only when society actively backs them up . . .'.[15] Whether in hindsight or in foresight, the problem remains the rudimentary one of our concep-

---

[10] *Ibid.*, p. 18; Buzan, *People, States and Fear* (1991), pp. 35ff.
[11] Waever *et al.*, *Identity, Migration*, p. 187.
[12] *Ibid.*, p. 189.   [13] *Ibid.*, p. 26.   [14] *Ibid.*, p. 185.   [15] *Ibid.*, p. 188.

tion of society as process or as object. How do we know when *society* 'actively backs them up'? We cannot unravel the concept of society in action by appealing to the same problematic concept in hindsight.

The problem of identity

We must ask why the authors choose identity from among the countless values which people are concerned about, and which can be attributed to the collectivity of society, thus coming under the umbrella of 'societal security'. It is clear that 'societal security' is the object of an *assumption* about its referent, not the object of inquiry. That would entail an inquiry into which of the indeterminate values susceptible to threat – including identity – may be vulnerable and require security. A society's survival *is* a matter of identity, they assert. No evidence or argument is offered in support, other than the comment that 'this is the way a society talks about existential threats: if this happens, we will no longer be able to live as "us"'.[16] This observation is made analytically true, of course, if we accept the definition of society in terms of 'individuals identifying themselves as members of a community'.[17] But that is to reduce our conception of society to its most ephemeral and empirically contentious component and to ignore other elements.

The authors briefly acknowledge that economic threats to particular groups within a society can affect the security of society as a whole.[18] But this passing interest in the multi-dimensionality of threats is not sustained. Neither does it reflect interest in the multi-dimensionality of *values* susceptible to threat. The only value which they can conceive as vulnerable in the event of economic threats is societal identity.

If, rather than assuming that identity is the unique value vulnerable to threat, the authors had posed as a problem – 'What is the focus of the security concerns of the people who comprise 'society'? – the intuitive evidence alone would have suggested a range of values, with economic welfare prominent. This would force the level of analysis down from society as a whole to its social-group components. That would open up, not just a methodological can of worms for the authors – as they realize[19] – but a theoretical one also. Their focus on the domestic dimension of the security problem could no longer remain at the macro level of society, and a new conceptual schema

---

[16] *Ibid.,* p. 26.   [17] *Ibid.,* p. 24.   [18] *Ibid.,* p. 20.   [19] *Ibid.,* p. 20.

would be required to deal with the dynamics of sub-societal, societal and state interaction. This would have resulted in a quite different approach, in which the apparent fact of societal identity was exposed as an integral, political aspect of the security problem, rather than a taken-for-granted reality which defined the problem.

Identity is not a fact of society; it is a process of negotiation among people and interest groups. Being English, Irish, Danish is a consequence of a political process, and it is that process, not the label which symbolizes it, which constitutes the reality which needs explication. We cannot decide the status, or even the relevance, of identity *a priori*. Where it is relevant, it is not necessarily the cause of a security problem, as the authors assume. It is just as likely to be its effect. Which is the chicken and which is the egg can only be explicated by deconstructing the process of identity-formation at the sub-societal level, but the authors reject this approach as leading inevitably to individualism. For example, a conflict of interests and a problem of security have coexisted with a conflict of identity between unionists and nationalists in Northern Ireland, between Serbs and Croats in former Yugoslavia, between Jews and Palestinians in Israel, between republics in the former USSR. The security problem is not there just *because* people have separate identities; it may well be the case that they have separate identities because of the security problem. Nationalism in the Soviet republics was not a cause of repression, according to Rogers Brubaker; it was an effect.[20] Contrary to the authors' claim,[21] identity is not to be taken as an independent variable, *tout court*; it is often the outcome of a labelling process which reflects a conflict of interests at the political level.

The concept of interests readily invokes the idea of human choice and moral decision. Anticipating more detailed discussion later, it is useful here to make some philosophical observations on choice and decision in relation to identity.[22]

Identity and moral judgment

In the view of Waever *et al.*, identity is a property of society, not to be confused with human beings. It 'emerges' (a frequently used term)

[20] Rogers Brubaker, *Nationalism Reframed: Nationhood and the National Question in the New Europe*, Cambridge University Press, Cambridge, 1996, p. 17.

[21] Waever *et al.*, *Identity, Migration*, p. 185.

[22] On the relation between identity and interests, see chapters 7–9.

from the peculiar interactions of people and institutions in each society, fixed and incorrigible like the computer output of a complex arithmetic. Identity describes the society and society is constituted by identity. Since its computation or construction does not crucially depend on human decisions, it makes no sense to speak of correcting it. Societal identity just is. We are stuck with it. There is no way we can replace it, except by adopting multiple identities, each of which is, in principle, as inviolable as the next.[23] It follows that we are stuck with every other community's accounts of their identity also, and have no intellectual means of passing judgment on them. We may not like who they are, but if they think that way, so be it, according to this school of identity theory.

This is to take an objectivist and reified view of what is a contingent, social construction. Collective identity and security share a similar dependence on subjective awareness and the need for objective verification. Collective identity is first a matter of perception, just as security and insecurity also begin in our perception of vulnerabilities and threats. A critical difference appears, however, when we consider that the perception and fear of threats to security can, in principle, be checked by observing and evaluating the facts external to the subject. To privilege perception would, in effect, turn security policy over to demagogues and paranoiacs. It is plainly critical for security, both that we take perceptions seriously and that we have some criteria for correcting them, for assessing their objectivity. Paranoia – or complacency – can be challenged by evidence.

There seems to be no parallel in regard to identity. There is no court of appeal which can perform the same epistemological task for our sense of identity, personal or collective. The authors acknowledge part of the problem in their concluding reflections.[24] They see that not everyone who claims to articulate the identity of a society must thereby be accepted as the authority. In other words, they recognize that there may be an empirical problem. Their choice of examples to illustrate this – fascism, racism, xenophobia – hints at awareness of a

---

[23] Though the authors raise the question: 'When (if ever) can national identity be replaced by another identity?' '(p. 28) the only discussion of this possibility concerns the overlaying of a European on a national identity: Waever *et al.*, *Identity, Migration*, chapter 4; see also Buzan *et al.*, *The European Security Order Recast: Scenarios for the Post-Cold War Era*, Pinter, London, 1990, pp. 36ff.

[24] Waever *et al.*, *Identity, Migration*, pp. 187–189.

deeper, normative problem,[25] but the discussion is not extended to explore it. When a claim is made about collective identity, their solution is to wait until hindsight reveals the truth.[26] Waever *et al.* offer no basis or criteria by which to arbitrate between competing identity claims. Faced with the fact that identity disputes are a special case, not susceptible to objective resolution by empirical observation, they conclude, in effect, that they are beyond all resolution.

Their case studies, their style and their apparent intention stand solidly within a neorealist tradition which is not noted for its affinity to relativism. Ironically, their solution to this problem of identity disputes – or rather their failure to offer any solution to it – leaves them, and us, in something of a postmodernist maze, celebrating difference, but powerless to pass critical judgment on the interests motivating its construction, or on the security claims which are derived from it.[27]

The problem of resolving disputes about identity is, at root, a philosophical one in which moral judgment inescapably intrudes. An analogy between identity and individual freedom will serve to illustrate the point. The test of freedom cannot be reduced to a test of the absence of obstacles to the fulfilment of desires. By that criterion, a happy slave might be judged free and a frustrated professor enslaved. Neither can it be reduced to perception. The slave may perceive himself more free than the professor, but it is obvious that the concept

---

[25] *Ibid.*, pp. 187–189.   [26] *Ibid.*, p. 188.

[27] In their response to the published version of this critiqe, Buzan and Waever seem to have missed the irony – signalled in inverted commas – which accompanied my comment on the need to 'correct' identity claims. Correcting identity claims in this sense does not mean establishing which are 'authentic' and which are imagined, socially constructed (Buzan and Waever, 'Slippery? contradictory?', p. 246). It means making a moral judgment to arbitrate between the competing *moral decisions* which underlie all claims to collective identity and all security policies which flow from them. If, as I noted, the imaginary character of all identity claims leaves no objective basis for epistemological evaluation, we are left with the same choice in respect of rival identity claims that we face in regard to the questions of race or human rights: between our capacity to pass critical judgment on the moral values of others and a relativist impotence to move beyond observation, disapproval, or celebration of difference. The critical judgment required is not one of evaluating the authenticity of the boundaries of a particular identity, but the moral values which give rise to them. It does not intimate a naive 'universalism and harmony-of-interest' in the sense implied by Buzan and Waever (p. 247) to insist that there are grounds for criticizing the ethical positions underlying the identity claims – or the human rights claims – of other cultures.

of personal freedom loses the meaning we invest in it if we limit it to the perception of either.

We need a test to judge the needs which are relevant to personal freedom if we are to rescue the concept from being merely an expression of taste. The test of freedom must begin from a positive judgment about human needs and rights, not from a negative assessment of obstacles. The philosophical starting point must be some ideal of human nature.[28] The fact that we have no authoritative, epistemological basis for constructing such an ideal is no argument against its necessity. We can, and we routinely do, make judgments about personal freedom. But they are not judgments which can be validated by empirical observation alone.

If we want a test allowing us to transcend individual perception and to judge personal freedom in the light of the human competence to which the concept refers, then we are in the business of making a moral decision. We stand some chance of making a more reasoned judgment if we address its normative character explicitly, than if we hide it from view behind a veil of false respect for the authenticity of the person.

The implication for personal and collective identity should be clear. The basis of judgment about personal identity overlaps closely with the judgment about personal freedom. The question 'Who am I?' clearly does not rest simply on empirical evidence, though the factual, historical data collected in our passport, our diary and our past experiences are very relevant. Neither can it be decided exclusively in terms of subjective perception. We routinely 'correct' identity claims, not only of others, but of ourselves. It rests also on the contrast and balance between a normative view of human nature and the facts of personal biography. It entails an element of moral judgment as well as self-observation.

Similarly, the collective question: 'Who are we?' cannot be answered simply by reference to opinion polls, ancient myths, folk music or other measures of collective history. It too entails a decision based on a theory which relates some of the countless biographical facts of our collective past and present to a view of who we want to be. 'We are who we choose to be', overstates our freedom in the matter,[29] but it

---

[28] See the discussion of personal freedom from which this analogy is drawn in Martin Hollis, *Invitation to Philosophy*, Blackwell, Oxford, 1989, pp. 138ff.

[29] The voluntaristic emphasis in this and other references to identity as human choice should not be taken to deny the variable constraints which *limit* our freedom to

76

makes the point forcefully that collective identity is a choice made by people, not a property of society which transcends their agency. We *choose* from an array of possible identities, so to speak. (Clearly, this is to analyse identity-formation in the abstract. No society exists which would allow us to observe this process from the *tabula rasa* of a group without an already existing identity and the consequent pressures of socialization to adopt and to affirm it.) The question is how these diverse individual choices come to cohere in a clear or vague collective image, and how disputes about identity, with security implications, are settled. If we reify the notion of societal identity, in the manner of Waever *et al.*, the answer is that it just happens; identity 'emerges', and with it, the security claim. If sub-societal groups see things differently from the majority, Waever *et al.* offer no criteria by which to judge and resolve the dispute. For them, society *has* an identity by definition. People do not choose it; they recognize it, they *belong* to it.[30]

This is sociologically untenable. It is blind to the moral choices which go into the melting-pot of the process of identity-formation. To answer the question raised above: individual and group choices come to cohere in a societal identity – when they do – only by virtue of higher-level *moral* decisions about what counts and what is not to count in the image we want to have of ourselves and the correlative image we want to construct of others.

In Buzan (1991), as noted, the state was not only given the political mandate in relation to security. It was also ontologically identified with the needs and rights of the people whose security was at stake. The moral judgment entailed in his account is hidden within the function of the state. In the new focus on societal identity, there are no criteria for legitimizing decisions about identity. In effect, the construction of identity and the resolution of identity disputes are left to emerge, incorrigible and beyond assessment, from the mysterious workings of society. The element of normative judgment in the negotiations which constitute the permanent process of identity-formation is lost.

Collective identity is not out there, waiting to be discovered. What is 'out there' is identity discourse on the part of political leaders,

choose. These constraints are integral to structure. Identity as structure, and the sense in which human freedom to choose identity is constrained by structure will be explored in chapter 11.

[30] Waever *et al.*, *Identity, Migration*, p. 21.

intellectuals and countless others, who engage in the process of constructing, negotiating, manipulating or affirming a response to the demand – at times urgent, mostly absent – for a collective image. Even in times of crisis, this is never more than a provisional and fluid image of ourselves as we want to be, limited by the facts of history. The relevance of this argument to the concept of societal security should be clear.

The importing of 'identity' into a neorealist perspective makes for an unlikely synthesis. Either objectivism is modified beyond the boundaries of neorealist tolerance and identity is made a variable, rather than a fixed, property of states, or a reified concept of identity is just added on to that of state. Buzan and Waever take the latter course; two referent objects of security are better than one.

Mixing Durkheim into the ingredients only serves to flavour the analysis with a dash of social constructionism.[31] Durkheim is no less objectivist than Waltz. By imputing a Durkheimian notion of identity to 'society' and making it an equal referent of security *as distinct from the state*, Waever and Buzan have pulled the rug from under Buzan's earlier thesis. The earlier argument rested on the state's capacity to control the domestic elements of social cohesion – including societal identity – as a condition of becoming a strong state and a candidate for membership of a mature anarchy. If it was hard to see how the weak became strong in Buzan's earlier work, the later compounds that difficulty.

Though Buzan and his Copenhagen School of security studies did not provide the needed break with neorealism and open the way to a study of security which respects its human reference and comprehensive scope, their systematic analysis has made an important contribution to our understanding of its relational character and the inadequacy of its narrow definition. Due to them more than the other forerunners examined, it is second nature today for most scholars to affirm the necessity of a broad concept of security within a variable structure of anarchy, and to disavow the uncomplicated certitudes of security orthodoxy. In the chapters of part II, which follow, the attempt to rethink the concept and develop a more adequate schema of analysis is indebted to these insights.

---

[31] The relevance of a Durkheimian approach to international relations theory is discussed in chapter 6.

Part II
Theorizing security: the turn to sociology

5   A conceptual discussion

The examination of the objectivist tradition of security studies in part I brings the story up to the beginning of the 1990s, with a return to an old idea of 'common' in place of 'national' security, and implicit reference at least to an image of human security in place of the material one of the 'political science' period.

With the collapse of the bipolar system of the Cold War, and the need to define a new international order in the face of the uncertainties of transition, the concept of security came into sharper political focus. In the early 1990s, President Clinton repeatedly referred to 'human' security and called for 'a new understanding of the meaning and nature of national security and of the role of individuals and nation-states'; the United Nations Secretary-General noted: 'The United Nations was founded fifty years ago to ensure the territorial security of member states . . . What is now under siege is something different.' He urged a 'conceptual breakthrough' on understanding security in terms of 'people in their homes, jobs and communities'.[1]

Recalling the discussion in chapter 1, everyday usage of the term 'security' tends to reinforce the idea that the concept is ambiguous beyond remedy. On the one hand, it refers to something hard, objective and unproblematic. But the word also has a common 'soft' meaning, referring to intersubjective relations and covering a bewildering array of values which acquire a degree of authenticity and imperviousness to challenge, similar to that associated with the

---

[1] President Bill Clinton, 27 September 1993; Boutros Boutros-Ghali, "International Herald Tribune", 10 February 1995 – both cited in Emma Rothschild, 'What is Security?', *Daedalus*, 124/3, 1995, pp. 55/56.

concept of identity. It embraces all the areas of personal relations in everyday life which are subject to anxiety.

Any attempt to define the term threatens to collapse into the same confusion as that which attends 'peace', 'justice', 'power'. One solution is to abandon the attempt to capture the comprehensive meaning of the concept in favour of an operational definition, rather as 'absence of war' reduces the concept of peace to more manageable proportions. This can be of value as long as we are clear about the restricted sense of peace being conveyed, and do not allow the label to smuggle in the full meaning of the concept.

In the 'national security' tradition, and in some attempts to reform it discussed in the preceding chapters, the definition of security and of the entity to which it refers are both simplified and operationalized to make analysis easier. The 'balance of threats and military capabilities in respect of the state' serves to draw a boundary around 'security' with two important implications: it guards against the collapse of the concept into the confusion whereby a comprehensive notion of security means everything which is humanly beneficial, and it delineates clear avenues of policy which is relevant from that which is not. Logically, policy direction derives from the meaning of a concept.[2] The question arises: is a state-focused, threat-centred understanding of security a meaningful boundary to draw in philosophical terms and in terms of the policy prescriptions which flow from it, and is it the only alternative to conceptual confusion? And if humans are placed at the centre of security as its primary reference point, does this not commit us to the equation of security with individual welfare and the impossible task of aggregating subjective feelings into a collective concept?

If the statist side to the dispute accepts that human beings are 'ultimately' the grounding of security, and the 'human' side rejects methodological individualism, what is the dispute about? This chapter is an attempt to clarify what it means to adopt a deeper, human-centred idea of security in place of the state focus, and a broader concept instead of a narrow, militaristic one. It will be argued that the point at issue in the individual-state question turns on a normative judgment about the policy implications. We shall return to

---

[2] In the concrete, policy may be driven by the interests of actors, resulting in the reverse causal sequence. One's interest in a particular policy can be a powerful motive for defining the concept underlying it in terms restricted to that policy.

this at the end of the chapter. Before that, it is necessary to discuss some distinctions related to the questions raised above.

Security as an 'essentially contested' idea

In his discussion of the definitional problem, Buzan leans on W. B. Gallie's now-famous article for support in excluding the individual focus and in declining to define his central idea.[3] This has given rise to a widespread myth of the 'essentially contested concept' of security – repeated ritually in the literature – concerning the peculiar intractability of security, and implying that other concepts of the social order are different. Gallie's discussion refers to conceptual disputes 'which, although not resolvable by argument of any kind, are nevertheless sustained by perfectly respectable arguments and evidence'.[4] They are used in ideological mode, 'against other uses . . . aggressively and defensively'.[5]

Buzan's needs bear too heavily on an article which does little more than reiterate the commonplace observation that certain ideas in the social sciences easily lend themselves to ideological purpose. This is the interpretation offered by Richard Little in his discussion of ideology and change:

> The debates cannot be resolved because the concepts employed contain an ideological element which renders empirical evidence irrelevant as a means of resolving the dispute. It is this ideological element which ensures that the concepts will be 'essentially contested'.[6]

Little is correct in identifying the ideological element in debate as *one* source of dispute, though it is not clear how a proclivity to ideological distortion renders empirical evidence 'irrelevant', unless this is taken to be a comment about ordinary lay practices, as distinct from the practices of scholars. Buzan elevates it to a judgment about the 'essential' character of the concept and its consequent intractability for analytical purpose by professional theorists.

---

[3] W.B. Gallie, 'Essentially contested concepts', in Max Black (ed.), *The Importance of Language*, Englewood Cliffs, New Jersey, 1962, pp. 121–146.
[4] Gallie, 'Essentially contested concepts', p. 123.
[5] *Ibid.*, p. 125.
[6] Richard Little, 'Ideology and change', in Barry Buzan and R. J. Barry Jones (eds.), *Change and the Study of International Relations*, Pinter, London, 1981, p. 35. Since Buzan cites Little approvingly, one can assume that he shares this interpretation.

It is not denied that concepts like 'security', 'justice', 'peace' or 'freedom' are particularly prone to ideological interpretation. What is contended is the implication that other concepts, like 'state', are not essentially contested. All concepts of the social order are contested, in the sense that they are inherently unstable models of order from which we – as lay actors – negotiate meaning. The problem with adopting operational definitions as the meaning of social concepts is that they are thereby rendered *uncontested* by theorists of 'state', 'sovereignty', 'democracy', etc. Even if we unravel the ideological distortion of particular usages of such ideas, we are left with concepts which cannot be traced to an essential or core meaning, cleansed of the disputes and contestations which mark their history.[7]

Concepts like 'security' and 'justice' are additionally disputed because, in normal usage, they bear a heavy normative weight and expose this burden in everyday transactions. That is to say, their meaning entails a judgment of value or standards from within a particular moral framework more explicitly than that of other ideas. No exercise in unpacking the ideological clothing, or the social context, in which such terms are used can render them factual and susceptible of objective measurement. Buzan avoids explicit discussion of moral judgment in relation to security, as he avoids explicit definition, to the same effect: an implicit operational definition of security applied to a concept of *state*, itself stripped of its 'essentially contested' meaning.

Subjects, objects and instruments

The contested nature of the concept of 'state' arises from its multi-faceted character as a structure, a collectivity, an organization, a policy instrument – or as the supreme value to which others are subordinate. This last perspective on the state mirrors the commonplace rivalry between institutions and the people who sustain them in existence. Roman Catholicism, for example, has long had its own version of the same analytical problem as that relating to the state. Is the church a collectivity and a means of organizing the welfare of the laity – in which case its form, and even its continued existence, must be subordinated to a calculation of lay interests and needs? Or is it

---

[7] On the fluid and contested character of social concepts, see the theoretical discussion in chapter 8.

more than that – a subject of values in its own right, still resting on a notion of the 'human' for its legitimacy, but subsuming lay interests and values within its own calculus? It is, then, the supreme value, to which all others are subordinate, and without which there is no salvation (the ecclesial version of 'security') for anyone. The Reformation served to problematize the concept of 'church', uncovering the practices of individuals and the pursuit of interests which constitute it. This helped to restore a balance between the church as instrument and the individuals as the subject and referent of the value desired.

Like the church, the state is a structure, a collectivity, and an organization. As an organization, it is a powerful instrument for the promotion of values and the pursuit of interests. How the interests are balanced between competing interest groups at any time, and between the requirements of the organization and the needs of its members, is a matter of judgment within the context of the *human* referent of security. To say that security policy must be formulated with reference to human individuals is not to say that each individual or any particular group is privileged. It is to say that some assessment of human needs derived from empirical observation and philosophical analysis must be the reference for security policy; and it is to deny that the collective good can be subsumed under the needs and requirements of the organization of the state. It is also to say that such a judgment must be understood as a normative assessment, corrigible only in respect of moral criteria of appraisal. Ontologically, the state is an instrument of security, and human individuals are its subject.[8]

The conceptual and normative problem of defining state security can be illustrated further by reference to the idea of 'economic growth'. The question analogous to that of security poses itself: growth for whom? The 'rising tide' assumption that policies which produce growth in the economy also produce a growth in national prosperity cannot be sustained. Economic growth for people (national

---

[8] See the point made by Walker in his critique of Buzan, for whom sub-state security issues 'are recognized to be legitimate concerns, [but] they are simply translated into the familiar even if modified routines marked by claims about national security'. R.B.J. Walker, *Inside/Outside: International Relations as Political Theory*, Cambridge University Press, Cambridge, 1993, p. 139. See also Barry Buzan; *People, States and Fear: An Agenda for International Security Studies*, 2nd edition, Harvester Wheatsheaf, London, 1991, pp. 375 and 377.

prosperity) necessarily entails a measure of social justice in order to remove distortions to wider participation in the economy, just as economic growth for many states within the international economy cannot rely on the rising of an international tide, but requires policies designed to eliminate structural obstacles to participation in the wider economy.

The concept of state security disguises a 'rising tide' assumption of its own. The defence of the state apparatus and territory is assumed to be the guarantee of the security of the majority, and of significant minorities, of the people. This is problematic, not axiomatic as is implied, but the necessary inquiries are precluded by the normative assumption built into the concept itself. By excluding people from the discussion of economic growth and of state security, we simplify the model, and escape the task of investigating growth and security in all their complex, value-laden respects as concepts which have meaning only in relation to people and their needs.

Security is indivisible. Understood in one sense, this idea represents a departure from the 'national security' tradition, a departure heralded in Deutsch's 'security community' and in the 'common security' of the 1980s, and receiving sophisticated treatment in Buzan. But his idea of indivisibility is restricted to state-to-state relations horizontally, and excludes the vertical dimension which contains the bearers of security and insecurity – human individuals.[9]

The distinctions alluded to here can be clarified. Ken Booth argues that 'it is illogical to place states at the centre of our thinking about security'.

> An analogy can be drawn with a house and its inhabitants. A house requires upkeep, but it is illogical to spend excessive amounts of money and effort to protect the house against flood, dry rot and burglars if this is at the cost of the well-being of the inhabitants. There is obviously a relationship between the well-being of the sheltered and the state of the shelter, but can there be any question as to whose security is primary?[10]

---

[9] This is the restricted sense in which Buzan understands the security relationship, or what he calls 'the seamless web'. Security is relational only in the sense that 'one cannot understand the national security of any given state without understanding the international pattern of security interdependence in which it is embedded'. Buzan, *People, States and Fear* (1991), p. 187.

[10] Ken Booth, 'Security and emancipation', *Review of International Studies*, 17, 1991, pp. 319–320.

It is not a question of logic. There is nothing illogical about the process of objectification, whereby human practices take on an objective, independent meaning in everyday discourse, or the consequent reification of this phenomenon whereby the state (or house) is transformed from a valued instrument into the referent subject. It is the moral judgment, not the logic, which is in dispute, and which has elevated the state from an instrument into a subject, thereby settling the question *a priori* of the balance between competing interests and values in the formulation of security policy.

In traditional security discourse, the state is accepted unproblematically as the primary referent of security analysis, and the principal instrument of attaining security is military force. In effect, the state is not allowed to be open to inquiry along the lines of Booth's analogy of the house and its inhabitants. There cannot be any question as to whose security is primary, since that question has been decided *a priori*, in favour of the state.[11]

In the alternative ontology proposed here, the state is not the subject. It is an instrument, as are military forces, weapons, bank vaults, guard dogs and alarm systems. They cannot be considered a primary referent, or subject, of security. Their significance, and our assessment of their ranking in a hierarchy of security instruments, rests on a moral judgment in respect of the human individual, who is the proper focus, and can be the only subject, of security policy.

These distinctions are not discrete. Instruments of security may also become indirectly objects. Banks are an instrument of security, but the negotiable value of the money they protect makes them indirect objects also. Similarly nuclear weapons and their component materials can represent a valued resource in the context of a particular security policy, thus raising the need for other security instruments to protect them from theft and other threats. The higher the significance we attribute to particular instruments, the more easily their instrumentality shades into being valued as an object of security in its own right. It is important to be clear, however, that they are still primarily instruments, and it is their instrumental worth, not their value which they represent as object, that determines their significance within the security equation.

---

[11] Buzan's use of the term 'referent *object*' in relation to the primary orientation of security is confusing; in the terminology adopted here, the state, for Buzan, is the subject.

It is particularly important to bear this in mind when it comes to viewing the state both as instrument and indirect object of security. Among the range of security instruments in any society, the state is unique, with its command of coercive, political, financial and economic resources. It represents a valued resource in the hands of those who control it and on behalf of those – putatively the whole society – whose interests it serves. Its unique position, and its ambiguity as instrument and object, allow us to slip easily into misconceiving it as the answer to the question 'Security for whom?'. The state can no more be a subject of security than it can be a subject of justice. Whatever its importance, even in times of crisis – and perhaps especially in times of crisis – a declared need to secure the state always requires primary reference to, and justification in terms of, the individual subjects under threat.

What constitutes an instrument of security for some, finally, may be *directly* an object – a value in itself – for others. Religious or ethnic identity, can be an object of security for those who share it. It thus becomes an answer to the question 'Security for what? What is at risk and must be secured on behalf of the human subject?' Identity can also be an instrument or weapon in the security policies of others – as, for example, in the stimulation of ethnic unrest for the purpose of destabilizing a foreign government, or in the instrumentality of national identity in the interests of the state. Whether we see something as instrument or as object cannot always be determined in abstraction from the context and the various communities to which it is linked.

To claim that the cultural properties of individuals, such as religious belief, language, collective identity, can be a direct object of security, and not merely its instrument, raises a problem, however. Material entities, such as territory, weapons, buildings, have no value in themselves; cultural entities, such as language, or identity, only exist as objective properties by virtue of the social practices and social relationship which constitute them. A 'dead' language is one which has lost its community and, thus, its value as an object of security. It cannot be an object of threat, since its survival has already been determined in the negative. It is the relationship of members to each other, and of the community to other communities, which stands as the irreducible object of security, not the cultural properties chosen to express it.

Natural and social threats

The call to broaden and deepen the concept of security carries the risk that threats are expanded to include all the vicissitudes of life, and that security – like the idea of 'positive peace' – will be extended to include all possible sources and causes of insecurity, resulting in a security policy so wide that it lacks the focus necessary to direct the allocation of scarce resources to it.

The problem bears on a distinction between natural and social threats. In everyday usage, we speak of the need to secure the individual, the family, the society and the state from a range of identifiable risks – from ill-health, unemployment, economic recession, environmental damage, to the more familiar risks in the international realm of military aggression.

Judgments about security and insecurity are part of a wider set of judgments about danger. Individuals are at risk, and the territory of the state is at risk, from a variety of natural causes which we loosely refer to as 'threats'. It is not useful to include the risk of road accidents, debilitating illness, global disease and damage from volcanic eruption in a security policy which also includes the threat of military aggression by external forces. Those threats which are grounded in the purposive behaviour of other actors – social threats – are distinguishable in terms of the policy required to address them from those which arise from the chance occurrences of the natural order and which require different measures. An insurance 'policy' against natural risks is not necessarily a security policy in this sense, though it may provide us with a feeling of 'security'.

Natural risks are, by nature and definition, unintended. No purposeful behaviour by other actors directs the course of a meteorite, the flow of volcanic lava, or the spread of disease. The danger which they pose may be as real and more frightening than that represented by the proliferation of weapons in a neighbouring country. But the policy requirements to deal with the risks of the natural order are of a different kind to those which are needed to respond to purposive threats, and call for the mobilization of quite different resources. In so far as they arise from natural causes, environmental threats do not fall under the category of security. (But an accident at a nuclear reactor, or a volcanic explosion, or global warming, may be drawn into a security relationship, depending on how the danger is confronted.)

There are some threats, however, which do not obviously fit into the category of either natural or social threat. These are not the direct consequence of the purposive behaviour of other actors, though they may be sufficiently linked to their intentions, and to their capacity to alter their behaviour, as to warrant inclusion in a concept of security, in a way useful for policy formulation. I refer to the idea of 'structural' threats.

The discussion of the relational basis of security raises a problem with regard to threats which stretch beyond the boundaries of the relationship of the subject to a threatening party. Social action can have unintended consequences, for good or ill, and arms-racing is one among many activities of states which can take on an appearance of autonomy and lead to consequences different, or opposed, to those intended by the individual state actors. The 'security dilemma' is the consequence of the dynamic of structural threats at the military level.[12]

The distinction between 'structural' and 'intentional' threats is a familiar one, relating to the dangers inherent in malign structures of insecurity.

> The causes of insecurity are sought in the structural and relational dynamics of states and the system, such as fragmented and incremental decision-making procedures, misunderstanding and misperceptions, arms racing, and the sheer complexity of cross-cutting interests and attitudes in a system of high-density interdependence.[13]

It is not clearly logical or analytically useful to separate structural from intentional. The implication is that structural threats are detached from human agency. Structures have no autonomy. The consequences which they embody may be unintended, but they emerge from, and depend for their existence on, deliberate and intentional social action.

Furthermore, all intentional acts are structured – from the declaration of war to the threat of divorce. Threats are meaningful actions

---

[12] John H. Herz, *Political Realism and Political Idealism*, University of Chicago Press, Chicago, 1951, and 'Idealist Internationalism and the security dilemma', *World Politics*, 2, 1950, pp. 157–180; Robert Jervis, 'Cooperation under the security dilemma', *World Politics*, 30/2, 1978, pp. 167–214; and 'Security regimes', in Stephen Krasner (ed.), *International Regimes*, Cornell University Press, Ithaca, 1983, pp. 173–194; *Perception and Misperception in International Politics*, Princeton University Press, Princeton, 1976.

[13] Buzan, *People, States and Fear* (1991), pp. 120ff.

which draw upon a structure of social rules embodied in the threatened relationship. They do not come spontaneously out of the ether as the creatures of pure agency.

The European Union is today an example of a security dilemma transformed into a security community. We can contrast the pre-1945 situation in which the core members, France and Germany, were mutually threatened by the structure of their relationship with one in which a benign structure conditions their actions. Neither in the earlier period of malign structure, nor in the current period of benign, can we say that their intended actions were disconnected from their structural consequence. It makes as little sense to assert that their actions fifty years ago emerged, unrelated to intention, from the constraints of a malign structure, as to claim that their current benign relations are detached from intentional actions today.

To claim that a malign structure itself poses a threat, over and above any specific aggressive intentions of its members, points to a particularly visible case of the grounding of security in the relationship rather than in threat. The difference between such a case and others less structured is one of degree, not of intention. Security policy within a malign and structured relationship must be directed towards changing the relationship. It cannot rest on the hope of directly changing the motives and intentions of the principal actors.

For the reasons discussed, it is useful to exclude natural threats and to restrict the meaning of security and the scope of security policy to the social relationships relevant to social threats, including the structural.

Limitation of operational definitions.

Positive and negative security

A narrow, operational definition of the concept of peace as 'the absence of war' excludes so much that is relevant that it is of little use in understanding the idea or the policy required to embody it. Similarly, a definition of security which restricts its meaning to the management of external threats to the state ignores much that is relevant to a policy designed to achieve security. Much of the concern driving the criticism of the narrow definition in the 'national security' tradition, stems from moral opposition to the policy prescriptions derived from it, as much as intellectual disagreement with the contents of the concept. A concept which dictated nuclear deterrence, arms escalation, the subordination of individual and collective rights to the needs of the state, and which gave primacy to the allocation of resources to the management of interstate rivalry during the Cold War, must be redefined in terms yielding more acceptable policy implications. This is a normative argument, implying that security is a choice we make, which is contingent upon a moral judgment about human *needs*, not just human fears; it is not simply an intellectual discovery based on objective observation of facts. Human needs encompass more than physical survival and the threats to it, and they raise the question of the positive dimension of security and security policy.

The analogy can be made with the concept of health. The state in many countries invests heavily in a 'health' policy. Where health policy is oriented to the provision and use of high technology, the tendency to think of health in terms of disease and its cure is reinforced. But there are other, more positive and arguably better, ways of conceiving of health, with corresponding differences in health policy and the organization of medicine as a profession. Disease is to health what material threat is to security: a significant hazard which cannot be ignored, but not its defining characteristic. Health is not just about disease and the threat of disease; neither can it be claimed that 'security is about survival' and security policy 'the pursuit of freedom from threat'.[14] A health policy formulated on the basis of a negative concept of health, will have the inevitable consequence of reducing the significance of positive factors directly bearing on health – nutrition, physical fitness – and structural factors such as public hygiene, health education. In addition, it is likely to encourage health professionals to construct threats to health and to promote the recourse to curative medicine without adequately balancing their significance in relation to the overall quality of life. Security professionals, narrowly focused on threat and military response, are similarly less disposed to consider what kind of policy is likely to prevent the threat arising in the first place.

It is not erroneous to view the cure of disease as a health matter, of course, or the military defence against threat as a significant security matter. Traditional defence measures to deter or resist aggression are a significant part of security policy. In the imagery of chapter 1, Rambo

---

[14] Ole Waever, 'What is security? The securityness of security', in Birthe Hansen (ed.), *European Security 2000*, Copenhagen Political Studies Press, Copenhagen, 1996, p. 227; Buzan, *People, States and Fear* (1991), p. 18.

has a place alongside the Mother and Child. The error rests in the view that Rambo says it all, that defence is all that matters, and that it is not choice, but scientific observation, which restricts and determines the definition.

But how do we limit a positive conception of security and security policy? If we widen the definition of health to encompass the welfare of the individual in all its dimensions – physical, mental, spiritual – we weaken our ability to allocate limited resources to a coherent and manageable health policy. Similarly, an exhaustive concept of security embracing all that contributes to human wellbeing, as well as the perceived threats to it, would indeed be comprehensive, but useless. We need to draw the boundaries of the term in a way which avoids the distortions and difficulties inherent in the narrow and the comprehensive alike.

The Welfare State, drawing its central concept of welfare from the needs of individuals and allocating welfare to individuals according to their needs, is not the model of international security. Not all human needs are suitable candidates for inclusion in a security policy; only those which are capable of being viewed or accommodated as objects of collective threat – or instruments in the response to threat – by one community or state against another.

The concept of human needs functions as the basic rationale for security and security policy in the state-centred approach to security studies. It is, after all, the human need for physical survival – translated into the survival of the state – which provides the basis of the claim for the supremacy of state security over all other values in the traditional approach to security.

As with freedom and identity in the discussion in chapter 4, so with human needs: objective empirical evidence is relevant, but it is only a normative judgment which can finally establish their ranking in a hierarchy of needs. It is a moral judgment, disguised as an objective discovery or an axiom of common sense, which grounds the hierarchy of needs on which state security rests in the primacy of the survival of the state. Since a state cannot have needs, the plausibility of this judgment, and the legitimacy of the mobilization and allocation of resources to state security consequent on it, depend on the attribution – by scholars and policy-makers – of the same primacy of survival to the human individuals who comprise the state. The judgment appears somewhat distorted, if not absurd, when measured against the hierarchy of human needs experienced daily by most people most of the time. Nevertheless, the primacy of the state in realism is founded on subsuming the needs of individuals under those of the state, and it rests as inescapably on a moral judgment about human needs as a definition of freedom is grounded on a moral judgment about human nature.[15]

There is no easy answer to the problem of what to include or exclude under the category of security comparable in its simplicity to the idea of 'survival' in the orthodoxy of security studies. Social welfare would be much simpler if the state's role as the major provider of it were restricted to an operational definition of the *national* welfare, the common good. It is not made impossible by the linking of an idea of general welfare to individual rights and human needs; just more complex and morally more defensible. We need to rid ourselves of the notion that a deepening of the concept of security to locate its meaning at the level of the human would make the study and practice of international security impossible. Against a common charge to the contrary, a comprehensive understanding of security in its positive and negative dimension can indeed have policy implications for hard cases like the Middle East, the Indian subcontinent, or Rwanda in the early period of ethnic cleansing. Situations of security breakdown cannot be considered the only litmus-test of our conception of security. Nonetheless the Middle East and Indian cases, for all that they are charged with military-defence ideas, are also relationships between communities of conflicting interests and identities; as such they are as much the consequence of human choice as the conflictual structure of relations in Northern Ireland or Western Europe after World War II. As we shall see, these latter conflicts were intractable until a comprehensive understanding of security was applied to their resolution.

Critics of the broad-concept school of thought include, but are not restricted to, those defending the realist tradition. Simon Dalby questions the growing support in the academy for a wider conceptualization of security. The question for him is 'whether in the process of extending the ambit of threats requiring a military response, one is not further militarizing society . . .'.[16] It is not just an extension of threats

---

[15] See chapter 9 for further discussion of security and human needs.
[16] Simon Dalby, 'Contesting an essential concept: reading the dilemmas in contemporary security discourse', in Keith Krause and Michael C. Williams (eds.), *Critical Security Studies: Concepts and Cases*, UCL Press, London, 1997 p. 5.

that is required, however, but a widening of the range of appropriate responses.

Mohammed Ayoob warns against 'the temptation to make the concept of security so broad that it comes to mean all things to all people because this is certain to render the concept analytically useless'.[17] This is not very helpful unless he makes it clear where the boundaries should be drawn and, thus, which issues are excluded. The environment and human rights seem to be two such issues. His worry appears to be that broadening security means *adding on* new problems to traditional concerns, not *conceptually widening* what security means. His own narrow definition of security in terms of the vulnerabilities of state structures and regimes clearly entails the exclusion of what I have called the 'positive' dimension, in favour of a practical emphasis on military means of countering threats. Similarly, Robert Dorff resists broadening our understanding of security to embrace problems other than threats to the state, on the grounds that the wider range of human problem constitute 'problems', not a concept, and '"problems" provides us with no ordering of reality that we can use to create a common understanding of what it is that we are talking about and the range of possible policy approaches to addressing those problems'.[18]

These criticisms focus on the *quantity* of issues and a consequent loss of clarity and analysis if they are included in a wider understanding of security. If 'all large-scale evils will become threats to national security . . . we shall soon drain them of meaning', as Daniel Deudney writes.[19]

The grounds for attaching the label 'security' to a threat has nothing logically to do with the need to elevate its importance, as some critics imply. The threat of Aids, cancer, and other natural phenomena can be given priority without security being invoked. The broadening of security threats and responses is anchored in the judgment that they

---

[17] Mohammed Ayoob, 'Defining security: A subaltern realist perspective', in Keith Krause and Michael C. Williams (eds.), *Critical Security Studies: Concepts and Cases*, UCL Press, London, 1997, p. 125.

[18] Robert Dorff, 'A commentary on *Security Studies for the 1990s* as a model core curriculum', *International Studies Notes*, 19/3, 1994, p. 27.

[19] Daniel Deudney, 'The case against linking environmental degradation and national security', *Millenium*, 19/3, 1990, p. 465. Note, however, that this is a different question to that of 'methodological individualism'; conceptual clarity relates to the range of human concerns, while individualism/holism relates to the kind of entity capable of such concern.

arise from, and relate to, the quality of the relationship between communities, collectivities, states. The decision to base our conception of security on these grounds is a normative one, of course, as is the realist decision to narrow it to the military capabilities of the state. In either case, conceptual clarity demands that those dimensions be included which fall within a defensible definition, even if this complicates the task of measurement and analysis.

Consideration of the positive dimension of security raises the question of gender bias and the invisibility of women in international relations theory. As I speculated in chapter 1, the emphasis on negative security in mainstream security studies owes something to the exclusion of women from the policy-making and theory-building community, which sets the conceptual terms on which security is pursued and the topic is studied. There is scarcely an area of academic research in which women have been so inhibited from participation as security studies.[20] Left to themselves, men have an intuitive recourse to the masculine version of the human condition: the breadwinner, the competitor in the rat-race, the protector in the jungle of life. Such an animal is not without the need for human security, but he is unlikely to conceptualize the requirements of the collectivity in this way. It is easier for him to see security in the terms traditionally allocated to him – as a competition, a game of Chicken, with relative gains, winners and losers.

Fred Halliday attributes the invisibility of women in international relations theory to institutional inertia, disciplinary isolation, the presumption that women are ill-suited for international security responsibilities in diplomacy and government, and the unwarranted assumption that 'international processes are gender neutral'.[21] There is a need to reveal how gender issues and values play a role within international relations, and to analyse the gender-specific consequences of such processes. In particular, he argues, the core concepts of security and national interest need to be examined in regard to gender bias.[22]

The problem of conceptual bias, as distinct from that of the equitable distribution of power, seems to be of fundamental importance in respect of security. Women and men conspire to reproduce

---

[20] Physics is comparable to security studies in this respect. See Margaret Wertheim, *Pythagoras' Trousers: God, Physics, and the Gender Wars*, Fourth Estate, London, 1997.
[21] Fred Halliday, *Rethinking International Relations*, Macmillan, London, 1994, p. 149.
[22] *Ibid.*, p. 152.

gender difference, as a consequence of which women are systematically denied access to those areas of power and decision-making which may determine how we conceptualize international security and how we formulate policy in regard to it. It is not immediately clear why women in power would necessarily bring to bear upon institutional thinking a different set of values to those which have guided national and international security for so long.[23] It is clear, however, from the conceptual analysis of security and the dominance of the negative dimension discussed, that those elements associated with female attitudes and values are missing, while the masculine are projected as the defining reality, with little awareness of the distorting effect of gender.

Greater access to power in the security world would, of course, redress a basic injustice to women. But it is likely to have a more profound effect. In the world of art, for example, the absence of women was not only an injustice to women; it resulted in a distorted idea of art being promoted as a universal, objective reality. Women artists, excluded by contingent circumstances from the world which defined high art, were judged not to 'represent significant expressions of the human spirit, nor symbolize the highest ethical or philosophical values of a culture'.[24] As a consequence, the art world lived for centuries deprived of the richness of human art, under the delusion that the fundamental concept which informed it reflected an objective reality.

As with art, so in the world of security, it is not the injustice of women's exclusion which is of fundamental importance. It is the injustice to men and women as a consequence of excluding the perspective and values of half the human race from influencing the formulation of the controlling concept.

The special contribution of the women's movement in respect of security has been to focus attention on differential gender experience of militarization and war, thereby raising the old question in a gender context in regard to the national security tradition: security for whom?[25] The concern to widen the scope and instruments of security

---

[23] For a provocative attempt to clarify this point, see Francis Fukuyama, 'Women and the evolution of world politics', *Foreign Affairs*, September/October, 1998, pp. 24–40.

[24] Norma Broude and Mary D. Garrard, 'Feminism and art history', in their edited *Feminism and Art History*, Harper Row, London, 1982, p. 13.

[25] Among the prominent writers addressing this question, see Jean Bethke Elshtain, *Women and War*, Harvester Press, Brighton, 1987; Cynthia Enloe, *The Morning After:*

and to make it more responsive to the needs of people is as much a human value as the traditional 'male' emphasis on military preparedness and defence of the state.

Women have no monopoly on the positive elements of security, nor are they absent from playing a significant role in the militaristic sphere at the negative end.[26] The stress on the positive dimension of security, which we associate with the feminine, owes its growing prominence in contemporary security discourse to the influence of social movements in general, including peace and environmentalist activism. It is not the greater proportion of individual women in positions of power which is likely to cause a fundamental change in the way we think about security, but the continued progress of social movements – including the women's movement – which can generate public pressure both to support gender equity and to rethink the gender bias in the concepts which govern policy.

It seems clear that the perception of the security problem in the negative terms of the realist school of national security is biased in favour of promoting those human values linked with male attitudes and behaviour and against other human values, oriented towards cooperation, inclusiveness, and the positive amelioration of intergroup relations, associated with female behaviour. Most of the males in the human race have an interest in countering the bias towards the state and a militaristic conception of its security needs, by an infusion of 'feminine' values into security policy. While justice towards women demands their wider participation in the exercise of power, a more profound justice towards men and women requires that the ideas which dominate our thinking about international security be informed by a wider range of *human* values than those conventionally associated with male needs and proclivities.

The greater participation of women in the academic and policy-making communities concerned with international security could have a salutary effect in debunking the claims to gender neutrality

Sexual Politics at the End of the Cold War, Berkeley CA, 1992; Adam Jones, 'Does gender make the world go round? Feminist critiques of international relation', *Review of International Studies*, 22, 1996, pp. 405–429; V. Spike Peterson (ed.), *Gendered States: Feminist (re)visions of International Relations*, Lynne Rienner, London, 1992; Christine Sylvester, *Feminist Theory and International Relations in a Postmodern Era*, Cambridge University Press, Cambridge, 1994; J. Ann Tickner, *Gender in International Relations*, Columbia University Press, New York, 1992.

[26] On this point, see Elshtain, *Women and War*.

and universality in the conceptualizing of security and its related policies. It is the values differentially allocated to men and women which constitute the stock from which theorists and policy-makers need to draw in their understanding of international security; if women's more equitable participation in decision-making restores balance to our thinking about the nature of state security and to the relation between the security of state and people, then men and women will be the beneficiaries. As Irish President Mary Robinson commented: '[a] society that is without the voice and vision of a woman is not less feminine. It is less human'.[27]

Finally, to draw together the main lines of this conceptual discussion and propose a working – if not operational – definition, there are three aspects to the notion of a broad concept of security: that it is grounded in the human individual as its primary referent, that it encompasses the positive as well as the negative dimension, and that it is focused on the relationship, not exclusively the self, as the source of security or insecurity. This excludes natural threats to human welfare, including threats to health and the environment – on conceptual, not normative or methodological, grounds.

To say that security must be grounded in the human individual means that our understanding of the concept must be drawn from a judgment of human needs, not assumed to be so linked and read back into human needs on the basis of state institutional requirements; that our calculation of threats – internal and external – must be referred to the criterion of human needs in their positive, as well as negative, dimension; and that our choice of the appropriate response to threats (security policy) must likewise be rooted in a judgment about its impact on human needs – both those of the threatening and of the threatened.

The adoption of a broad and positive conception of security undoubtedly complicates the task of policy-making. But that in itself is no argument against it and in favour of the straightforward, tangible realities of the 'political science' approach. The case rests on identifying the ontological referent of security: how complex or simple is the primary referent from which we must derive our understanding of security and the appropriate policy to achieve it? If

---

[27] Cited in Alida Brill (ed.), *A Rising Public Voice: Women in Politics Worldwide*, Feminist Press at the City University of New York, New York, 1995, p. 156.

that is a simple, observable entity like the neorealist state, a relatively simple conception and policy follows from it.

This understanding of security relates to a quality of a relationship, grounded in human needs, which encourages confidence in the participants that their legitimate values are protected in a manner compatible with the capacity of others to do likewise. Such a definition includes, as an integral part, the traditional role of the defence of self and others by violent means and the readiness to employ it in cases of security breakdown. A richer conception of human security does not mean its replacement by pacifism; such an approach could be defended philosophically, but it could not be defended as a policy grounded in, and responsive to, the wide spectrum of human concerns. On the other hand, we cannot expect to find a security policy, restricted to the negative confines of state and material threats, adequate to the complexity entailed in the assumption of the human referent.

The search for ways of replacing the negative conception of security by a wider and more positive one is already taking a central place in academic and policy-making circles. Some practical steps towards this end can be discerned in the policy projections of the major security organizations. In the attempt to formulate a credible security policy for post-Cold War Europe, both the Western European Union and NATO have moved in the direction of a wider and more positive policy, which links the so-called 'Petersberg Tasks' of crisis management, humanitarian responsibilities, peacekeeping and peacemaking, to the traditional military readiness to respond to external threat.[28]

That this is still an inadequate response to the requirements of security policy will be argued in later discussion of particular problems, in the context of developing a social-theoretical framework for the analysis of security and security policy.

[28] Petersberg Declaration of the Council of Ministers of the WEU, Bonn, 19 June 1992.

6 The social constructionist approach

Security cannot be reduced to defence, to a balance of threats and vulnerabilities, or to any such objective and material equation, it has been argued. Security and insecurity are a quality of a relationship, and reflect stability or change in the identity of the collectivities involved. Secondly, security relates to interests which need to be secured. The identification of the self and the identification of one's interests are problematic for the human agents involved in security policy-making at every level – from the individual infant in the nursery to the state leadership with a finger on the nuclear button. The resolution of this problem is complicated by the variable constraints and opportunities afforded by material resources and structural factors – both for the infant and the state – and it is a matter of empirical enquiry to define the degree of freedom of choice among alternatives. That there is choice, however, and that neither a fixed human nature nor an independent structure determines the direction of security policy, is a fundamental conclusion to be drawn from the analysis of this and the following chapters.

To highlight the contrast, a brief discussion of the positivist view of causality and structure in neorealism is presented before outlining a sociological approach which has become a significant source for contemporary critics of neorealism. The 'social constructionist' perspective is examined with a view to assessing its links with the ideas claimed to represent the anti-positivist shift in international relations theory.

Causality and structure in neorealism

For Kenneth Waltz, states are the unit actors within an international system the structure of which is an objective reality, independent of the acting units. This structure, in its essentials, is a material entity, not an ideational one. As a contemporary champion of realism puts it:

> Realists believe that state behaviour is largely shaped by the *material structure* of the international system. The distribution of material capabilities among states is the key factor for understanding world politics.[1]

Mearsheimer depicts the relationship between agents and structure in terms of dominance: 'in the final analysis, the system forces states to behave according to the dictates of realism, or risk destruction'.[2] There is no logical difference between this conception of causality and that applicable to the natural order. 'Structure' has an independent existence; it makes things happen, makes states conform to its laws in spite of themselves and in spite of the reasons they may have for their behaviour. There is no adequate account in Mearsheimer or Waltz of where such an entity comes from; just the assumption that the predictability of state behaviour must have an independent cause, and that the resemblance between states in the international system and firms in a market economy warrants the analysis of states as if they were physical units in the natural order.

It is questionable whether state behaviour is as predictable as realism implies; the alleged sameness of state actions depends upon the description under which action is characterized. The characterization of the behaviour of physical units in the natural order is a relatively simple matter of quantitative measurement. The behaviour of states – even for realists who disregard the domestic dimension of the concept of state actor – can be characterized for the purpose of comparison only by freezing and isolating segments of action temporally and spatially, and applying to them a descriptive label drawn from an already existing stock of knowledge about how states behave. Thus we can describe the behaviour of Germany and Britain in the 1930s as 'mobilization for war' and 'appeasement'. Since both descriptions are the products of theoretical accounts of state behaviour they cannot serve as neutral denominators for all theoretical needs. On such labels realists rest their case for the objective regularity of state behaviour, from which to derive a naturalist conception of causality and to infer its corollary, an independent structure.

This is not to deny regularity, or to say that the apparent sameness

---

[1] John Mearsheimer, 'A Realist reply', *International Security*, 20/1, 1995, p. 91.
[2] *Ibid.*, p. 91.

of state behaviour is immune to any description justifying the perception of regularity and predictability. States do mobilize for war, balance power and join alliances under specifiable conditions, though the empirical evidence would not allow that we have more than a crude grasp of the conditions even in those periods and regions where the apparent regularity occurs. The point is not whether we can observe regularity of behaviour but whether a pattern of regularity is caused by an external force – the structure of the international system – independently of the motives, intentions and preferences of the state actors, so that one could say, with Mearsheimer, that 'the system forces states to behave according to the dictates of realism, or risk destruction'.[3]

The observation that collectivities and individual human beings behave predictably under certain conditions has encouraged the search for law-like generalizations to account for it, in much the same naturalistic way as that pursued by neorealism. Regularity looks the same whether we perceive it in the natural world or in the social. There are strong grounds for the scientist to assume that the regularity observed in natural phenomena is caused by forces external to them. But there is another interpretation of pattern and sameness in human behaviour which makes the actor co-author of regularity and denies the need to postulate an external, and independent, causal force. Actions look the same because actors participate in creatively moulding them as such – not by way of imitation but as a practical need to make them comprehensible. The construction of routine is a condition of being able to act, and it is an accomplishment of the actor, not an effect of an independent force. It is redundant to look outside for the independent cause of sameness when the analysis of agency reveals it within action itself.

What applies to agency at the individual level must apply at the collective level of states. It is the human beings who constitute the state as actor who ensure that state behaviour will follow a pattern, because they have appropriated ideas – including realist ideas – about the relation of conditions to behaviour, leaving the professional theorist without the raw, untheorized facts from which to infer a scientific law. Regularity is imposed on behaviour, not by conditions independent of the actors, then to be inferred, or 'discovered', by professional theorists, but by the condition of action itself.

[3] *Ibid.,* p. 91.

These points are central to the theoretical approach developed in these chapters and will be further discussed in some detail. They are introduced here in advance in order to focus sharply on the gap in the understanding of structure and causality between the positivist position of neorealism and the sociological approach which will be developed. This difference is fundamental, representing not simply a fine point of philosophy but giving rise to the two quite different social worlds which were noted in the Introduction setting out the security puzzle. In both worlds there is agreement that regularity of behaviour can be observed and that this pattern is caused by structural factors which can be inferred by the observer.[4] The disagreement turns on the nature of structure and social causation.

The social constructionist perspective under review in this chapter promises a decisive break with the idea underlying Waltz – and shared more or less by all the approaches hitherto reviewed – that the social and the natural worlds belong to the same continuum of reality, while the international order constitutes a discrete world within the social, with its own laws, system and structures separating it as an object of inquiry from society. In practice, however, schools of thought employing the method and language of social constructionism will be seen to have seriously compromised the anti-determinist principles which it offers. But the shift from the material to the cognitive content of structure and the emphasis on the causal role of the human agent provide a base which has stimulated a more radical critique.

The social constructionist approach

The idea that the social order, the object of inquiry in the social sciences, is differently constituted to the natural order of material reality, is a core theme of Marx, Durkheim, Weber, Parsons, and specifically of the 'sociology of knowledge' school. The concepts and institutions which make up social reality owe whatever existence they have to the practices of individual human beings, and in that sense we can speak of the 'social construction of reality', – to use a term popularized by Berger and Luckmann, who are often invoked in international relations theory to characterize the new departure from

---

[4] Here I part company with some postmodernist scholars who reject the idea that we can sensibly infer causality in the social order.

positivism.[5] Implicit in this view is the idea that the object of study in international relations is the social order, an object which encompasses the domestic sphere no less than the international, the intersocietal no less than the societal. If organizational demands and historical contingencies have carved up separate territories, issue-areas, and methodological preferences for each, this is defensible only in terms of a division of labour in respect of a common object.

For two decades, the problems posed within sociology have forced that discipline to rethink its traditional boundaries and to redefine itself by drawing upon a wider range of intellectual skills bearing upon the broad spectrum of social interaction and its institutional framework. Philosophical and historical insights have been brought to bear on problems which earlier had bifurcated sociology into its macro and micro specialisms, this general trend contributing to a growing acceptance that our understanding of the social order can never attain success measured by the empirically exacting standards of natural science.

The social order, as the common object of the social sciences, is inherently unstable in respect of any attempt of the professional observer to capture it in a model capable of natural scientific procedures of analysis. As will be explained, this is not merely the consequence of data complexity, or the intrusion of values into the research process, or the so-called 'saturation' of facts by theoretical assumptions. All of these obstacles to explanatory laws or generalizations are multiplied in the task set for the social theorist. But they are obstacles also to the achievement of law-like generalizations for the natural scientist. The problem lies in the nature of the irreducible unit of the social order itself – social action – the constitution of which makes it impossible to detach theorist from action, explanation from what is to be explained, structural components from structured.

It is necessary at this stage of the discussion to insist that such a radical disjunction between the natural and the social order, and between the self-image of sociology which dominated the discipline

---

[5] For example, see John A. Vasquez, 'The post-positivist debate: reconstructing scientific enquiry and international relations theory after enlightenment's fall', in Ken Booth and Steve Smith (eds.), *International Relations Theory Today*, Polity Press, Cambridge, 1995, pp. 220ff.; Alexander Wendt, 'Constructing international politics', *International Security*, 20/1, 1995, p. 76; Nicholas Onuf, *World of our Making: Rules and Rule in Social Theory and International Relations*, University of South Carolina Press, Columbia, 1989, pp. 54/55.

until roughly the early 1970s and that which today enjoys comparable status, does not imply the rejection of scientific method or the abandonment of any pretension to independent criteria of validity. The scientific norms of evidence and inference based upon the observation and interpretation of empirical data and the rigorous application of the laws of logic apply equally to the social as to the natural order, affording to empirical social research a standard of falsifiability which holds a line against relativism of a Winchian or Garfinkelian provenance.[6] A qualified foundationalism, in other words, as far removed from radical postmodernism as it is from objectivism of the empiricist and structural-functionalist schools, is taken here to represent the implicit epistemology of the emerging trend in sociological theory and research, and of much of the work in international relations theory which can be identified as 'social constructionist' in its approach.

This perspective can be illustrated by particular studies relevant to international security, which employ a common rejection of key tenets of realism, a subscription to a broadly sociological approach, and a common emphasis on the reflexive, cognitive element in the determination and explanation of actors' behaviour. Though they draw on quite diverse insights of Durkheim, Marx, Schutz, Habermas and Foucault, the more immediate literary sources which inspire these social constructionist accounts of international relations are the works of Berger and Luckmann, Robert Cox, and Anthony Giddens. A brief examination of the first two of these sources is necessary in order to understand both the background and the limitations to the adoption of this approach in international relations.[7]

In their classical theory of 'the social construction of reality', as they titled it, Berger and Luckmann developed a phenomenology of social action, adapting insights of Durkheim, Marx and Schutz concerning the relation of ideas to everyday practices and to the process by which social institutions acquire their capacity to constrain individual thought and behaviour. Their work played an important role in drawing the attention of sociologists to the ontological grounding of institutions in social practices, and to the concept of 'objectivation' – the process by which such practices are reproduced and given

---

[6] Peter Winch, *The Idea of a Social Science*, Routledge, London, 1958; Harold Garfinkel, *Studies in Ethnomethodology*, Prentice Hall, New Jersey, 1967.
[7] A discussion of the work of Anthony Giddens follows in the next chapter.

apparent independent existence in the rules, norms, values, which structure social action.[8] Distancing themselves from the functionalist theory of Parsons,[9] they saw their work as restoring to the human agent the creativity which, in their view, Durkheim had accorded it. 'It is important to keep in mind that the objectivity of the institutional world, however massive it may appear to the individual, is a humanly produced, constructed objectivity.'[10] Emphasizing what they termed the 'three dialectical moments in social reality', they characterized the social world in terms of a tripartite division:

> Society is a human product. Society is an objective reality. Man is a social product. . . . an analysis of the social world that leaves out any one of these three moments will be distortive.[11]

It is clear that they saw the first of these 'moments' as their major contribution to the critique of the dominant American sociology of the period, when Parsonian objectivism ruled, and human agency was reduced to puppetry.[12] It is this recovery of the agent from the bondage of structure which Berger and Luckmann promised, and which, allied to their focus on knowledge and the cognitive dimension of structure, made them an exciting read for sociologists in the mid 1960s; and no less a stimulus to scholars of international relations who, two decades later, were eager to shake off the determinism and materialism of Waltz and the neorealists and to make room for ideas and values within a new conception of structure.

Despite the range of sources cited as authoritative, from Marx to Husserl, Hegel to Scheler – uncommon in American sociology at the time – Berger and Luckmann's overwhelming debt is to Durkheim. They saw their work as an exposition of the insights of the French sociologist, informed by the Weberian emphasis on subjective meaning which, they understood, was implicit in Durkheim. Durkheim's famous injunction to 'consider social facts as things' is cited as compatible with Weber's view that 'the object of cognition is the subjective meaning-complex of action'.[13] The 'dialectical moments' which these perspectives represent are seen by Berger and Luckmann as a dualism or opposition of two separable dimensions of social

---

[8] The term 'objectivation' is central in Peter L. Berger and Thomas Luckmann's work, *The Social Construction of Reality*, Allen Lane, London, 1967, chapter 2.
[9] *Ibid.*, p. 29, p. 224 n.52.   [10] *Ibid.*, p. 78.
[11] *Ibid.*, p. 79.   [12] *Ibid.*, p. 222 n.29.   [13] *Ibid.*, p. 30.

reality. This raises for them the key problem of how agency becomes structure. As they express it:

> It is precisely the dual character of society in terms of objective facticity *and* subjective meaning that makes its 'reality *sui generis'*, to use another key term of Durkheim's. The central question for socio-logical theory can then be put as follows: How is it possible that subjective meanings *become* objective facticities. . . . How is it possible that human activity (*Handeln*) should produce a world of things (*choses*)? . . . This inquiry, we maintain, is the task of the sociology of knowledge.[14]

For Berger and Luckmann, their work constitutes an inquiry into how the social order is constructed by human activity.[15] This disclo-sure, however, still leaves social action under the determining influ-ence of social structure. The ontological priority of social action is not allowed to modify the Durkheimian emphasis on structure as the reality, or 'thing', which determines it. In effect, the actor is made to internalize the values which constitute the social system. The indi-vidual is the prisoner of the system, since Berger and Luckmann fail to account for any transformation of values through the only agency which is capable of it – the creative capacity of the acting subject. In other words, while they acknowledge the role of agency in reprodu-cing structures, it does so for them – as for Durkheim – only at the level of the *generalized human community* and constrains the individual within this community deterministically.

Theirs is a theory which starts with human agency and ends in structural determinism, since they view structure only as a *constraint* on action, never as a channel of creativity. Only at the level of *individual* action does it make sense to speak of human creativity.

Like Durkheim and Parsons, they acknowledge human agency in general as the ontological basis of structure and the social system, but lock the individual agent – via the concepts of 'socialization' and 'role', in the case of Parsons and Berger and Luckmann – into a determinative world. Berger and Luckmann emphasize the depen-dence of institutions on the human practices which 'objectify' them. But their analysis of the origin of 'objectivation' displays the paradox which gives the lie to institutional dependence. Once institutionalized, human institutions turn the tables on human practices.

Only in the case of a hypothetical couple, socializing outside the

---

[14] *Ibid.*, p. 30 (emphasis in original).   [15] *Ibid.*, p. 30.

framework of history – *'de novo'* – does Berger and Luckmann's social order allow for the creative input of the actors in the generation of institutions. When real people come into the real world, it is they, rather than the institutions, who emerge from Berger and Luckmann's theorizing as the dependent entities.[16] The fable of two actors emerging from a social vacuum to begin socializing is true to the theory which follows it, but it is an impossible hypothesis. Such a couple could not make sense of their world or their attempts to communicate in it without the facility to do so afforded by structural rules, norms, and a mutual understanding of the symbols of communication. To hypothesize a structurally uninhibited couple is as pernicious for the understanding of human agency as the similar hypothesis of our common ancestry in a unique couple for the understanding of human evolution.

For Berger and Luckmann – as they themselves stress in the citation above – the real world confronts the theorist as a dichotomy of subject *and* object, of independent structure and dependent agent: 'It is precisely the dual character of society in terms of objective facticity *and* subjective meaning.'[17] They fail to see that the structural elements which theorists infer as the constraints on human behaviour are, at the same time, the facility by which actors exercise their reciprocal dominion over structure. As in language, so in all social institutions, we cannot separate structure from agency, constraint from enablement.

Berger and Luckmann's work helped to sensitize many to the complex, cognitive construction of the social order ignored by the mainstream sociology of their time. Their theory of the 'dialectical moments' in social reality compounded this complexity by confusing analytical distinctions with temporally-discrete concrete entities. This had the inevitable consequence for them, as for Durkheim, that the 'moment' which Berger and Luckmann emphasized as their major contribution to sociological theory – the actor's production of structure – was surrendered to the logical entity of humankind in general, represented in the hypothesis of a pre-structured original couple. Berger and Luckmann can be portayed as essentially Durkheimian in reducing human agency to its logically necessary role in explaining the emergence of the social order and elevating its product thereafter to the position of dominance which denies the part of human agency in concrete historical and institutional development.

[16] *Ibid.*, pp. 73ff.   [17] *Ibid.*, p. 30.

Given the emancipatory intention of Berger and Luckmann to uncover the source of social constraint (and the consequent exhilaration their work engendered at the time) – that knowledge of the human process in constructing the social order would bestow human control over that process – one must attribute to the knowledge which they uncovered the pathos of nineteenth-century social thought which Giddens attaches to Comte and Durkheim:

> Yet that knowledge discloses that we are in the thrall of 'external' societal causes which bring about mechanically events that we suppose to be under our rational control; the subject initiating the investigation is rediscovered as an object.[18]

A second, and independent, source of inspiration for IR theorists seeking a framework to replace that of neorealism was furnished by the work of Robert Cox. In particular, his much-cited critique of neorealism, first published in 1981, provided an accessible source for questioning the objectivism and underlying positivism of much mainstream theorizing in international relations. Through Marx and Gramsci, Cox arrived at a similar position to that of Berger and Luckmann via Durkheim, and to the similar realization that the social order, and with it the international order, was a construct of social practices. Understanding the concepts and institutions which constrained state behaviour – including the concept of state itself – required an institutional analysis which proceeded by deconstructing them, and uncovering the social practices from which they derived their apparent objectivity.

Both the epistemological and moral arguments against traditional conceptions of international relations are represented in his writings. For Cox, 'theory is always *for* someone and *for* some purpose'.

> All theories have a perspective. Perspectives derive from a position in time and space, specifically social and political time and space . . . Of course, *sophisticated theory is never just the expression of a perspective. The more sophisticated a theory is, the more it reflects upon and transcends its own perspective*; but the initial perspective is always contained within a theory and is relevant to its explication. There is, accordingly, no such thing as theory in itself, divorced from a standpoint in time and space. When any theory so represents itself, it is the more

---

[18] Anthony Giddens, *New Rules of Sociological Method*, 2nd edition. Polity Press, Cambridge, 1993, p. 161.

important to examine it as ideology, and to lay bare its concealed perspective.[19]

Cox understands positivism as the effort to conceive of social science on the model of physics, positing a separation of subject and object. This stance results in what he calls 'problem-solving theory', which takes the world as it finds it and works within *ceteris paribus* assumptions to construct law-like generalizations. 'Critical theory', on the other hand, 'stands apart from the prevailing order of the world and asks how that order came about.'[20] It deals with changing reality and so must continually adjust its concepts to that reality.

Cox counterposes positivism to this critical theory, which views social institutions as the construct of people, making 'collective responses to a collectively perceived problematic that produce certain practices'.[21] 'Institutions and practices are therefore to be understood through the changing mental processes of their makers.' The objective reality is intersubjective meaning. These realities do not exist as individuals exist:

> but individuals act *as though* these other realities exist, and by so acting they reproduce them. Social and political institutions are thus seen as collective responses to the physical material context (natural nature) in which human aggregates find themselves. They in turn form part of the social material framework (artificial nature or the network of social relations) in which historical action takes place.[22]

The scholarly capacity to stand apart from the context in which we theorize about social and political institutions is implied, though it is never clearly explained how we attain the sophistication lacking in positivism:

> Social and political theory is history-bound at its origin, since it is always traceable to a historically-conditioned awareness of certain problems and issues . . . while at the same time it attempts to transcend the particularity of its historical origins in order to place them within the framework of some general propositions or laws.[23]

---

[19] Robert W. Cox, 'Social forces, states and world orders: beyond international relations theory', in Robert O. Keohane (ed.), *Neorealism and its Critics*, Columbia University Press, New York, 1986, p. 207. My emphasis (first published in *Journal of International Studies: Millenium*, 10/2, 1981, pp. 126–155).

[20] Cox, 'Social forces', p. 208.   [21] *Ibid.*, p. 242.   [22] *Ibid.*, p. 242/3.

[23] *Ibid.*, p. 207. Among those drawing inspiration from Cox, see Claire Turenne Sjolander and Wayne S. Cox (eds.), *Beyond Positivism: Critical Reflections on Inter-*

The work of Berger and Luckmann would presumably fit into Cox's idea of 'critical theory', since it 'stands apart from the prevailing order of the world and asks how that order came about', as Cox recommends.[24] But one might make much the same comment on Durkheim and Parsons, neither of whom would comfortably fit the 'critical' label as Cox understands it. To restrict the characterization of social theory to a choice of problem-solving versus critical is unhelpful, since some analyses of the social and political order are uncritical in his sense, and some problem-solving ones are critical. The constraints of working within '*ceteris paribus*' assumptions bear upon all theorizing, and it is particularly unclear how the wider lens of a critique of the social order could escape them.

But Cox employs institutional analysis in the service of a more radical epistemological point than either his or Berger and Luckmann's argument can support. As cited above, he stresses the importance of reflecting on problem-solving theory in order 'to lay bare its concealed perspective' and to provide instead a 'range of possible alternatives'.[25]

Two points arise from Cox's contention. First, it is clear that he subscribes to some of the tenets of the positivism which he decries, since otherwise he could not speak with confidence of the critic's capacity to expose the concealed perspective of traditional theory. His contention, however, that theory is *always* distorted by normative and epistemological factors is, to say the least, unclear. He seems to imply that moral concerns and unconscious preconceptions are inextricably bound up with the theoretical process. If this is so, there can be no criteria for establishing the validity of the kind of institutional analysis which Cox himself offers. But he is confident that theorists cannot only 'stand apart from the prevailing order of the world' to engage in institutional analysis, but can immerse themselves in the theory of others and separate the subject from the object in a plausible critique. Cox appears to avail himself of the ordinary rules of reason, evidence and inference, in order to argue the case against positivism.

The implication that Cox accepts the application of such rules as the criterion for assessing the validity of social theory is placed in

national Relations, Lynne Rienner, London, 1994; Mark Neufeld, *The Restructuring of International Relations Theory*, Cambridge University Press, Cambridge, 1995; Jim George, *Discourses of Global Politics: A Critical Re(Introduction) to International Relations*, Lynne Rienner, Boulder, 1994.
[24] Cox, 'Social forces', p. 208.   [25] *Ibid.*, pp. 207 and 209.

question by his claim that his preferred theoretical perspective 'allows for a *normative* choice' in favour of a different social and political order:

> Critical theory allows for a normative choice in favour of a social and political order different from the prevailing order, but it limits the range of choice to alternative orders which are feasible transformations of the existing world. A principal objective of critical theory, therefore, is to clarify this range of possible alternatives.[26]

It is not clear what is the import of 'allows', or by what criteria we are to judge the 'feasibility' of 'alternative orders'. In allowing for a normative choice is he excluding criteria of evaluation other than the normative? One can read Cox as a critical institutional analyst concerned to falsify the claims of realists that there is no alternative to the 'objective' political order as they conceive of it. This ethical impulse leads, positively, to the need to posit other feasible structures which serve different interests. As he writes, the 'utopianism' of critical theory 'must reject improbable alternatives just as it rejects the permanency of the existing order'.[27] This is to place international theory at the service of ethics in a wholly appropriate way; it is not to substitute moral judgment for rational inquiry. But Cox is not clear on the question of how we judge the limits of 'feasible' or 'improbable' alternatives, and this raises a doubt as to the rationalist basis of his argument.[28] If all observation is theory-laden and all theory is value-laden, how can Cox, the critical theorist, escape the circle of comprehensive distortion in which his own enquiry is located?

Sociology and the sociology of knowledge

Although by no means all the social constructionist writing in international relations theory is expressly indebted to the two works discussed, they stand as a fair representation of two sociological influences converging in a mode of analysis variously labelled

---

[26] *Ibid.,* p. 209. [27] *Ibid.,* p. 210.
[28] Neufeld is in no such doubt. He interprets the passages cited, as clear evidence that Cox 'extends the grounds of assessment to include the politico-normative dimension of rival theoretical enterprises'. Mark Neufeld, 'Reflexivity and international relations theory', in Claire Turenne Sjolander and Wayne S. Cox (eds.), *Beyond Positivism: Critical Reflections on International Relations*, Lynne Rienner, London, 1994, p. 30.

'constructivism', 'critical theory', 'constitutivism', 'reflexivism'.[29] These terms were coined to characterize the break with positivism within the discipline, sometimes referred to as the 'third debate'.[30] A constructionist approach which specifically addresses the problem of international security and which draws eclectically on diverse post-positivist perspectives is that of 'critical security studies'.[31]

Some confusion surrounds the labels used to characterize the new approach in the literature, and the claim here that this approach marks a *sociological* turn in international relations theory requires some justification in terms of developments in sociology in the past two decades. After all, sociology is by no means a unitary academic pursuit, and various shades of the neorealists' objectivism would find a comfortable home among the competing methodologies and epistemologies which still populate it.

International relations theory and sociology share a common focus – the social order – and a common fundamental problem from which other areas of inquiry derive their coherence. This was articulated by Hobbes, Durkheim, Parsons and others in terms of how social order is possible. The same question is implicitly posed in the various

---

[29] Applied to the new wave of international relations theory, the term 'constructivism' was coined by Nicholas Onuf – following Goodman – to characterize what he understands to be its theoretical core and to mark its radical departure from the international relations tradition. (N. Onuf, *World of our Making*, chapter 1. Onuf describes Giddens's theoretical work as 'constructivist social theory' (58)). This is somewhat odd, since Giddens characterizes his own approach as 'social theory' and, with Garfinkel, refers to 'constructivism' as akin to structuralism (Giddens, *New Rules*, pp. 45, 47). This is also the meaning employed by Johan Galtung, noted in Peter Lawler, *A Question of Values: Johan Galtung's Peace Research*, Lynne Rienner, London, 1995, pp. 126ff. This is the normal epistemological usage, the label describing how the theorist understands rather than what the actor is believed to be doing. In this convention, Wendt and Berger and Luckmann are 'deconstructionists', Kaplan and Waltz 'constructivists'. Onuf reverses the convention; his label 'constructivism' is ontological – drawing its sense from what the actor is believed to be doing (constructing social reality), rather than the theorist (deconstructing social concepts). Despite the ambiguity, the term appears to have gained ground in the United States. The continuing dominance of neorealism in the US inhibits radical challengers from displaying the void between their 'constructivism' and the IR orthodoxy, encouraging them to portray it rather as an extension of liberal institutionalism (see chapter 11 for further discussions).

[30] Lapid Yosef, 'The third debate: on the prospect of international theory in a post-positivist era', *International Security Quarterly*, 33/3, 1989, pp. 235–254.

[31] See Keith Krause and Michael C. Williams (eds.), *Critical Security Studies: Concepts and Cases*, UCL Press, London, 1997, and the definition of critical security studies in the contribution of Booth and Vale to this collection.

approaches which characterize anti-positivism in sociology and the 'third debate' in international relations theory, though the understanding of its terms of reference is coloured by philosophical developments since the 1960s. How is the regularity of human behaviour patterned, or ordered, in relation to the institutional framework in which it takes place? The question concerns the relation of human agency to social structure – posed empirically in respect of historical events and institutions, and theoretically in regard to the ontology of social action, captured by Touraine's 'self-production of society' and Giddens's theory of 'structuration'.[32]

The sociology of knowledge seeks to explain systems of ideas in terms of social context, and owes its impulse to Marx – with his theory of superstructure determined by economic realities – and Mannheim. Whereas Weber and Durkheim explained institutions by reference to cognitive patterns – capitalism in terms of religious ideas, religiosity in terms of social organization rather than class – the sociology of knowledge asks how such patterns come about in the first place. Marx relates ideas, art and cultural developments in general to class systems and historical contingencies. In his *Ideology and Utopia*, published in 1936, Karl Mannheim extended this approach to all ideas, including Marxism.[33]

The modern concern with the problem of order locates the source of order in the primal concept of social action, and the debate in the relationship of agency and structure. With Goffman, Garfinkel (see below) and Berger and Luckmann, the sociology of knowledge is extended to cover all knowledge, and the analysis of everyday life is seen as an important path to understanding it. The focus on agency in relation to structure moves the sociology of knowledge from the sub-disciplinary fringe to the centre of disciplinary practice. That the social order and our knowledge of that order are socially constructed is a thread linking Marx, Durkheim and Weber and finding different expression in the schools of symbolic interactionism and structural functionalism which marked the great divide in the growth period from the 1930s until the mid 1960s. Contemporary sociology can thus be understood as a development of the sociology of knowledge which

---

[32] Alain Touraine, *The Self Production of Society*, University of Chicago Press, Chicago, 1977.

[33] Volker Meja and Nico Stehr, 'Sociology of knowledge', in William Outhwaite and Tom Bottomore (eds.), *The Blackwell Dictionary of Twentieth-Century Social Thought*, Blackwell, Oxford, 1995.

has brought it to the centre of disciplinary concern. The production and reproduction of knowledge is today a core issue of the sociological project in a way which cannot be compartmentalized as a sub-disciplinary concern.

The pervasiveness in contemporary sociology of this development since the beginning of the 1970s has altered the character of the discipline, from one dominated by structural concerns in the 1950s, to the 'interactional' approach of today which has swept its critique of the mainstream throughout the discipline, in the view of one reluctant convert. That critique, he writes, 'can now be judged, from the standpoint of the 1990s, to have been successful. For one can say that most contemporary sociologists, at least in Britain, now accept this critique as valid.'[34]

It is this shift in sociology which characterizes the common core of the various anti-positivist positions in international relations theory today. For that reason, in my view, it is more appropriate and meaningful to represent their emergence in IR as a turn to sociology than to focus on differences suggested by disparate labels.

International relations theorists cannot ignore the advances in the social sciences, and in sociology in particular, which have brought together the explanatory and interpretative concerns of the classical tradition in an eclectic approach to understanding human behaviour and institutions. The international order, as part of the social order, is a construct of ideas, values, norms and interpretative schemes, which yields understanding only to a procedure of decoding or deconstructing it.

Deconstructing security

Two examples of the application of a sociological approach to the deconstruction of concepts relevant to international security provide the contrast between this approach and that of the security studies tradition.

Alexander Wendt argues that the explanatory work in Waltz's model is done by properties of the state – its identity and interests – which are assumed to be fixed and constant. But this assumption cannot be supported as the necessary consequence of anarchy. The

---

[34] Colin Campbell, *The Myth of Social Action*, Cambridge University Press, Cambridge, 1996, pp. 1ff.

structure of anarchy and the nature of states, for Waltz, are two sides of the same assumption, resulting in the behaviour of states being seen as wholly determined by structural elements (the distribution of capabilities) and having no causal role in respect of anarchy.

For Wendt, anarchy is what states make of it. Though the real world may in fact be accurately described as one in which states interact with each other as self-help or egoistic actors, this is not a consequence of logical necessity, but of process. There is no 'logic' of anarchy apart from the practices that give rise to one kind of structure rather than another.[35]

Against the materialism of Waltz, Wendt posits what he terms a 'fundamental principle of constructivist social theory': all actors, including states, interact with one another on the basis of meanings.

> The distribution of power may always affect states' calculations, but how it does so depends on the intersubjective understandings and expectations, on the 'distribution of knowledge', that constitute their conceptions of self and other. . . . It is collective meanings that constitute the structures which organize our actions.[36]

Actors acquire identities – defined as 'relatively stable, role-specific understandings and expectations about self' – by participating in collective meanings. Identity is inherently relational and identity is the basis of interests.[37] An institution is 'a relatively stable set or "structure" of identities and interests'.[38]

> Institutions are fundamentally cognitive entities that do not exist apart from actors' ideas about how the world works. This does not mean that institutions are not real or objective, that they are 'nothing but' beliefs . . . institutions come to confront individuals as more or less coercive social facts, but they are still a function of what actors collectively 'know'.[39]

Identities and collective meanings are 'mutually constitutive'.

What kind of thing states are in relation to other states – their identity – can be mapped, for Wendt, on a continuum of identities from egoistic to cooperative. Where a state is located on such a continuum is not pre-determined by a structure of anarchy, but is caused by the process of interaction.[40] In this process, states may well

---

[35] Alexander Wendt, 'Anarchy is what states make of it: the social construction of power politics', *International Organization*, 46/2, 1992, pp. 394/395.
[36] *Ibid.*, p. 397.   [37] *Ibid.*, p. 398.   [38] *Ibid.*, p. 399.
[39] *Ibid.*, p. 399.   [40] *Ibid.*, p. 403.

learn to adopt an identity of self-help, and thereby present the kind of observable evidence of state egoism from which the realist infers – incorrectly – that such identities are given prior to, and outside of, the interaction process.

Wendt applies his 'constructivist' perspective to the analysis of the end of the Cold War, in order to argue the case for the transformation of state identities over the period. Four decades of cooperation have transformed West European states into a collective 'European identity' which will be as resistant to change towards an egoistic identity now as it was towards a cooperative one before the process began. There is no 'inherent, exogenously given interest in abandoning collective security if the price is right'.[41] 'Through participation in new forms of social knowledge, in other words, the European states of 1990 might no longer be the states of 1950.'[42] What has changed in regard to their 'being', Wendt implies, is not just their behaviour but the fundamental properties of interests and the identity which determines interests.

David Campbell's account of the determinants of US foreign policy starts 'from the position that social and political life comprises a set of practices in which things are constituted in the process of dealing with them . . .'.[43] This study represents an attempt to problematize the perception of insecurity on the part of the American state, showing how – through the process of foreign policy formulation – it has interpreted danger and secured the boundaries of the identity in whose name it operates.

Though drawing primarily on the sociological and philosophical work of Foucault (and perhaps too copiously on Foucault's penchant for the obscure and the metaphorical), Campbell offers a perspective on American foreign policy close to that of Wendt on anarchy, aiming to deconstruct the terms and concepts historically embedded in foreign policy discourse. His unfolding of the social practices conventionally ignored as irrelevant to the conceptualization of security and security policy, places the cognitive and reflective dimensions of action at the centre of analysis. Though owning to postmodernist, rather than sociological provenance, Campbell's work – like some of the postmodernist literature – is an exploration of the focal themes of the sociology of knowledge as described above. Moreover,

---

[41] *Ibid.*, p. 418.   [42] *Ibid.*, p. 418.
[43] David Campbell, *Writing Security: United States Foreign Policy and the Politics of Identity*, Manchester University Press, Manchester, 1992, p. 4.

there is a strong tone of foundationalism throughout his work, hinting that his is not merely a take-it-or-leave-it account in the postmodernist stereotype, but a more rationally defensible one which acknowledges a language of logic and inference enabling us to make such evaluations.[44]

Current security policies dependent on objectifying danger must be understood as an effect, for Campbell, not a cause, of political practices.[45] The conventional understanding takes as unproblematic that foreign policy is the action of fixed states with fixed identities; Cold War foreign policy sees an independently existing hostile world to which it is a reaction. If we problematize this, then the Cold War can be seen 'in terms of the need to discipline the ambiguity of global life in ways that help to secure always fragile identities'.[46]

The conventional approach to the international order sees theory as outside the world it purports to observe. Bull's proposition that international relations theory was concerned with the political relations *among* states underlines this perspective, according to Campbell. The interpretative approach, by contrast, sees theory as practice serving to discipline ambiguity.

Experience has to be arrested, fixed or disciplined for social life to be possible.

> The form that emerges through this process is thus both arbitrary and non-arbitrary: arbitrary in that it is one possibility among many, and non-arbitrary in 'the sense that one can inquire into the historical conditions within which one way of making the world was dominant so that we now have a world that power has convened.'[47]

Both orthodox interpreters of the Cold War and their critics share the view that 'there exists a non-discursive realm outside of the purview of their interpretation which confers authority and legitimacy upon their argument'.[48] 'In contrast, if we accept that there is nothing possible outside of discourse . . . the way is open to reconsider what was at stake in the Cold War.'[49]

---

[44] This dash of foundationalism is noted – albeit with some irritation – in his book review of Campbell by Ole Waever in *Millenium*, 24/1, 1996, p. 140.

[45] Campbell, *Writing Security*, p. 18.

[46] *Ibid.*, p. 18.

[47] *Ibid.*, p. 19, citing Michael Shapiro, *The Politics of Representation: Writing Practices in Biography, Photography, and Policy Analysis*, Madison, 1987, p. 93.

[48] Campbell, *Writing Security*, p. 22.

[49] Campbell, *Writing Security*, p. 23.

Running through the official secret documents establishing the basis of US foreign policy from Truman to Reagan is the theme of the potential for anarchy and the intolerable absence of order in the post-war years which could be exploited by totalitarian forces. If the Soviet Union was the threat, it was not the primary threat. That was disorder. To see the Soviet Union as the threat 'involved more than the absorption of sense-data by an independent and passive observer'.[50] In top-secret documents, the frequent refrain of national values, God-given rights, the principles of European civilization, the fear of cultural and spiritual loss and the duties entrusted to America was clearly 'the scripting of a particular American identity'.[51]

> . . . just as the source of danger has never been fixed, neither has the identity which it was said to threaten. The contours of this identity have been the subject of constant (re)writing: not rewriting in the sense of changing the meaning, but rewriting in the sense of inscribing something so that that which is contingent and subject to flux is rendered more permanent.[52]

The fundamental question is posed:

> how was it that we . . . came to understand foreign policy as the external deployment of instrumental reason on behalf of an unproblematic internal identity situated in an anarchic realm of necessity?[53]

Campbell examines conventional foreign policy theory and its representation of history. Here the focus of foreign policy is 'the policies of states oriented towards the external world', underlining the perception that 'the state is prior to the policy'.[54] On the contrary, he holds, the state and the identity of people in it must be seen as the effects of discourses of danger. 'Foreign policy thus needs to be understood as giving rise to a boundary rather than acting as a bridge.'[55] 'Foreign policy creates the very dangers to which we are supposed to accommodate ourselves.'[56] Like the creature in Kafka's 'The Burrow', it cannot distinguish the noise of danger from the noise it creates in securing itself against danger.[57]

> In this context, then, we might be able to think differently about the Cold War; as another episode in the on-going production and reproduction of American identity through the practices of foreign policy, rather than as simply an externally induced crisis. Indeed, if

---

[50] *Ibid.*, p. 32. [51] *Ibid.*, p. 33. [52] *Ibid.*, p. 33. [53] *Ibid.*, p. 43.
[54] *Ibid.*, p. 44. [55] *Ibid.*, p. 56. [56] *Ibid.*, p. 77. [57] *Ibid.*, p. 77.

the nexus of internal and external threats was so ubiquitous that 'it was writ large on the birth certificate of the United States of America', it should not be surprising to find this logic operating each time the birth records are updated.[58]

He argues that 'it is not possible to explain the Cold War by reference to the objective threat said to reside in the Soviet Union'.[59] The events which punctuated it were real, not fabricated by either superpower. 'What is denied is not that . . . objects exist externally to thought, but the rather different assertion that they could constitute themselves as objects outside of any discursive condition of emergence.'[60]

The Cold War represented a process of the reproduction of American identity, which was influenced, but not directly caused, by the Soviet Union. Whether or not it is over depends therefore on whether we see its ending as a stage in the reconstruction of identity or as a unique event. The view that its ending heralded a new international order presupposed that it was an external event independent of the action of the surviving participant. In Campbell's neat formulation, it 'ignored the debt that subjectivity owes to otherness and the role the requirements of identity play in giving rise to discourses of danger'.[61]

The main policy challenge arising from the analysis is 'to address the process whereby the subjectivity of the United States is continually in hock to strategies of otherness'.[62] (For 'United States', Campbell would have us read all states, in some measure. His account of American foreign policy is not intended to explain a unique case. America is the same as everyone else only more so; it is 'the imagined community *par excellence*'.[63])

The contrast between Campbell's analysis and that of the security studies orthodoxy is sharp, and instructive for our understanding of security and its relation to identity. He shows that American concern with the construction of security for identity purposes signifies a markedly different concept of security from that of the foreign policy community – not military threats but cultural; not military

---

[58] *Ibid.*, p. 145, citing Richard Drinnon, *Facing West: The Metaphysics of Indian Hating and Empire Building*, New York, 1990, p. 99.
[59] Campbell, *Writing Security*, p. 156.
[60] Campbell, *Writing Security*, p. 157, citing Ernesto Laclau and Chantal Mouffe, *Hegemony and Socialist Strategy: Towards a Radical Democratic Politics*, London, 1985, p. 108.
[61] Campbell, *Writing Security*, p. 249.
[62] *Ibid.*, p. 250.   [63] *Ibid.*, p. 251.

vulnerability but political; not external threat but domestic; not a policy determined by independent laws of realist 'structure', but one co-determined by history and the agency of people.

The analysis of anarchy by Wendt is representative of the general approach in the rest of his work since his discussion of the agent-structure problem in 1987.[64] The theoretical position outlined in his account of anarchy is focused on the critique of Waltz's concept of structure, and his work as a whole on the development of a socio-logical theory of international relations – or, as he prefers it, a 'constructivist' perspective.

Some points of criticism directly relevant to his treatment of identity, and that of Campbell, will be addressed in the next chapter, in which the principal focus is on the relationship between identity and interests. Here a more general point must be noted, which touches on Wendt's core perspective *vis-à-vis* Waltz and the neoreal-ists, and which is relevant to the theoretical position developed in later chapters.

Constructivism emphasizes the malleability of collective identity and the variability of the constraints of anarchy as a consequence. States are not like units, each endowed with an egoistic identity by virtue of the structure of the international system. Nor is the structural constraint of anarchy always and everywhere necessarily the same. A cooperative structure can develop to replace one of self-help.

Wendt's account of the malleability of state *identity* and the varia-bility of international *anarchy* should sound familiar to students of security studies. Buzan had made a similar break with Waltz almost a decade earlier. His idea of weak and strong states within a mature or immature anarchy can be translated into Wendt's terminology of egoistic or cooperative states shifting along a continuum of anarchy without any resolution of the problem of agency which was noted in respect of Buzan. How do weak states become strong? How do egoistic states become cooperative? The answer of Wendt's constructi-vism is as unsatisfactory as the implicit one of Buzan: through the learning process of state interaction at the cooperative end of the

---

[64] Alexander Wendt, 'The agent-structure problem in international relations theory' in *International Organization*, 41/3, 1987, pp. 335–370. Wendt's more recent writing on constructivism include 'On constitution and causation in International Relations', *Review of International Studies*, 1998, pp. 101–117 and *Social Theory of International Politics*, Cambridge University Press, Cambridge, forthcoming 1999.

anarchy continuum. As in the Durkheimian school of sociology, however, the stress on the cognitive element of ideas still leaves the actors as determined by the structure of ideas as they are by a material structure of Waltz's anarchy. The Durkheimian learning process was structured through the concepts of socialization and role through which actors internalized the ideas and values of the collective conscience as mechanically as states in the Waltzian system. The concern of both Buzan and Wendt to avoid a radical break with the explanatory model of neorealism is more pronounced in Buzan, but the failure of Wendt to follow through the logic of his earlier work on agency and structure has left its mark on the constructivist project.

As stated above, it is on the understanding of structure and causality in the social sciences that the gap can be measured between the positivist approach of neorealism and that of the post-positivist schools which today challenge it. Wendt's first contribution to the critique of neorealism in his work on agency and structure drew on the social theory of Anthony Giddens to provide the basic insights into a new understanding of structure and causality in international relations theory.[65] On structure Wendt writes:

> Neorealists think it is made only of a distribution of material capabilities, whereas constructivists think it is also made of social relationships. Social structures have three elements: shared knowledge, material resources, and practices. . . . [they] exist, not in actors' heads nor in material capabilities, but in practices . . .[66]

Thus social structure cannot be considered an independent force, external to the acting unit. On causality, Wendt's earlier writings offered only a footnote to clarify his preference for the term 'constitute' over 'cause':

> A constitutive relationship establishes a conceptually necessary or logical connection between X and Y, in contrast to the contingent connection between independently existing entities that is established by causal relationships.[67]

These views, following Giddens's theory of structuration, represent more than a revision of positivism, and much more than the mixing of

---

[65] Wendt, 'The agent-structure problem'; and Wendt, 'Constructing international politics', pp. 71–81.
[66] Wendt, 'Constructing international politics', pp. 73/4.
[67] *Ibid.*, p. 72.

the cognitive with the material structure of Waltz. As Wendt himself rightly notes, Giddens's theory

> *radically* reconceptualizes the fundamental properties of agents and social structures in such a way [as] to make them *ontologically interdependent*.[68]

Wendt's view of structure and causality is, thus, incompatible with that of Durkheim and Berger and Luckmann who, as we have seen, leave the human agent as much the puppet of a cognitive structure as Waltz makes the state in relation to his material structure. Yet Wendt appears not to recognize this, since he frequently cites these objectivist sociologists as authorities on structure.[69]

Durkheim and Berger and Luckmann hold the same view of causality and of the independence of structure from agency as Waltz. Mead's interactionism was at the other extreme – so far on the subjectivist side that he scarcely qualifies as structuralist. Merely to add ideas to matter or even to exchange a material structure for an ideational one can indeed qualify the theorist for the label 'social constructionist', but to no radical purpose in terms of Wendt's core position.

This inconsistency in Wendt is compounded by his affirmation of realist principles of method and his commitment to the project of bridging the gap between the neoliberal version of realism and the multi-labelled family of 'reflectivists', within which he counts constructivism as the bridge-builder.[70] There is certainly a bridge of sorts which can be built between them under the heading of 'social constructionism', or 'constructivism'. As stated, this requires only that neorealists add more Durkheim to Waltz and recognize that values, norms and ideas are elements of the structure of international politics. If this is the price of becoming a constructivist, many neoliberal theorists should have no difficulty in joining the club.[71]

Whether Wendt's radical view has yielded to this diluted version of Giddens is not completely clear from a reading of his writings prior to

---

[68] Wendt, 'The agent-structure problem', p. 361 (my emphasis).
[69] Alexander Wendt, 'Collective identity formation and the international state', *American Political Science Review*, 88/2, 1994, p. 385.
[70] Wendt, 'Anarchy', p. 424 and pp. 393/394.
[71] Indeed many have joined already, particularly in the US academy, where a form of diluted 'constructivism' appears to have disciplined the critical thrust of Wendt's early interpretation of structure and causality and seems so eirenic as to challenge little more than the school label.

1998. But my remarks above suggest an unresolved difficulty about agency and structure, while his views on 'where neorealist and constructivist structuralisms *really* differ' about structure are hardly radical: they really differ, he asserts, in that the former think it is only material while the latter think it is also social.[72] More recent writings of Wendt seem to confirm that the 'constructivism' of which he is a notable representative, far from mediating the philosophical differences between varieties of rationalism and the dissident schools of the post-positivist family, is more appropriately identified with the former.

The interpretation and critique of constructivism merits further discussion. I shall return to the subject in the concluding chapter, in the light of the intervening attempt to develop a more sound basis for a sociology of the international.

---

[72] Wendt, 'Constructing international politics', p. 73.

7 The limits of identity theory

From different backgrounds, Wendt and Campbell bring the cognitive dimension of collective identity to bear on the formulation of foreign policy in a mode of inquiry relevant to security and in contrast to the materialist, structural mode of security studies. That tradition, it will be recalled, effectively ignores collective identity as a dynamic factor in the construction and analysis of security, since it assumes that all states share a common identity, fixed and given prior to interaction and immune to change through any learning process in which the state actors may engage.

Their approach can be characterized as a kind of cultural determinism, however, pressing identity beyond its explanatory weight. In the identity theory of Wendt and Campbell the cognitive is stressed to the point that they lose sight of an essential material feature of all questions of security and identity-formation. This concerns the place of interests in the perception of security and in the management and transformation of collective identity.

Several points of criticism may be noted, which bear upon later discussion of a theoretical framework appropriate to the understanding of security. These points will be illustrated by concrete example to highlight the deficiency of identity theory in general. This is followed by consideration of an alternative approach, marking a different turn to sociology, which escapes the limits of identity theory and – with some modification – can be seen to offer a richer conception of social constructionism.

First, Wendt criticizes Waltz's assumption that states are like units, their properties irrelevant to the explanation of their behaviour. These properties are state identities and state interests. Interests are synonymous with preferences and are seen by Wendt as arising from, dependent on, identities.[1] Thus a transformation of identity from self-help to cooperative is a necessary prerequisite of a change of interests and a consequent change of behaviour.

It seems logically correct to prioritize identity over interests in this way. This may, however, be a necessity imposed by language. The 'I', or subject, who formulates preferences, wants, interests, is linguistically placed prior to the action of satisfying them. What kind of entity I am is made to determine what kind of wants I have. What we want follows from who we are. This is an anti-behaviourist way of expressing the issue.

Philosophically and empirically, however, it is not clear that the causal connection is unidirectional. Biology certainly places limits on human interests – we could not rationally want to live like a mollusc. But it does not determine which of the range of rational and available interests we pursue. It is certainly the case empirically that what we want can also modify what we become in identity terms. (Nowhere is this exemplified better than in the practices which make up the Northern Ireland peace process and in the management of identity-transformation which lies at the heart of European integration. These processes serve to illustrate the dynamics of identity and interests, as will be shown below, and further in chapter 10.)

The range of interests available to us can cause us to reinvent the social identity appropriate to them. We can become more self-assertive, egoistic, kind or cooperative individuals if we choose to pursue interests consonant with such a definition of self. The collective self is, similarly, defined in relation to what it does and, conversely, constrained in what it does by how it is defined. Interests can play the decisive role in triggering the process of identity transformation. We are who we want to be. Thus we can analyse the relationship without embracing a behaviourist ontology. The relation between identity and interests is probably best conceptualized as *recursive*, following the logic of structure and agency.

A second point relates to the concept of state identity and the source of its change or stability which Wendt correctly locates in the inter-action process. The difficulty here is one which points up the problem of adopting the state actor as the unit of analysis. The state is a

---

[1] 'Interests are dependent on identities', Alexander Wendt, 'Collective identity formation and the international state', *American Political Science Review*, 88/2, 1994, p. 385.

collectivity, and collective identity-formation is an appropriate and necessary topic if we are to make sense of actions which flow from, and carry with them, the power and resources of the state. But it is not only the process of *state interaction with other states* in the international arena which provides the school of learning by which collective identity, relevant to foreign policy, is fashioned. It is also the domestic process of *state interaction with sub-state actors* which influences the sense of commonality brought to bear upon international relations. Wendt notes the distinction in passing,[2] but does not allow it any purchase on his theoretical development of the determinants of state identity. This allows the working assumption that sub-state relations have no bearing on the process by which states learn to mould and modify their sense of statehood. Furthermore, it implies that the identity acquired in and from the process of interstate negotiation is necessarily consistent with that which characterizes the collectivity domestically at any particular time. In the light of evidence to the contrary, this appears to assume too much.[3]

A third difficulty concerns the hard question of how a change of identity can be inferred from the only observable datum which indicates it: a change of behaviour. It should be noted that such an inference is critical to establishing Wendt's thesis against the alternative inference of neorealists. For Waltz and the contemporary exponents of his theory, the fact that states cooperate is not in question. Where they differ from Wendt is in their interpretation of cooperative behaviour. Clearly Waltz's primary assumption – that states are like units – rules out *a priori* the possibility of fundamental change in the identity or interests of the state. The interpretation of cooperative behaviour as strategic cooperation on the part of egoistic

---

[2] Wendt, 'Collective identity formation', p. 388 – 'I shall limit my focus to factors at the systemic level, even though domestic factors may matter, as well'. This self-imposed limitation is justified earlier in the same article, where Wendt refers to domestic roots of state identities as 'systemically exogenous' (p. 385). This is to postulate a logical barrier between domestic and systemic which is familiar in neorealist literature, but cannot be justified within a sociological account of the interaction process of state identity-formation. There is an intimate and interactive – one might say 'recursive' – dynamic between the process of negotiation which engages the state at the international level and the process of learning and negotiation at the domestic level which respects a sociological conception of the state as actor.

[3] Compare my comments below and in chapter 9 with Wendt's assumptions regarding domestic and state identities in Germany and Serbia in his 'Collective identity formation. . .' p. 387.

states, follows from that assumption. But it is equally plausible socio-logically to make the alternative assumption to which Wendt sub-scribes: that state identity is the dependent variable in respect of the process of interstate relations, capable of being modified through this process and of becoming, in turn, a source of change in state interests and behaviour. Since this does not eliminate the possibility of strategic cooperation between egoistic states, the problem is to grasp con-ceptually the difference between behavioural and identity change indicated empirically in some forms of cooperation as distinct from others.

Wendt does not explicitly address this and his implicit criterion for inferring a change of identity is inadequately argued. At several points in his discussion, time seems to be of the essence. For example, he writes that egoists learn to cooperate '. . . *over time*', '. . . *four decades* of cooperation may have transformed' the European states into a collective identity; the evolution of cooperation '. . . is *slow*'.[4] However, if forty years of bipolar state egoism during the Cold War is not long enough for anti-realists to succumb to the attractions of realism, it is hardly likely to convince neorealists that behaviour in the European Community, which to them looks strategic,[5] is really ema-nating from a transformed identity. Some stronger basis for making the inference is required.

David Campbell's deconstruction of security raises a difficulty similar to the first problem noted in regard to Wendt. It is not so much the causal direction of the relation of identity to interests which is problematic, as the absence of any substantive role for interests in the formation of identity. One can detect an implicit causal argument in Campbell's study – notwithstanding his evident awareness of post-modern sensitivities in that regard. The perception of crisis (never satisfactorily defined), related to the fissiparous character of American society, generates a critical reflection within the state leadership to repair the threatened solidarity by recourse to the images and dis-course of external threat. Thus, American security policy is driven by the impulse for a coherent identity.

If we think in terms of societal solidarity instead of 'identity', this conclusion seems somewhat commonplace, and it immediately

---

[4] Wendt, 'Collective identity formation', pp. 417 and 418 (my emphasis).
[5] Kenneth Waltz, *Theory of International Politics*, Addison-Wesley, Reading MA, 1979, pp. 70–71.

evokes other variables conventionally associated with the solidarity argument and other domestic determinants of enemy images. Since there is no reason to suppose that 'identity' does more work in Campbell's study than 'solidarity', there is no reason to exclude the obvious factor of domestic *interests* from playing a causal role in the generation of American solidarity or identity. Foremost among such interests, one must include the complex of military and defence-industrial pressures in relation to the perception of external threat and the demands for increased military expenditure and weaponry to meet it. Studies of the relation between industrial interests and threat perception in the United States, together with Campbell's account of the relation between threat perception and identity formation, leave little doubt – *pace* Wendt as well as Campbell – that interests play a mutually constitutive role with identity.[6]

Both Wendt and Campbell can be charged with missing the facts on the ground through their exaggeration of the identity factor. Identity theory can be defined as the grounding of analysis in the causal potential of collective identity to the exclusion of material factors. It provides the implicit assumption behind identity politics – the claim that collective identity constitutes the moral basis of collective action. It feeds on certain superficially obvious features of inter-community and international conflict. Among several contemporary problem areas, the conflicts in former Yugoslavia and in Northern Ireland are fertile ground for this tendency.

In the past three decades, academics and activists appear to have discovered the ease with which conflict can be reduced to a dispute about tribe, religion or national belonging. The term 'collective iden-tity', scarcely heard prior to the 1960s, today comes intuitively to mind to account for the anomalies and complexities of communal

---

[6] The literature on the so-called 'military-industrial complex' in the United States demonstrates the causal impact of motivational factors (interests) on cognitive (identity) in the competition between various sectors of the armed services, of the defence industries, and media interests. See Fred Kaplan, *The Wizards of Armageddon*, Simon and Schuster, New York, 1983. See also Mary Kaldor and A. Eide, *The World Military Order:The Impact of Military Technology on the 3rd World*, Macmillan, London, 1979; A. Eide and Marek Thee, *The Problems of Contemporary Militarism*, Croom Helm, London, 1980; J. K. Galbraith, *How to Control the Military*, Doubleday, New York, 1969; Robert H. Johnson, 'Periods of peril: the window of vulnerability and other myths', *Foreign Affairs*, 61/4, 1983.

confrontation.[7] Aside from the moral ambiguity involved in the rhetoric of universalist principles to achieve self-centred gains, identity theory ignores the question of interests without which we cannot explain the genesis and transformation of identity.

We cannot make sense of the Northern Ireland peace process, for example, by focusing on the introspection of the main collectivities involved. As in former Yugoslavia, Northern Ireland teems with collective memories and ancient myths, making it a fashionable hunting-ground for identity politics. The burden of ancestry and the discourse of the past which gives it currency in the contemporary conflict, together with the high degree of cultural, social and physical segregation of the two communities, has encouraged observers to lean more heavily on identity as an independent variable than the evidence warrants.

The evidence on the ground in the Northern Ireland peace process is awash with state and sub-state interests also, jostling with the cognitive elements of identity to push some actors in the direction of change and others towards the imagined community of the past. There is no explanation of why the nationalist community in the North or their nationalist brethren in the South should abandon their historic demand for a united Ireland, and why the southern nationalists should secularize so rapidly and break the bond between nationalism and Catholicism, unless material interests are factored into the analysis. Money, political influence and international pressure are teaching the actors in the peace process – some, perhaps, slower learners than others – that we can be who we want to be.

Perhaps the most glaring failure of identity theory to explain the facts is evident in its application to European integration. Since the end of the Cold War, a literary industry has flourished on the real or illusory existence of a European identity and on the question of multiple identities coexisting with it.[8] Encouraged by the need of the

---

[7] 'Identity' has only one entry in International Encyclopaedia of 1968 and that is about psychosocial identity, by Erik Erikson. 'Ethnicity' in the Oxford English Dictionary of the same period is regarded as a rare word meaning 'heathendom'. See Eric Hobsbawm, 'Identity politics and the Left', *New Left Review*, 1996, pp. 38–47.

[8] For a sample, see David Bell (ed.), *The Development of the European Idea Since the Middle Ages*, Dartmouth, Aldershot, 1995; Gerard Delanty, *Inventing Europe: Idea, Identity, Reality*, Macmillan, London, 1995; Soledad Garcia (ed.), *European Identity and the Search for Legitimacy*, London, 1993; Sharon Macdonald (ed.), *Inside European Identities: Ethnography in Western Europe*, 1997; Anthony Smith, 'A Europe of nations – or the nation of Europe?', *Journal of Peace Research*, 30/2, 1993, pp. 129–135; Larry Wolff,

Community itself to make sense of its aspiration to embrace the whole continent, and by the vogue for identity politics following the emergence of newly independent states in Eastern Europe seeking to discard the identity imposed on them by their former links with the Soviet Union, this literature shows a similar tendency to cultural determinism to that displayed by Wendt and Campbell.

The empirical evidence of the strategy and practices involved in the construction of European integration gives the lie to two different kinds of identity theory and politics: that which treats identity as given in more or less essentialist or primordialist form – as in Waever *et al.*'s analysis of what they call 'the new security agenda in Europe' (discussed in chapter 4) – and that which accepts the malleability of identity as a social construct, but ignores the equally central place of interests in security perceptions and policy, in the manner of Wendt and Campbell. In the building of the European Community, the aim has always been to reconstruct the identity of the state and other key actors. But the primary means of achieving this – and the practical concern of policy-makers and bureaucrats – has always been focused primarily on interests. By transforming the practice of interest-definition through the medium of practical cooperation, it was held, collective actors would learn to transform their self-definition. This, in turn, would facilitate the upgrading of interest from self to community in a reflexive dynamic.

This duality of interests and identity has an intuitive appeal arising from commonsense understanding of their mutual constitution in everyday life.[9] It has also provided the basis for a formal theory of integration which can here be reinterpreted to refine the social constructionist school in general.

An alternative turn to sociology

The approach in question is not one which readily comes to mind in surveying the application of the sociology of knowledge to security problems, for reasons which should become clear in the course of these theoretical chapters. In its classical formulation, it belongs to the

---

Inventing Eastern Europe: The Map of Civilization on the Mind of the Enlightenment, Cambridge University Press, Cambridge, 1996.

[9] A more formal, philosophical discussion of this duality will be presented in chapter 9, while the derivation of a theory of collective behaviour from analysis of everyday life will be discussed in the following chapter.

school of neoliberalism, and its epistemological preferences lie firmly within the boundaries of positivism. It is important in this context, however, because it was formulated to provide an account of the emergence of a particular security policy – the security community of the EC; because an implicit sociology of knowledge can be discerned in its approach to interests and identity which provides a contrast with the works discussed above, and because its key conceptual innovation – the concept of spillover – can be employed to less positivistic ends than its theoretical progenitors imagined.

Neofunctionalism, the best-known and most elegant attempt to explain European integration, was neglected for over two decades before its qualified revival in 1989. First developed in the early 1950s, it offered an attractive alternative to the realist focus on the autonomy of the state.[10]

The theory is centred on the idea of spillover, the structural mechanism which supplies it with powerful explanatory and predictive promise. Integration is driven by a logic which Haas defined as the consequence of 'policies made pursuant to an initial task and grant of power [which] can be made real only if the task itself is expanded'.[11] This 'expansive logic of integration', as he called it, is activated by the trigger of spillover.

As integration progressed at the technical-economic level towards greater complexity, the technical spillover described would prove inadequate to the problems encountered and would yield to the demand of interest groups for a higher level of political control at the centre. Functional spillover would cause political spillover, which Haas defined as:

> the process whereby political actors in several distinct national settings *are persuaded* to shift their loyalties, expectations and political activities towards a new centre, whose institutions possess or demand jurisdiction over the pre-existing national states.[12]

(My emphasis underlines a voluntaristic element which coexisted with determinism in the early formulation of the theory.) Unlike

---

[10] The principal texts of the neofunctionalist school include Ernst Haas, *The Uniting of Europe: Political, Social, and Economic Forces,* Stanford University Press, Stanford, 1958; L.N. Lindberg, *The Political Dynamics of European Economic Integration,* Stanford University Press, Stanford, 1963.

[11] Ernst Haas, 'International integration: the European and the universal process', in *International Organization,* 15, 1961, p. 368; Lindberg, *The Political Dynamics,* p. 10.

[12] Haas, *The Uniting of Europe,* p. 16 (my emphasis).

traditional negotiations between states, which produce agreement on the basis of minimum common denominator, neofunctionalists saw integration proceeding on the basis of upgrading the interests common to member-states: problems of cooperation in one sector would stimulate cooperation in others.[13] This gradual expansion of tasks, enmeshing the participating states ineluctably into an ever-tighter web of integration, depended on the key role of the Commission in managing the process to that end.

Neofunctionalism provided a seductive and powerful way of grasping the complexities of integration in the early years of enthusiasm for the project. Instead of identifying the unit actors as the source of integration in the manner of classical diplomatic analysis, or the structure of the international system in the way of neorealism, it attributed causal power to the process of interaction itself. Cooperation created a learning process in which state actors, constrained by the existing web of relationships in which their interests were engaged, learned to identify themselves and their interests with higher levels of cooperation. Non-state actors, in particular the Commission, played a vital management role in the process, ensuring that spillover and the reconstruction of state interests and identity were progressive and incremental. The theory attempted to explain how incentives for personal gain at different levels of society could be managed by covert forces to bring about the consequence of integration, conditional upon voluntary acceptance of a change of identity. Despite the hints of voluntarism noted above, there is a strong tone of determinism in the account of the neofunctionalists, notwithstanding some reservations expressed by its leading theorists.[14] The weight of tight, formal analysis, and the general scientific objectivism of the theory made neofunctionalism hostage to the facts which it purported to explain, and gave to it an economic determinism which helped to bring down the whole intellectual edifice in the early 1970s. The proposition that a 'functional logic . . . may lead, more or less automatically, from a common market to political unification'[15] was not working by the end of the 1970s, when the Community had

---

[13] P.C. Schmitter, 'Three neofunctionalist hypotheses about international integration', *International Organization*, 23, 1969, pp. 162ff.
[14] Haas, *The Uniting of Europe*; Lindberg, *The Political Dynamics*.
[15] Ernst Haas, 'The uniting of Europe and the uniting of Latin America', *Journal of Common Market Studies*, 5/4, 1967, pp. 324/325.

patently not responded to the economic and political challenges in the manner predicted.

Neofunctionalist spillover reflects an over-socialized conception of state behaviour. States become the cultural dupes of the integration process, parallel to the individual actor *vis-à-vis* the central value system in the theory of structural functionalism, fashionable in sociology in the heyday of neofunctionalism. Just as Parsons and Berger and Luckmann, following Durkheim, trapped human agency in a structural scheme intended to emancipate it, so the sociology of knowledge implicit in neofunctionalism made collective actors the puppets of a cognitive and material structure in which interests were learned and identities refashioned almost mechanically.

For almost two decades following the decline of neofunctionalist theory, attempts to account for European integration took an atheoretical turn under the label of 'intergovernmentalism', a term employed, for the most part, as shorthand for the rejection of any theory which purported to explain the integration process as a whole, and as justification for the enterprise of piecemeal, empirical analysis.[16] It was only with the dramatic and quite unanticipated progress towards the achievement of the internal market in 1988/1989 that theorists revisited and revived elements of the discredited neofunctionalism.[17]

Elegant and sparse neofunctionalism may be, but it is perhaps too sparse, too simple, and certainly too deterministic, to account for the complex pressures which attend the building of an integrated community. In three respects, however, it draws attention to key features of the European phenomenon it was intended to explain and provides elements of a general theory of the ordering of social life which is relevant to our understanding of security and security policy.

The theory emphasizes interests almost to the neglect of identity, in contrast to Wendt and Campbell. In still sharper contrast to the shades of rationalism which make up the dominant tradition of neorealist descent, it does not take interests as given and unproblematic, but

---

[16] Carole Webb, 'Theoretical perspectives and problems', in Helen Wallace, William Wallace and Carole Webb (eds.), *Policy-making in the European Community*, 2nd edition, Wiley, Chichester, 1983, pp. 1–42. For criticism of this trend see Robert O. Keohane and Stanley Hoffman, 'Conclusions: community politics and institutional change', in William Wallace (ed.), *The Dynamics of European Integration*, Pinter, London, 1990, p. 284.

[17] Wayne Sandholtz and John Zysman, '1992: recasting the European bargain', *World Politics*, 42/1, 1989, pp. 1–30. See also Keohane and Hoffman, 'Conclusions', p. 289.

underscores their social construction. In Wendt's terminology, interests are endogenous, not exogenous to the process of social interaction. Interests are problematized in neofunctionalism in the sense that it conceives of collective actors coming to the school of interaction to learn and relearn – 'upgrade' in the jargon – what the sectoral or national interest is, rather than assuming it as a given in the manner of neorealism.

Secondly, the neofunctionalist view of collective identity-formation has an inner and outer dimension which respects the duality of identity observable in the real world. States learn to become cooperative or egoistic entities through the interaction with others of their representatives and bureaucratic delegates. But these are not free-floating individuals who transcend the complex business of domestic affairs. As Moravcsik insists, governments learn what is in the national interest through their interaction with sub-state groups.[18] The Danish government discovered to its cost at Maastricht that a domestic process of interest- and identity-formation had been going on which was at odds with the image of the state formulated by the political and business elites in the international sphere. The Irish government discovered, to its benefit, that a domestic process of secularization, independent of state management, had blunted the edges of egoism *viv-à-vis* the Unionist population of Northern Ireland to facilitate the peace process which led to the Belfast Agreement with Britain in 1998. In West Germany, the business of marrying the inner and outer dimensions of identity by managing domestic opinion in tandem with a transformation of the state's new international relations was remarkably successful until the end of the Cold War. The reunification of Germany put the core relationship with France on a more voluntaristic basis, however, placing in question the continued harmony between inner and outer spheres of learning. Identity-formation at the domestic level was always a feature of the neofunctionalist model which was regarded as critical to the success of the integration process. What was sometimes called 'informal' or 'cultural' integration[19] represented the attempt to promote domestically that transfer of loyalties and allegiances vital to the success of

---

[18] Andrew Moravcsik, 'Preferences and power in the European Community: a liberal intergovernmentalist approach', *Journal of Common Market Studies*, 31/4, 1993; 'Negotiating the Single European Act', in Robert O. Keohane and Stanley Hoffman (eds.), *The New European Community*, Westview Press, Boulder, 1991.

[19] William Wallace, *The Transformation of Western Europe*, Pinter, London, 1990.

European integration and critical to the triggering of political spillover.

The third point on which neofunctionalism offers a pointer to a richer conception of theory relevant to security policy concerns the central concept of spillover. As argued above, the deterministic application of spillover within the neofunctionalist literature exposed the theory inescapably to falsification by the facts. Theorists cannot play the game of determinism in the social sphere without revealing their vulnerability to the related game of empirical validation. But spillover can be reinterpreted to illuminate the dynamics of social action in a philosophically more interesting and empirically more satisfactory way.

All three approaches considered here display the constructionist approach which marks the sociological turn in international relations depicted in the previous chapter, even if the lineage of only one – that of Wendt – is clearly located in a self-styled sociological literature. The idea of spillover will be revisited in chapter 9 in order to integrate it in a reflexive theoretical framework for the analysis of security and its related concepts of identity and interests. Before addressing theory, however, the philosophical basis of a reflexive sociology must be clarified, bringing together several points already made in commenting on the various scholars who have contributed to clarifying the social constructionist approach. This is the task to which we now turn.

8 Agency and structure in social theory

That social structures are the product of social practices and, at the same time, the medium by which such practices are made possible is the insight derived from the confluence of philosophical and socio-logical perspectives in opposition to naturalism in sociology, brought together and formalized under the ugly label of 'structuration theory'.[1]

Within this literature, a central figure and the principal source of the ideas which follow is Anthony Giddens. His vast output has been overtaken by the quantity of critical literature addressed to it, mostly to his body of social theory published since 1976.[2] I am primarily

---

[1] For references see fn. 4 and 8 below. Among the theorists who have independently developed a 'structurationist' account of social action – though none as systematic as Giddens – are Alain Touraine, *The Self Production of Society*, University of Chicago Press, Chicago, 1977; Pierre Bourdieu, *The Logic of Practice*, Polity Press, Cambridge, 1990, and Roy Bhaskar, *The Possibility of Naturalism: A Philosophical Critique of Contemporary Human Science*, Harvester, Brighton, 1979.

[2] Giddens's principal writings on structuration theory are *New Rules of Sociological Method*, 1st edition, Hutchinson, London, 1976; 2nd edition Polity Press, Cambridge, 1993; *Central Problems in Social Theory*, Macmillan, London, 1979; *The Constitution of Society: Outline of the Theory of Structuration*, Polity Press, Cambridge, 1984; *Social Theory and Modern Sociology*, Polity Press, Cambridge, 1987; *Modernity and Self-Identity: Self and Society in the Late Modern Age*, Cambridge University Press, Cambridge 1991. Among commentaries and critical works, see Jon Clark, Celia Modgil and Sohan Modgil (eds.), *Anthony Giddens: Consensus and Controversy*, Falmer Press, Brighton 1990; Ira Cohen, *Structuration Theory: Anthony Giddens and the Constitution of Social Life*, Macmillan, London, 1989; Ian Craib, *Anthony Giddens*, London, 1992; Mark Haugaard, *Structures, Restructuration and Social Power*, Avebury, Aldershot, 1992; Christopher Bryant and David Jary (eds.), *Giddens' Theory of Structuration: A Critical Appreciation*, Routledge, London, 1991; David Held and John B. Thompson (eds.), *Social Theory of Modern Societies: Anthony Giddens and his Critics*, Cambridge University Press, Cambridge, 1989.

concerned with the application and extension of core concepts of his structuration theory to a theory of security. In this chapter I attempt to outline these concepts briefly, and in terms accessible to readers less familiar with the literature. In the following chapter, I shall apply this theoretical framework to the question of security and its relationship with identity.

Elements of social action

The novelty of a structuration, or reflexivist, theory of social action lies in the relationship it postulates between the agency of the unit actor and the structure which makes agency possible, constraining it and facilitating it at the same time. Against subjectivism which denies the constraint of structure in favour of the dominion of the subject, social action must be understood to take place within a framework of habit, or routine, not randomly in some process of creative imagination. We do not, and cannot, communicate meaning without the framework of rules and resources which enable us to do so and which simultaneously limit the performance of what we do. It is this limitation on our creativity which provides the basis of the predictability of human behaviour. But this regularity, or predictability, is also at the root of the misunderstanding of structure in objectivist perspectives, which reify the framework of rules and resources as an *independent* object capable of causing its dependent effect – social action.

We can distinguish structure from agency for the purpose of analysis, but each is realized and made actual in and through the other. We cannot conceive of one without the other, just as we cannot conceive of language (structure) without speech (linguistic act). Language exists only in the instances of speech. It is not *caused* by speech in a sense which logically entails the relation of dependence between two separable entities, and ontologically entails the reduction of structure to act. Nor is speech caused by language, in the obverse form of misinterpretation. Language is instantiated by, or constituted in, speech – rather as (in the metaphor of Bauman) the wind exists only in its blowing, or the river in its flowing.[3]

---

[3] Zymunt Bauman, 'Hermeneutics and modern social theory', in David Held and John B. Thompson (eds.), *Social Theory of Modern Societies: Anthony Giddens and his Critics*, Cambridge University Press, Cambridge, 1989, p. 44.

Reflexivity and the monitoring of routine

The idea of a 'reflexive' theory is grounded in the reflexiveness of its basic datum: social action. Actors monitor their own and others' behaviour, not as isolated acts but as instances of shared understanding of how to make sense. Their monitoring, however, is not just a passive check on the consistency of behaviour with given rules and standards, as might be the case in playing a formal game of cards, or chess. It is strategic monitoring, in which the exercise of power in accomplishing interaction, or the application of sanctions in legitimizing a modification or departure from standards, is part of the normal achievement of individuals and collectivities in their everyday relations with others. As Garfinkel and Goffman have shown, far from being passive receptors and reproducers of an assumed consensus about meaning and norms, actors draw strategically upon such consensus to establish agreement, to lie, to seduce, to dissimulate, to repair a relationship or to end one at least cost – in short, they manage the rules which make the game of interaction possible, with the resources at their disposal, and regenerate them in so doing.

The idea of reflexivity is best understood in its technical meaning within new developments in social theory, rather than loosely employed to denote interplay between subjective and objective dimensions of theorizing. This is not always clarified in constructionist and post-positivist writings on international relations, where 'reflexive' and 'reflective' are interchanged as if they were synonyms. This is a misuse which Robert Keohane has handed on, labelling as 'reflective' that body of theory which he sees as interpretative and constructionist.[4]

Social action is reflexive: this does not refer to the self-conscious and deliberate *reflection* on self, of which most actors are capable to varying degree. It refers, rather, to the unconscious and taken-for-granted skill which all display of necessity, in drawing on and producing the routine which makes action comprehensible to oneself and to others. It is a basic error to mistake this capacity for the

---

[4] Robert Keohane, 'International institutions: two approaches', *International Institutions and State Power: Essays in International Relations Theory*, Westview, Boulder, 1989, p. 161; see also Ole Waever, 'The rise and fall of the inter-paradigm debate', in Steve Smith, Ken Booth and Marysio Zalewski (eds.), p. 164; see also the editors' usage in Sjolander Claire Turenne and Wayne S. Cox (eds.), *Beyond Positivism: Critical Reflections on International Relations*, Lynne Rienner, London, 1994.

conscious, intellectual act of self-reflection, in which the self becomes an object of inquiry. Social life is only practically possible because we are *not* normally reflective, not normally aware of our monitoring of how to do it.[5]

It is in this sense of the reflexivity of social action that we must understand social theory as reflexive. A reflexive social theory is one which respects the monitoring of social practices as a fundamental datum of all social action. What actors are doing in monitoring the practices by which they 'do' action, theorists are doing in checking on, and recirculating, knowledge back into the world observed. This underlines the central importance of the idea which Giddens terms the 'double hermeneutic' – discussed below – for our understanding of the different world which social theory confronts in contrast to natural science, and which a reflexive theory offers in place of a naturalistic political science. It is not mutual interplay between facts and values, theory and practice, the thinking subject and the self, which is at issue here, but the chronic, irremediable instability of social concepts and the social order.

To illustrate in respect of the social constructionists already considered: there is no sense of reflexivity in the social theory of Durkheim and Berger and Luckmann. The actor's skill in managing or manipulating the social practices which are the carriers of routine is eliminated in the constraint predicated on 'role', 'internalization' and 'objectivation'; the theory reflects a world which differs from the natural order only in the cognitive elements of its structure. David Campbell, on the other hand, sees a reflexive world in which actors monitor significant elements of the everyday practices which are coded in foreign policy.

The routines and 'predictability' of life provide the essential order without which social action would be literally impossible. Just as we can only communicate verbally in any instance of time by drawing on the 'routines' and 'habits' of language outside these temporal boundaries, so we can only communicate socially in a concrete situation through the medium of existing structures of meaning transcending the immediate temporal boundaries of that situation. Just as language

---

[5] For the technical meaning of reflexivity see Harold Garfinkel, *Studies in Ethnomethodology*, Prentice Hall, New Jersey, 1967, p. 8; Ulrich Beck, 'The reinvention of politics: towards a theory of reflexive modernization', in Ulrich Beck *et al.*, *Reflexive Modernization: Politics, Tradition and Aesthetics in the Modern Social Order*, Polity Press, Cambridge, 1994, pp. 5–8; Giddens, *The Constitution of Society*, pp. 41–45.

is recreated, reproduced and modified unintentionally in usage, in repeated acts of speech, so with social structure in its relation to social action.

The sameness of human behaviour, its pattern, regularity, routineness – these terms capture the sense of 'order' in the concept of social order – is not something external to behaviour. It only exists in – is constituted in – the agency of individuals, acting in their own right or standing for collectivities of individuals.

This does not mean that the mutual knowledge, norms or resources which make action possible and repetitive – which enable and constrain – are always consciously available to actors in their reflexive monitoring of action. Actors are knowledgeable and skilled performers, without necessarily being able to give an account of what they are knowledgeable and skilled about. They know how things are done, how to get along, how to manage or 'do' complex tasks of sociability[6] without adverting to, or even being able to discourse on, the extent or basis of their competence. Everyday life for individuals and bureaucracies would be impossible if it depended on conscious recovery of the cognitive patterns which we call 'structure'. Furthermore, unconscious factors related to the interests which stimulate action, and unintended consequences of past actions, add an unknowable dimension to structure which it is not within the competence of the acting subject, by definition, to explain. Understanding the social order cannot be achieved simply by getting agents to account for their behaviour or by getting professional theorists to ignore the accounts of agents in favour of a reified structural determinacy. It can only mean respecting the reflexivity whereby social action is accomplished as the monitoring of habit in the presence of others, as the presentation of self in communication with others, as the regeneration of the very structural elements which make it possible. Routine, or institutionalized habits, is what makes social action possible and is, at the same time, the product of action and the creature of human agency.

---

[6] The term 'doing', for Garfinkel, captures the reflexive character of interaction, whereby it is managed and presented by actors as a social accomplishment in the performance of the act. Harold Garfinkel, *Studies*, p. 1. To 'do' social action also denotes the active sense of the term 'social practices', much in use in constructionist schools of IR. This is further discussed in chapter 10.

The duality of structure

Agency and structure are two sides of the same ontological coin, not two entities either of which can be accorded priority over the other *a priori*. Empirically, however, it is clear that configurations of material power, status, or communicative skills on the part of individuals or collectivities can be used to reinforce or to modify the common norms and meanings which bear upon action in a manner which constrains more than it enables, leaving some with less options than others. But this, to repeat, is an empirical question. It is the *a priori* assumption of the priority of structure over agency that feeds the impulse to bifurcate the social order into two separate entities in the characteristic perspective of objectivism. This entails a reification of a dimension of social action which can only analytically be conceived. To claim that structure 'determines', 'influences', or 'shapes' behaviour may be an acceptable figure of speech if it is clearly limited to the sense in which language constitutes speech and is, in the act, reproduced by it.

Agency and structure are misconceived in objectivist approaches to social theorizing as separate entities in a relationship of opposition. Structure is *used* by actors to produce meaningful conduct and, in that moment, it is drawn into the temporal, contextual dimension of action, thus to be reinforced and modified by 'usage' and repetition. In so doing, in adopting a mutually intelligible framework for interaction, actors subject themselves to the constraint of behaving within the confines of habit. Our assumption as observers of social behaviour that the confines of habit function as a force 'external' to action, in some quasi-physical sense, closes off the possibility of understanding social change in terms of the logically necessary part played by human agency.

This does not imply a subjectivism of agency against structure, or the idea that social change is grounded only in the intentional and conscious cognition of the actor. It is to say that the social order – and change in the social order – is rooted in cognition. If Spaniards stop believing in the conflict with ETA, westerners in the conflict with the Soviet Union, and British with the IRA, these conflicts are over. They do not depend simply on the deployment of material forces, but on the ideas and beliefs held in respect of such forces. Denuded of cognitive elements, material forces are simply matter.

Actors' intentions alone cannot guarantee the redefining of material forces, since it is clear that unintended consequences can, and often do, feed into the structure of relations in a manner quite opposed to the intentions of actors. The intention of liberalizing international trade can generate the conditions for greater inequality and result in trade wars; the intention of building a protection against poverty can result in a culture of dependency; the disparate intentions of state actors to protect immediate interests resulted in World War I which no one intended. Each of these changes in social structure resulted in new social conditions which became constraints on future behaviour, and which cannot be traced back without surplus to the intentions or consciousness of agents acting to procure such change. It must be emphasized that structural constraints include factors of which the agent may have no knowledge whatever, either because they represent an unconscious dimension of interests or the recursive pressure of unintended consequences, which can only be inferred by social scientific, institutional, analysis.

But neither can they be traced to factors *external* to agency. It is not a barrier to our understanding of the influence of unintended consequences on social action that we grasp the reasons which actors attribute to behaviour. This is a condition of being able to formulate any theory whatever about social behaviour, including the description of action and the identification of unintended consequences. Human agency and the structuring element of routine, the reflexive monitoring of which makes agency possible, are mutually constituted – not as cause and effect recursively being transformed into effect and cause, in the model of functionalism[7], but as a duality of 'instantiation'. (Giddens's 'duality of structure' could equally be analysed as a duality of agency or a duality of agency and structure. Each represents a different focus on the manner in which analytically separate elements of action are produced and reproduced in and through occasions or instances of action.)

To say that it is a condition of understanding human behaviour as a professional theorist that we grasp how actors understand it, how they know what they are doing, is to state the obvious. We can only generate generalized descriptions of action by inference from actors' accounts given of particular action. Without any means of knowing, assuming, or guessing how actors understand what they do, we could

---

[7] In the classic mould, see, for example, Robert K. Merton, *Social Theory and Social Structure*, Free Press, Glencoe, 1957; Arthur L. Stinchcombe, *Constructing Social Theories*, Harcourt Brace and World, New York, 1968.

never make sense of action in order to recognize regularity and pattern and elaborate propositional knowledge about it. Action must be credible in relation to agents' beliefs if it is to be meaningful to the observer. The cultural alien cannot begin to describe, much less to elaborate theory about, the behaviour of others. (This has implications for our understanding of security and security policy which will be discussed below.)

The double hermeneutic

The ordinary lay actor, as the unit of social theory, differs fundamentally from the unit of physical science in that he or she is a practical social theorist. The qualification 'practical' highlights the sense in which lay skills and knowledge are brought to bear on the situations of interaction: not the intellectual skills and discursive knowledge of professional theorists, but the practical skills and knowledge of how to get on in the complex variety of social life. From Schutz and Wittgenstein, through Goffman and Garfinkel, the awareness of the character and significance of practical knowledge for the understanding of social action has been brought to the forefront of social theory.[8] Ethnomethodology, the school of theory derived from the seminal work of Harold Garfinkel in 1967, was a radical statement of the subjectivist approach in opposition to the structural functionalism then reigning in the sociological academy. The centrality of everyday life and intersubjective meaning to our grasp of the social order, for Schutz, was taken further by Garfinkel with his stress on the continuity between professional and lay theorizing: the role of the analyst is to understand the 'methods' by which 'ethnie' (lay actors) make sense of – theorize about – daily life as the bedrock of the social order.[9] What lay actors do in accomplishing the social order is essentially no different from what professionals studying lay actors do, with the critical qualification that orthodox social science is not reflexive of its

---

[8] Harold Garfinkel, *Studies*, pp. 1ff. Garfinkel's principal intellectual mentors were his Harvard professor Talcott Parsons and the school of phenomenology associated with Edmund Husserl and Alfred Schutz. Ethnomethodology's radical departure from mainstream sociology was mostly influenced by Ludwig Wittgenstein, *Philosophical Investigations*, Blackwell, Oxford, 1968; Peter Winch, *The Idea of a Social Science*, Routledge, London, 1958; Alfred Schutz, *The Phenomenology of the Social World*, London, 1972.

[9] Harold Garfinkel, *Studies*, pp. 1ff.

own methods as lay actors are. On the contrary, it views the conceptualization of the social order by social scientists – what Garfinkel calls 'second-order' theorizing – as belonging to a different and superior order of knowledge to the first-order theorizing of common sense.[10] And lay actors are not generally as reflec*tive* of their methods as are professionals, but this does not disqualify them as theorists.

We can see the originality and the deconstructionist impulse in ethnomethodology, by contrast with the approach of Berger and Luckmann, in its emphasis on process, and on conceptual and institutional 'facts' of the social order as the accomplishment of 'members' (lay actors in Garfinkel's terminology). Against orthodox sociology's urge to freeze action and to assume the stability of the object for purposes of objective analysis and explanatory generalization, ethnomethodology understands action as a process in time, drawing its meaning from the temporal and spatial setting.

> Where others might see 'things', 'givens', or 'facts of life', the ethnomethodologist sees (or attempts to see) *process*: the process through which the perceivedly stable features of socially organized environments are continually created and sustained.[11]

The setting of action constitutes its context within which – and only within which, for ethnomethodologists of the earlier school – the meaning of action is revealed. In this sense, all social action is irremediably contextual, or 'indexical', to use the term which Garfinkel borrowed from linguistics.

The criticism, even opprobrium, heaped on ethnomethodology during the first decade of its growth was based as much on fear of its sectarian challenge to established perspectives in sociology as on considered judgment of its challenge to objectivism.[12] What has endured, in the gradual adjustments on both sides of the academic divide, is a growing acknowledgment of the creativity of the human agent in the construction of the social order and of the routine interaction between the lay concepts of social reality and those formulations of it which constitute professional practice.

Giddens adopted from ethnomethodology the key hermeneutic

---

[10] Harold Garfinkel, *Studies*; George Psathas, 'Ethnomethods and phenomenology', *Social Research*, 35, 1968, pp. 500–520.

[11] Melvin Pollner, 'Sociological and common-sense models of the labelling process', in Ralph Turner (ed.), *Ethnomethodology*, Penguin, Harmondsworth, 1974, p. 27.

[12] Jonathan H. Turner, *The Structure of Sociological Theory*, 5th edition, Wadsworth, Belmont CA, 1991, pp. 485/486.

point that 'lay actors are concept-bearing beings, whose concepts enter constitutively into what they do'.[13] It follows as a practical implication for professional observers that social science concepts are parasitic on those of the actors under observation. To discover what an actor does logically requires knowing what an actor knows.

> All social science is irretrievably hermeneutic in the sense that to be able to describe 'what someone is doing' in any given context means knowing what the agent or agents themselves know, and apply, in the constitution of their activities.[14]

But he makes the critical amendment to Garfinkel in his coining of the concept of the 'double hermeneutic'. Whereas Garfinkel and the ethnomethodologists, drawing on Schutz, Winch and Wittgenstein, correctly identified the logical barrier to naturalistic and objectivist inquiry in the practical skills and knowledgeability of the social actor, they closed off the world of social action from the influences of power and the unintended consequences of action which are, by definition, outside the agent's frame of knowledge and control.

Giddens defines the double hermeneutic as 'a mutual interpretative interplay between social science and those whose activities compose its subject matter'.[15] It must be understood in contrast to the single hermeneutical task of the natural scientist, who interprets and studies data which are not constructing themselves in the manner of the observer. The idea of the 'double hermeneutic' serves to balance the dependence of sociological observers on the theorizing of actors which constitutes the social order – as Garfinkel noted – with the converse 'slippage' and the dependence of actors on the discourse of theorists:

> Sociological observers depend upon lay concepts to generate accurate descriptions of social processes; and agents regularly appropriate theories and concepts of social science within their behaviour, thus potentially changing its character. This introduces an instability into sociological theorizing which inevitably takes it some distance from the 'cumulative and uncontested' model that naturalistically-inclined sociologists have in mind.[16]

Thus, he argues, it is not due to a deficiency of objectivity or of the

---

[13] Anthony Giddens, *New Rules*, p. 13.   [14] *Ibid.*
[15] Anthony Giddens, *The Constitution of Society*, p. xxxii.
[16] Anthony Giddens, 'Nine theses on the future of sociology', *Social Theory and Modern Sociology*, Polity Press, Cambridge, 1987, pp. 30/31.

control of complex variables – either of which is corrigible, in principle – that professional observers of the social order cannot achieve the standard set by objectivist schools of theory. It is due to the chronic instability of a social world, cognitively constituted, in which lay and professional concepts spill erratically into each other's domain, making the observer's access to an independent object of inquiry a chimera. This offers a different and more radical interpretation of the idea of the value- or theory-saturation of reality than that espoused by Cox or Berger and Luckmann.[17]

The task of the professional theorist is profoundly complicated by contrast with that of the natural scientist, whose object of inquiry is relatively stable. The response of the social science objectivist is to regard this instability of the social order as an irritation, a marginal complication which can be ignored, or disposed of in a *ceteris paribus* assumption. But such instability is not a barrier; *it is the key to understanding social action* and to explaining the self-evident fact that we can never succeed in generating the kind of stable explanations of human behaviour espoused by objectivists aspiring to cumulative knowledge – such as the practitioners of the security studies orthodoxy reviewed in chapter 2 – which can be transformed into a strategy of control. Social science and the behaviour viewed as its 'object' are recursive; like the duality of structure and agency, and for the same reasons, *social theory and social action are analytically distinct moments of the same reality.*

By way of example of conceptual spillover from professional to lay usage, one might cite the technical notion of alienation, which has become adopted as a lay idea used to organize urban life,[18] or the manner in which theories of sovereignty arose from the study of social trends into which they were, in turn, fed back. As Giddens writes, our

---

[17] Gillian Slovo, *Every Secret Thing: My Family, My Country,* Little, Brown, 1996. Gillian Slovo elegantly recounts her discovery of the chronic instability of the social order. After searching to make sense of the disparate events in the lives of her famous anti-Apartheid parents, Ruth First and Joe Slovo, Gillian finally discovers a philosophical truth about human agency and its interpretation:

> I'd realized that memory, experience, interpretation could never be fixed or frozen into one, unchanging truth. They kept on moving, relentlessly metamorphosing into something other so that the jagged edges of each fragment would never, ever slot together.

[18] Richard Kilminster, 'Structuration theory as a world-view', in Bryant Christopher and David Jary (eds.), *Giddens' Theory of Structuration: A Critical Appreciation,* Routledge, London, 1991, p. 81.

modern sovereign state necessarily incorporates 'a discursively articulated theory of the modern sovereign state'.[19]

The double hermeneutic reveals the element of human autonomy which escapes determination by structure conceived as external to agency. Ethnomethodology's insight into one side of the conceptual slippage – from the theorizing of the agent to the second-order theorizing of the observer – exaggerates the autonomy of the subject, but has contributed to reinstating the balance of autonomy and constraint logically present in all social interaction: social scientific knowledge is parasitic on the knowledgeability and skills of human agents, who construct, sustain, and modify the social order which provides the data for the models of social scientists. It is through grasping the double hermeneutic of the social order that we understand the place of self-fulfilling prophecy in international relations theory, which will be further discussed below.

The state as actor

We misunderstand the international order if we consider it as an object *sui generis*, set apart by its own logic from domestic society and from the social order in general. We can speak of collective decisions, or state intentions or policy, but this can only be understood as a shorthand way of referring to decisions and policy formulated by individuals in a certain representative capacity in relation to others. There are laws, rules, norms, applicable to states and their conduct which set them apart from other collectivities and individuals. But there is no logic governing their behaviour or generalizations which can explain it apart from the logic and practices which pertain to individuals in the different modes of individuality or positions which they occupy in society. For example 'anarchy' relates to a structural condition which only makes sense for states because it makes sense for individuals. It is individuals who bestow on states the apparent peculiarity of the properties which structure state relations – properties which are meaningful only because they are not peculiar to states. Like 'intention', 'purpose', 'rationality', the qualities of 'sovereignty', 'security' and 'self-help' must first be grasped as images of human behaviour frozen in time and space to make them susceptible to analysis.

---

[19] Giddens, *The Constitution of Society*, p. xxxiii.

It follows from the analysis of social action as purposive, reflexive, monitored, routinized, that collective actors, including states, cannot strictly be agents. It makes sense, however, and for some purposes is essential, to treat the state and other collectivities as unit actors, as if they were agents. Their action is subject to the same logical and sociological analysis as that of individuals or other collectivities.

It makes sense to speak of states as if they were agents when the agency of individuals in a representative capacity carries the allocative and authorititative resources of the state with it. The power of a business tycoon, like Rupert Murdoch, rests not just on whatever personal skills he may bring to interaction, but on his control of wealth and property and on the norms by which we accord him this control. His interaction with other individuals is clearly qualified by his greater power to reward or punish than that possessed by others. In such interaction, he is partly a collectivity – representing the combined interests of his shareholders – and partly an individual in his own right. It would make no sense to ignore the power which his resources give him and to analyse his interaction with others as if it were simply the unproblematic communication of one individual with his peers.[20] It therefore makes every sense to speak of Murdoch's action as the intersection of an individual and a collectivity: that of an individual with exceptional command over collective resources.

Similarly, it would make no sense to ignore the resources which the agency of individuals, charged with state leadership, bring to bear on interaction with others. Margaret Thatcher was a powerful individual in her own right. To say that Britain committed itself at the Milan Summit in 1985 to the signing of the Single European Act is to adopt a shorthand for the behaviour of Thatcher and many other individuals, whose actions entered into a causal nexus which ended with the signature of the British Prime Minister. Uncovering the number and degree of influence of the individuals involved is a complex research problem, but we can assume that the action is not the aggregate of individual decisions embracing the population of the United Kingdom. In that sense, we can – and must for some purposes – adopt the shorthand of describing the action as that of the state. Only under that description does the action at Milan carry the power which

[20] It is the major failing of subjectivist schools of social analysis like ethnomethodology and the 'symbolic interactionism' of George Herbert Mead that they treat social action only at the level of communication of meaning, and ignore factors of power and the constraints of habit not immediately present to the acting individuals.

Thatcher as representative brought to it, and which an aggregation of all individuals represented would lose.[21]

The theoretical issues discussed above are drawn primarily from the systematic theory of structuration in Giddens in order to provide a basis for elaborating a reflexive framework for the understanding of international security. The discussion is not intended to provide a summary of his overall position, accounts of which are available in the substantial secondary literature, nor to adjudicate between Giddens's approach and other attempts to articulate a more plausible relation between agency and structure than that offered by objectivism and subjectivism.[22] In their radical rejection of the dualism of agency and structure, and their break with a naturalistic idea of causality, Giddens and other 'structurationists' represent a significant point of departure of contemporary social theory with its past. In my view, they provide the richest philosophical resource from which to mount the critique of positivism and establish a firm basis for a theory of international affairs emancipated from its scientific pretensions and failed objectives.[23] A more modest task of the next chapter is to extend the foregoing discussion to the area of international security and identity.

[21] On the idea of collective actor, see Giddens, *The Constitution of Society*, pp. 220/221.

[22] Some secondary literature is noted in fn. 2 above. Among alternative accounts, see Margaret S. Archer, *Culture and Agency: The Place of Culture in Social Theory*, University of Cambridge Press, Cambridge, 1989.

[23] Contrasting objectivism with structuration, the image of Plato and Aristotle in Raphael's mural, 'The School of Athens', comes to mind – if somewhat playfully – to illustrate the agency-structure debate: Plato, the 'objectivist', points up to independent essences (structures) to account for the data of experience (human agency); Aristotle, the 'structurationist' points instead to the data as the site of essences. The link between the Greek debate and the contemporary one may not be as fanciful as it appears.

9 Seeing a different world: a reflexive sociology of security

To see how the framework of the last chapter applies to the topic of security and, through security, to the concepts of identity and interests, it is useful to return to the question of agency and to 'mutual knowledge' as its condition. The argument is that we can only understand how *international* security can be meaningfully grounded in and organized for *individuals* by first understanding the security impulse in the individual, who stands as its ultimate point of reference.

Individual concerns with security are diverse with respect to the differential interests arising from material possessions, institutional commitments and the threats and vulnerabilities to which they are exposed. From this point of view, the majority of poor and isolated have less to secure. All can be recruited to the general cause of collective security more legitimately by identifying the level at which a common interest, arising from a common need, can be located.

The language of needs, and the idea of a hierarchy of human needs, plays a significant part – often implicit – in theorists' accounts of the motivation of action and the sources of conflict. The plausibility of a hierarchic table of human needs, with physical survival in the highest rank, helps to legitimize the allocation of resources to the means best suited to ensure it. Common sense dictates that if there is a primary concern which can be generalized to all individuals – let us say, a 'fundamental' human need for survival – it should be met by an appropriate response in the collectivity charged with security. Paranoia or complacency in the individual or collectivity is the condition of those who are perceived to lack a sense of balance in apportioning resources to securing their 'primary' over their other basic needs.

The stress on security in international relations theory underlines a hierarchy of needs assumed to govern the behaviour of states in

152

realist thought. The nature of states in an environment of anarchy raises the security of the state to the highest rank, above other interests of an economic, political, or cultural kind. Within the interest of security, the threat to the physical survival of state territory, institutions and people is the major focus selected to lend legitimacy to this hierarchy, and gravity to the issues defined as state security. Any threat perceived by the state is thus projected as potentially a threat to physical survival, as if this were the elemental condition of insecurity in relation to which our daily life is organized and against which the apparatus of the state must be mobilized.

In a sense, of course, our physical survival is the bottom line. A car bomb or a Russian missile can destroy the fabric of our lives more comprehensively than a fall in share prices, an unwanted pregnancy, a street mugging, or any of the countless lesser threats which visit us on a regular basis. If a street mugging worries us, the realist story implies, how much more will an ICBM twenty minutes after launch from its base. The logic is unassailable. The problem is that ICBM threats do not visit us on a regular basis. Most of us do not live our lives in the terror of the London blitz, but in the presence of the network of risk attendant on ordinary everyday life in an urban setting.

If we allow that physical survival has a *logical* priority over other needs, this makes it 'primary' only in the uninteresting sense: it is a logical pre-condition of doing anything that we remain physically alive and capable of doing it. It becomes significant for the allocation of resources only if we live in a jungle where this level of security is empirically the most pervasive and common concern. If we *assume*, with Robert Gilpin, that wherever we live we live in a jungle, then it is reasonable to conclude that it is complacency rather than rational assessment not to elevate physical survival to the highest rank in the hierarchy of human needs.[1] Conversely, it is paranoia to organize our lives on that assumption without compelling evidence to support it.

The division of human needs between the social, cultural, psychological, biological, and their ranking in an abstract hierarchy is notoriously contentious. Which need is 'primary' is not resolvable by

---

[1] 'As Thomas Hobbes told his patron, the Second Earl of Devonshire, and realist writers have always attempted to tell those who would listen, "it's a jungle out there". Anarchy is the rule; order, justice, and morality are the exceptions.' Robert G. Gilpin, 'The richness of the tradition of political realism', in Robert O. Keohane (ed.), *Neorealism and its Critics*, Columbia University Press, New York, 1986.

empirical observation. As stated in chapter 5, it is a normative judgment to rank human needs in a hierarchy. It may be sociability for some, at some times, basic education for others, physical survival for others still – each depends upon a judgment about human nature and the particular environment. In the attempt to locate the meaning of security in the common experience of individuals, it is better to abandon the search for a universal league table in favour of a judgment about the pervasiveness or spread of the security impulse. A good candidate among the identifiable human needs is that which presents itself, problematically in some measure, in every instance of interaction which goes to make up the social order.[2]

The need for security

That security is problematic in everyday social interaction is noted in several sources, and is given the label 'ontological security' in the work of psychiatrist R. D. Laing.[3] The impulse to achieve and to manage the security of one's being is present as an unconscious element even in the youngest infant, socially skilled enough to display the capacity to experience relational stress and to negotiate its repair, though lacking the linguistic skills necessary to monitor and reflect upon them. This interest arises from unconscious, organic, needs,[4] and it is plausible to assume that it represents the elemental experience of security and insecurity common to all individuals at every stage of development, though differentiated in its problematic character for some, and in some environments.

The idea of 'ontological security' or existential trust is grounded in the secure or trusting relationships which respond to the fundamental

---

[2] For discussion of human needs in sociology see Jonathan Turner, *The Structure of Sociological Theory*, 5th edition, Wadsworth, Belmont CA, 1991, chapters 30/31.

[3] R.D. Laing, *The Divided Self*, Penguin, Harmondsworth, 1965; A line of sociological analysis, from Husserl, through Schutz, Goffman and Garfinkel, can be traced in the use Giddens makes of the concept of 'ontological security': Edmund Husserl, *Phenomenology and the Crisis of Western Philosophy*, Harper and Row, New York, 1965; Alfred Schutz, *The Phenomenology of the Social World*, London, 1972; Erving Goffman, *Encounters*, Bobbs-Merrill, Indianapolis, 1961; Harold Garfinkel, *Studies in Ethnomethodology*, Prentice Hall, New Jersey, 1967; Anthony Giddens, *The Constitution of Society: Outline of the Theory of Structuration*, Polity Press, Cambridge, 1984.

[4] Roy Boyne, 'Power-knowledge and social theory: the systematic misrepresentation of contemporary French social theory in the work of Anthony Giddens', in Bryant Christopher and David Jary (eds.), *Giddens' Theory of Structuration: A Critical Appreciation*, Routledge, London, 1991, p. 70.

want or interest from which other needs – such as the need for sociability – are derived. We acquire this trust and avoid anxiety or insecurity, the fear of which drives the interest, through the early interplay of presence and absence of the parent.[5] 'The generation of feelings of trust in others, as the deepest-lying element of the basic security system, depends substantially upon predictable and caring routines established by parental figures.'[6] This sense of security is relational, but is not tied to the preservation of intimacy, or even positive relations, from which it is pychologically derived.

Trust and ontological security concern the acquisition of confidence in the routines of daily life – the essential predictability of interaction through which we feel confident in knowing what is going on and that we have the practical skill to go on in this context. From his different analytical perspective, as noted in the etymological discussion of chapter 1, Nietzsche made the link between knowledge and security, 'this need for the familiar', leading to 'the restoration of a sense of security'.[7] Garfinkel and Goffman have shown the centrality of such a link, conceptualized as ontological security, to the maintenance of social life; Garfinkel in particular used experimental methods to demonstrate this through breaching trust in different situations[8] – rather as the television series 'Candid Camera' occasionally disrupted the ontological security of victims for the amusement of viewers.

It is the routine, habitual character of social action which structures it, enabling and limiting the creativity of the actor. This sameness, or ordered pattern, is represented for the individual in the stock of mutual knowledge 'accompanying' different contexts of action, allowing individuals to comprehend the basis on which interaction is to take place. To know what is going on so that an actor can participate in interaction is to know what all other skilled actors know, and is the condition of being able to reaffirm it or change it. What is done habitually or routinely is the very stuff of the social order.

---

[5] Erik Erikson, *Childhood and Society*, Norton, New York, 1963, cited in Giddens, *The Constitution of Society* pp. 50ff.
[6] Giddens, *The Constitution of Society*, p. 50.
[7] See chapter 1, fn. 5.
[8] Harold Garfinkel, 'A conception of, and experiments with, "trust" as a condition of stable concerted action', in O.J. Harvey (ed.), *Motivation and Social Interaction Cognitive Determinants*, Ronald Press, New York, 1963; see also Garfinkel, *Studies in Ethnomethodology*.

'Routinization is vital to the psychological mechanisms whereby a sense of trust or ontological security is sustained in the daily activities of social life.'[9]

Routine is neither an accident nor a gift of nature, still less an object imposing itself on interaction from outside, in the model of objectivist 'structure'. It comes from actors, is sustained, modified, and, in Goffman's term, 'repaired' when threatened, by individual actors.[10]

Security is a central condition for action. The basic sense in which we must understand the order of 'the social order' is one of pattern and regularity affording the confidence of being able to function, to go on, to get by, to make sense of our particular segments of activity. While material conditions critically affect ontological, as well as any more conventionally conceived, security, they only do so informed by the cognitive dimension of structure – the pattern of meaning or mutual knowledge in relation to which we feel secure or insecure. This structural dimension of security refers to our sense of the situation as ordered; but it is the social aspect of the situation, not merely its physical aspect, that is ordered or disordered, secure or insecure.

Ontological security relates to the sense that the social order as practically conceived is normal, consistent with one's expectations and skills to go on in it. It is a security of social relationship, that is to say a sense of being safely in cognitive control of the situation. It is thus an elemental idea of security, universal in its incidence, which embraces both the negative and positive senses of the concept (outlined in chapters 1 and 5), and to which the other contingencies of social life can be related.

How we relate this common experience of the problem of ontological security in the individual to collective security and security policy will be argued schematically in the following points.

Security and identity

For Ken Booth, 'the issue of identity – what makes *us* believe we are the same and *them* different – is inseparable from security.[11] In what

---

[9] Giddens, *The Constitution of Society,* p. xxiii.
[10] Erving Goffman, *Interaction Ritual: Essays on Face-to-Face Behaviour,* Anchor Books, 1967, pp. 135ff.
[11] Booth Ken, 'Security and self: reflections of a fallen realist', in Keith Krause and Michael C. Williams (eds.), *Critical Security Studies: Concepts and Cases,* UCL Press, London, 1997, p. 6.

sense can we speak of an inseparable link between these two ideas? Ontological security relates to the self, its social competence, its confidence in the actor's capacity to manage relations with others. It is a security of social relationship, a sense of being safely in cognitive control of the interaction context. It is relational at the most basic level of interaction: that of the mutual knowledge which is a condition of action, and which derives from a sense of *shared* community.

At this level of the security-of-being, it is not just a question of confidence that *we* are the same and *they* are different, but a prior confidence that we and they share in a common, fundamental identity, as the condition for being able to construct differences between self and other, us and them. We, as humans, are the same; different from inanimate objects and animate ones which lack our capacity for self-reflection, ordering, theorizing, habit-monitoring.

All human beings share a fundamental sense of collective identity, against which ethnic and group divisions are defined as a breach of solidarity. An ethnic division acknowledges a fundamental identity which is *divided*. It would make no social sense to divide into groups of us Americans and them baseball hats. We could not divide into family groups, regional groups, ethnic or national groups unless we first shared a sense of common identity. The study of social division and conflict of identity must start with the common identity which makes the communication of meaning in social action possible. The fracture of common identity into self and other, with often violent consequences, is a second-order accomplishment, achieved by virtue of the fundamental sense of sameness. (Thus understood, the instruments and the process by which social divisions are brought about are revealed as human skills creatively employed in a human choice which could have been expressed otherwise.)

The elemental problem of security entailed in all social action is, therefore, a problem of collective identity: order is disrupted and ontological insecurity engendered insofar as we sense a cleavage or dissonance in the patterns of mutual knowledge, common norms and standards binding us in a condition of solidarity with others. What is rendered insecure in a condition of ontological insecurity is fundamentally our common ties and shared knowledge with others involved in the interaction in which it occurs: our identity. The remedy, and the common response in everyday life – if not in international relations – is to negotiate, to try to 'repair' the 'defective' communication in the practical knowledge that this will repair the disrupted order and its underlying collective identity. This is not to suggest that actors always want to repair defective communication and that the reproduction of order is necessarily paramount in every interaction. Actors can manipulate meaning to bring about disorder and breach of common identity. Candid Camera, again, is the humorous example, and Garfinkel's experiments the research model, to demonstrate this fracture of identity and the insecurity which it entails. Nationalist elites are engaged in the same business at the institutional level – disrupting order in one direction while recreating it by constructing a collective identity in the other. But even the manipulation of meaning to bring about disorder and fracture of common identity requires, as it implies, a prior and fundamental capacity to perceive identity as common.

The inner-outer dimensions of identity

The parallel between individual and collective actors can be applied also to help clarify a distinction made between two different aspects of collective identity.[12] I refer to these as 'societal identity' and 'state identity', or inner and outer.

Again, the starting-point to understanding the collective phenomenon is the individual. As individuals, we can distinguish analytically between the image of self in interaction with similar others, and the understanding of the self as distinct from others. The former relates to a conception of a generalized *human nature* and its capacities and limitations; the latter to the *particular character of an individual*, based on a judgment about his or her biography. Identity as human nature entails a view about all entities which share the property of being human, and is typically grounded in a set of philosophical or religious beliefs. The optimistic view of Marx and Rousseau, and their sense of the positive capacities of the individual which must be released from the restrictions of a contingent, social, development, is often contrasted with the pessimism of Augustine and Hobbes, for whom such constraints are demanded by the nature – not the contingency – of individuals as morally corrupt and egoistic.

---

[12] Alexander Wendt, 'Collective identity formation and the international state', *American Political Science Review*, 88/2, 1994, pp. 384–396. Wendt distinguishes between 'the corporate and social constitution of state actors' parallel to Mead's 'me' and 'I' (p. 385) but he does not sustain the tension in the analysis here or in his later version in Lapid Yosef and Friedrich Kratochwil (eds.), *The Return of Culture and Identity in IR Theory*, Lynne Rienner, London, 1996, chapter 3.

By contrast, we can speak of the distinctiveness of the self, an aspect of identity more familiar in popular psychological discourse, and related to the idea of role and position in society. This is the understanding of identity which lends itself to a further distinction between ascription and achievement – both of which should be understood in social terms as differing degrees of constraint and freedom to choose; it makes no sense to think of ascribed roles or identity as bereft of agency and achieved roles as free of structural constraint. Some aspects of self, such as gender, could be viewed as part of nature – hence under the first category of identity – or, more commonly today, as a product of nurture. One's ethnic character is normally viewed as a position of ascription; one's character as a rebel or conformist, or one's position as a parent or a surgeon, as one of achievement. Both, however, are socially constructed.

This distinction between the identity of the self as human and the identity of the self as distinctive does not normally affect our discussion of individual identity.[13] A Hobbesian view of human nature is unlikely to co-exist with a personal identity as rebel. Where the two dimensions of identity are experienced as incompatible – as typically occurs in reflection on gender – the individual requires a new account, or narrative, of identity to sustain the contradiction, or to bring one dimension of his or her self-image into harmony with the other.[14]

The parallel distinction, at the level of the state as a collective actor, introduces a layer of identity-formation which is more problematic. The nature of the state, what kind of thing the state is, affects our understanding of the limits and possibilities of interaction among states – whether we see them as capable of sustained cooperation or not. This is a generalized category, and as such it applies to all states, analogous to the category of human nature in individuals. But states as collective actors also have a distinctive identity overlaying their 'nature', and there is no necessary coherence or compatibility between the two. A society of individuals within the boundaries of a state may be characterized as tolerant, chauvinist, democratic, extroverted, or

---

[13] It may be significant in regard to questions tied to religious discourse – such as abortion or euthanasia – where dispute about the nature of the person is explicitly at issue.

[14] Betty Friedan, *The Feminine Mystique*, Pelican Press, Harmondsworth, 1965, offers a biography of identity which illustrates the gap, and the new narrative to close it, between the two dimensions.

reserved – each of which can affect its understanding of other societies and be converted into pressure on the state to qualify its relations with other states.

The management task which multiple identities present to the state is more complex than that posed to the individual. The individual who learns to define his or her 'nature', or natural identity, in association with others is the same individual who constructs a pattern of distinctive identities in the diverse encounters of social life. Collective actors such as the state must negotiate their two dimensions of identity with different constituencies: with other states, on the one hand, and with the people who comprise the domestic constituency, on the other.

The individuals mandated to act on behalf of the state, and to enter into international negotiation with other states, are thereby exposed to the interaction process by which states learn and construct the limits and possibilities of their 'nature'. A strong power has greater capacity to influence this learning process than a weak one, making the latter more a consumer than a producer of meaning.

The same state actor, personified in the same, or other, individuals, is also exposed to the domestic interaction process – between individuals, social and interest groups and the state – in which a quite different learning procedure is at work. In the domestic interaction process the state – even a weak one – is the strong unit, commanding greater resources to ensure that its societal identity is consistent with its 'nature' as a state in the international arena.

 In modern conditions, the spread of democratic values and the interpenetration of global culture and institutions add significantly to the burden of political leaderships to manage their state and societal identities in a harmonious way to ensure legitimacy in foreign policy.

In the comparison of Campbell's study of US foreign policy with Wendt's analysis of anarchy we saw the problem of assuming that 'identity' can be assimilated to its domestic or international expression. Campbell demonstrates how the moralism of American domestic identity influenced a particular foreign policy in relation to communism, but it tells us little about American state identity which may have changed over a historical period during which this moralism was relatively constant. Surely the state learns in the international process of interaction, just as it learns in the domestic? Otherwise, we must read Campbell as implicitly adopting the assumption of Morgenthau and Waltz that states are by nature egoistic and their identity is hence fixed prior to, and outside of, interaction with other states. This would be absurd, given the sharp hostility to neorealism of Campbell's overall perspective.

Wendt, in effect, restricts collective identity to the state as the only unit of analysis within a systems approach, limiting state properties to the continuum of self-help to cooperative. This makes his idea of identity analogous to that of human nature for the individual – though he allows that the units can change under the influence of interaction. Wendt locates the source of identity change in factors endogenous to *international* interaction, but exogenous to *domestic* conditions, while Campbell sees it the other way round.

There is need to address both sources of identity-formation. We cannot explain how collective identities are formed and reformed by focusing exclusively on the socialization of the state actor. What happened in the 1992 referenda on the ratification of the Maastricht Treaty in Denmark and France, and seems to be a growing phenomenon in Germany, is the popular expression of discontent with the identities and interests which their state elites have learned through negotiation in the international forum. To bias integration policy towards the state within the interstate arena is, effectively, to fall into the practical error of neofunctionalism – notwithstanding its inclusion of sub-state elite groups in its school of learning – and to ignore the domestic conditions of societal identity which must be synchronized with the international if foreign policy is to have sufficient legitimacy to make it effective.[15] To focus only on the domestic arena, on the other hand, is to ignore the malleability of state identity through international negotiation and to imply, at least, that state identity is fixed and unproblematic. States are not irreducible actors. They are an expression of the international *and* the domestic. They are structure to domestic actors, and actors to international structure.

Identity as structure and action

Social actors, individual and collective, routinely address the project of their identity through space and time. That is to say, they are faced with the task of distinguishing their selves spatially from others and of accomplishing their sameness, their continuity with their different selves, temporally. Neither the sameness of our identity through time

---

[15] Neofunctionalism and its shortcomings will be further discussed in chapter 9.

nor its distinctiveness through space can be given to us as an unproblematic property to be discovered and appropriated. Whether we live in a culture of fluid identities – a feature of modernity or, as some would say, of postmodernity – or in one of traditional ascription of self and community, identity is an idea in search of a person. It has no content, no fixed dimensions which we can customize and which exist independently of human choice.

An analogy can be made with the concept of race. It is a familiar liberal interpretation of race to distinguish between the fact of phenotypical attributes which visibly distinguish different human groups, and the value-judgment which politically organizes them in a hierarchy of being or performance. On this liberal view, skin colour, hair structure and facial features are self-evident facts which link people into different groups whether we are made aware of it or not.[16] The process of social construction, in this view, applies to race, not to phenotypes.

Similarly, it is often claimed that collective identity, while socially constructed, nonetheless has certain basic elements or ingredients – analogous to phenotypes – which provide the objective stuff, the template on which we write identity. Place of birth, language, religion, a shared culture, are deemed to be the principal attributes.[17] The reasoning seems intuitively compelling. Just as a black man cannot escape membership of the group which has been defined in racial terms, so a woman born in Croatia, sharing the majority religion and language, cannot extricate herself from being a Croat.

But there is no compelling reason to assume that phenotypes present themselves to us already organized in groups. The British anthropologist, Peter Wade, argues persuasively that the physical ingredients of racial distinctions are no more objective and independent of our observational activity in constructing them than are the mental attributes which racial theory adds to them.[18] Of the countless phenotypes available to our perception, and standing as candidates for selection into categories, we choose which ones to organize into distinctive groups; not blue eyes, short legs, or long chin – all of which

---

[16] See, for example, Rex John and D. Mason (eds.), *Theories of Race and Ethnic Relations*, Cambridge University Press, Cambridge, 1986; Michael Banton, *Racial and Ethnic Competition*, Cambridge University Press, Cambridge, 1983.

[17] Anthony Smith, 'The ethnic sources of nationalism', *Survival*, 35/1, 1993; and *National Identity*, Penguin, London, 1991.

[18] See Peter Wade, ' "Race", Nature and Culture', *Man*, 28, 1996, pp. 17–33.

remain self-evidently as facts which do *not* link people into different groups – but other physical attributes which history and politics had already grouped for us.

Similarly with identity: place of birth and language may be common to the story of most collectivities, just as skin colour is common to racial groups. But there is no intrinsic reason why my place of birth must provide a central – or even peripheral – element of my identity. We only see phenotypes as a group property after we have been directed to see them by imputations of race. One's birth-place and one's skin colour only appear to be objective *after* they have been chosen from countless other properties as being relevant to identity or race. Collective identity, like race, is no more than an organizational idea in search of a community to embody it.

Like race, collective identity can be considered as a theory or, more to the point, as a story or narrative. Its capacity to stand as an object of inquiry or a fact of politics depends entirely on the capacity of the group to sustain the story of belonging and solidarity which defines it in space and time. In that sense, identity is a project, in Giddens's term.[19] Like social action, the project of identity is a continuous stream of experience monitored by the actor as a reflexive endeavour. The task is to sustain the narrative through time and across space, to keep it going in the face of countless events and experiences which challenge its coherence.

This should not be taken to mean that particular identities always and necessarily present themselves to actors as stories to be sustained against all challenge, still less that the narrative relates to a uniform self or identity. On the contrary, a change of identity or the adoption of multiple identities or the transition from multiple to uniform identity all demand the reflexive attention of the actor to appropriate the new or the modified story, and to keep it going.[20]

In all cases, the narrative of identity must not be understood as the

---

[19] Anthony Giddens, *Modernity and Self-Identity: Self and Society in the Late Modern Age*, Polity Press, Cambridge, 1991, pp. 32/33.

[20] Slavenka Drakulic, in her biographical account of the transition of Croatia to independence and statehood, describes her experience of trying to resist the imposition of a new identity, the sense of being 'overcome by nationhood'. 'The trouble with this nationhood, however, is that whereas before, I was defined by my education, my job, my ideas, my character – and, yes, my nationality too – now I feel stripped of all that.' Drakulic found it hard to sustain the old narrative in the face of overwhelming public demand to tell a new story. See her *The Balkan Express: Fragments from the Other Side of War*, W.W. Norton, New York, 1993, pp. 50–51.

private individual account of the self. As the term 'narrative' suggests, the story told of identity is neither out there to be discovered nor inside us as individuals to be externalized in a creative act. In a sense, it is both. It has to make sense to others, not only as common language, but as a meaningful account of the self which draws on a stock of such accounts. To sustain a narrative means to sustain an account of a self which is already in the public domain and can therefore make sense to others. For it is clear that the project of keeping a story going has critical reference to an audience other than the self. It is to others, as much as to oneself, that we must make sense of our identity. To ignore this is to adopt the position of the fantasist or insane.

To say that the constraint of structure and the production of meaning by agents are equally significant is to express a philosophy of social action in the abstract. It is not to deny that actors in concrete situations may experience greater liberty to adopt a new identity than in others, or a heavier burden of constraint to appropriate the identity traditionally ascribed. This is always an empirical question and one which requires us to judge the balance of constraint and personal freedom on a case-by-case basis. But it is to claim that this balance can never be calculated *a priori*, and that we cannot judge the weight of constraint bearing on individuals with regard to one particular social concept in the abstract rather than another.[21]

For example, it seems clear that women and men today enjoy a greater freedom to refashion their gender identity than they did in the 1950s, when it was difficult to conceive of any alternative to the distinctive identities ascribed to them. The manipulation of national identity in former Yugoslavia illustrates the ambiguity of constraint: a new national identity is 'discovered' and voluntarily embraced by some as the resurrection of the old, while others experience it as the denial of freedom.[22] As in Yugoslavia, the interplay of interests and identity in Northern Ireland has bequeathed to unionists, as distinct

---

[21] It makes little sense, with respect to Buzan and Waever, therefore, to contrast the socially constructed character of security with the objectivist character of identity in the abstract: that is, without reference to the empirical evidence demonstrating the extent of freedom or constraint in a particular social setting. See Barry Buzan and Ole Waever, 'Slippery, contradictory? sociologically untenable? The Copenhagen School replies', *Review of International Studies*, 23/2, 1997, pp. 241–250 and Barry Buzan, Ole Waever and Jaap de Wilde, *Security: A New Framework for Analysis*, Lynne Rienner, London, 1998, chapters 2 and 9.

[22] See the reference to Slavenka Drakulic in fn. 20.

from nationalists, a different experience of constraint and freedom to choose. It is clear that moral choice for change on the part of unionists is more severely constrained than for their neighbours.

Doing identity

To analyse identity in terms of narrative, and to speak of narrative as, in part, an act of communication which draws from a stock of knowledge which we share with others, is at once to focus on an important characteristic of the concept of identity and, I shall argue, of all social concepts.

Identity is a social act as well as a structure of meaning. As act, it refers to the capacity of individuals to sustain a story about the self or the collective self. As structure, it relates to the story or narrative sustained, from which individuals draw to enact identity. The term which best captures this dual sense of identity is becoming a familiar one to students of international relations: social practice. Social practices are habitual or regularized *types* of action which link, or mediate between, structure and agency. In social practices we 'do' concepts: that is to say we draw upon typified behavioural patterns to reproduce meaning in a particular setting or situation and, in the same act, to reaffirm or modify its sense. Thus, we can 'do' ending an interview, signing off a telephone conversation, saying goodbye at the airport, or 'state sovereignty'.[23]

We have no verbal form of 'sovereignty' to express the social practice in which it is constituted as action. In a discipline notorious for its tendency to reification, theorists of post-structuralist or post-modernist leanings have had to resort to neologisms to capture the sense in which certain concepts of the social order exist only in their doing. The concepts of sovereignty and security are perhaps the best-known examples of the application of this insight to central ideas of international relations theory.[24]

---

[23] For examples of the extensive literature on 'doing' social behaviour, see Paul Drew and John Heritage (eds.), *Talk at Work: Interaction in Institutional Settings*, Cambridge University Press, Cambridge, 1992; A. J. Wootton, *Interaction and the Development of Mind*, Cambridge University Press, Cambridge, 1997.

[24] Ole Waever, 'Securitization and desecurization', in Ronnie D. Lipschutz (ed.), *On Security*, Columbia University Press, New York, 1995; James Der Derian, 'The value of security: Hobbes, Marx, Nietzsche and Baudrillard', in David Campbell and Michael Dillon (eds.), *The Political Subject of Violence*, Manchester University Press, Manchester, 1993; R.B.J. Walker, *Inside/Outside: International Relations As Political Theory*,

The limitation of this literature, however, is one of omission – of failing to see that the verbal translation of the standard nominal form of, for example, 'security' applies equally to all social concepts and to the social order as a whole. We 'do' security. There would be no security without human individuals to 'securitize' their relations with others. But the point applies equally to 'justice', 'war', 'marriage', and 'the social order'. Just as we cannot restrict the idea of an 'essentially contested concept' to security (as shown in chapter 5), so we cannot assume that only some concepts of the social order are constituted by human practices. Without the social practices of individuals *ordering* our world in a regularity or pattern which enables us to know how to go on in it, there could be no social order, no action to observe and no structure to infer.

The relevance to identity should be clear. Brubaker's reframing of nationalism criticizes the substantive character of national identity in most of the literature, even the anti-primordialist. He wants to see nation as practice, and nationness as event.[25] Since there is no verbal form which adequately expresses the social action involved, 'doing identity' expresses the idea satisfactorily, and locates it in a fertile sociological tradition, without adding to the neologisms of contemporary IR theorists. As in all social concepts, the emphasis on social practices in respect of identity draws attention to the role of the agent in the production of identity without making the subjectivist assumption that structural constraints are not equally significant in its reproduction. We can only do language – speak – if we can draw on what is already done. We can only order the social order if it is already ordered for us. We can only do security, or do identity, if there is a body of typified actions, mediated by structure, from which to draw in order to make sense.

The duality of identity and interests

How do states learn to sustain or refashion their identities? Our concern about identity relates to its practical impact on behaviour. To understand what actors do, and are likely to do in the future, we must understand what kind of entity they are. Interests, wants, preferences

Cambridge University Press, Cambridge, 1993; and his 'Security, sovereignty, and the challenge of world politics', *Alternatives* 15/1, 1990, pp. 3–27.

[25] Rogers Brubaker, *Nationalism Reframed: Nationhood and the National Question in the New Europe*, Cambridge University Press, Cambridge, 1996.

– I use the terms interchangeably – are the mediating elements between identity and behaviour. If identity is learned through the dual processes of domestic and international interaction, as argued above, where do interests come from and how are they related to identity? Logically, they derive from identity, suggesting the priority of identity over interests which has been criticized in relation to Wendt (see chapter 7):

> I argue that interests are dependent on identities and so are not competing causal mechanisms but distinct phenomena – in the one case, motivational, in the other, cognitive and structural – and, as such, play different roles in explaining action.[26]

We should be cautious in stressing the independence of identity in relation to interests in the manner of Wendt, however. As a logical inference, it is clear that we formulate the values which inform policy in relation to others on the basis of a perception of self and other as positively or negatively interrelated. But this does not mean that identity cannot be altered, in practice, through a change in the interests which logically flow from it. We can be led to perceive ourselves differently – to choose a different position on the continuum of identities – by the opportunities which may be offered to satisfy new interests. This is the principle underlying the practical strategy of neofunctionalism, as illustrated in chapter 7, and it expresses the theoretical relationship of base and superstructure in Marxism.[27]

Campbell, as we saw, does not allow the state to learn in the domestic process – only to teach. This follows from his emphasis on the role of the National Security Council, and other bodies which comprise the institutions of state, in defining crisis and articulating the state response for public consumption. The people, in Campbell's analysis, are only consumers of meaning produced by the state. Campbell comes close to analysing human agency out of the picture, by ignoring the role of sectional interests in the production, as well as the consumption, of national identity-formation.

It is the dual possibility to reconstruct identity directly, *and* through the medium of interests, which lies at the core of the integration process in the European Community. It manifests the process in all social behaviour whereby social interaction and the agency of the unit

---

[26] Alexander Wendt, 'Collective identity formation', p. 385.
[27] Karl Marx and Friedrich Engels, *The German Ideology*, Lawrence and Wishart, London, 1970.

actors are fused, enmeshed, in a duality which cannot be resolved by *a priori* judgment of ontological privilege in favour of one or the other. It displays the particular aspect of managed identity-formation which characterizes an integrated security policy – one which, by its compre-hensive strategy for the positive as well as the negative requirements of security, may also be termed a peace process.

It is useful analytically to distinguish identity from interests – if only to get some critical purchase on the issues raised in identity theory and politics. But it is not clear how we can make a coherent case for separating the two concepts empirically. As already noted, the rela-tionship between interests and identity is best conceived as a recursive one, inseparably linked and 'feeding back' reflexively one upon the other. The example of European integration illustrates the point and extends this general theoretical outline to the reassessment of neofunc-tionalist spillover.

A reinterpreted concept of spillover can help in making sense of change, and the source of change, in the identity and interests of states, relevant to their security and security policy. The concept of spillover can be revised to draw on the philosophical analysis of agency and structure discussed in the preceding chapter, and to construct a sociology of security grounded in the interrelation of identity and interests.

The theory of neofunctionalism predicted that state interests would become gradually entangled in a web of relationships together with the interests of people and interest groups within and across states, so that their loyalties, their allegiance, would be refocused on the Community. The gradual expansion of tasks consequent upon func-tional cooperation would persuade states not only to 'upgrade' their interests to those common to other member states, but persuade domestic actors also 'to shift their loyalties, expectations and political activities towards a new centre'.[28] This move is better expressed as a change in identity (loyalties) and interests (expectations and political activities). It is difficult to make sense of the qualitative change implied in the shift from technical to political spillover without incorporating the concept of identity to express it.

The discredited baggage of neofunctionalism invites the search for

---

[28] Ernst Haas, *The Uniting of Europe: Political, Social, and Economic Forces*, Stanford University Press, Stanford, 1958, p. 16.

an alternative term to express its core concept of 'spillover' and to allow a fruitful idea to be detached from its deterministic history. Spillover is sometimes expressed in the French *engrenage*, or the more colloquial English 'enmeshment'.[29] The concept of enmeshment is preferable to the standard metaphor of 'spillover': 'enmeshment' denotes the entanglement in a web of relationships which is at the root of the neofunctionalist idea, rather than the mechanical and material connotations of 'spillover'.

There is a simpler, more familiar and evocative, term, however, which captures the sense of enmeshment and which has the merit of highlighting the continuity of everyday interpersonal relations with those between communities and states in line with the sub-thesis of this book: that the social order is a unity, and the logic and dynamics of international politics are of a piece with the routine interactions of individuals. It is not a term which would appeal to policy-makers needing to legitimize their management of an integration, or peace, process – for obvious reasons – but it more accurately describes that process and underlines the continuity of the international with the interpersonal which is critical to its success.

The commonsense meaning of the term 'seduction' loses nothing of the subtlety implicit in spillover and requires no technical redefinition to extend it from its everyday context to the world of politics. Seduction hints at conspiracy, at the conscious manipulation of others' identities and interests, as it hints also at human agency – influenced, but not determined, in its role as co-conspirator. Seduction also points to the processual character of the project in question – integration – rather than the discrete moment suggested by spillover. Although a romantic sense of 'seduction' invites us to anticipate the end-product of submission with the implied loss of agency which this entails, this is a particular, vulgar usage – and even 'submission' does not necessarily involve the abandonment of freedom. On the contrary, the imbalance of power suggested by the term 'seduction' exactly captures the imbalance required in the management of an integration

---

[29] See Paul Taylor, 'Supranationalism', in A.J.R. Groom and Paul Taylor (eds.), *Frameworks for International Cooperation*, Pinter, London, 1990. In the same volume, Harrison speaks of integration by stealth – 'incremental, concrete, economic achievements which build up *de facto* 'engrenage' or enmeshment of one national political and economic system with another.' R.J. Harrison, 'Neo-Functionalism', in A.J.R. Groom and Paul Taylor (eds.), *Frameworks for International Cooperation*, Pinter, London, 1990, p. 140.

process in which actors are tempted, led, entangled in a web of relations from which it becomes too costly to extricate themselves – and all in pursuit of their own self-interest, and with the essential definition of human agency intact: the option to do otherwise.

A seduction model

A seduction model of integration can be expressed in neofunctionalist terms without the closure which the classical theorists imposed for the misguided purpose of achieving a scientific standard of explanatory rigour. In this model, the concept of spillover is reinterpreted in the service of a reflexive sociology of integration: one which analyses the building of an integrated security community as the partly unintended product of reflexive agents monitoring their interactions with other agents in terms of the impact on interests and identities which are made vulnerable to change. The question arises in international politics as in interpersonal relations: Who is the seducer and who is being seduced? In that form, the question implies a zero-sum game beloved of romantic moralists and political realists, and neofunctionalists came close to modelling integration according to zero-sum rules. While spillover envisaged everyone as a gainer, its automaticity trapped member-states in a determinate process inexorably leading to their decline, by their submission to the operation of a mechanical trigger. Classical neofunctionalism saw the European Commission primarily as the agent of spillover and member-states as its target; the former as the seducer and the latter as victim.

But the historical evidence of integration in no way demonstrates the game of masters and puppets, played with the predictable outcome of state submission to a law of spillover. The strategy of conscious management of the enmeshment process to the end of achieving a shift towards a more collective identity and interests is fully compatible with the sovereign choice of the actors to cooperate with it, or to resist. In respect of European integration, the management is part of the learning process whereby agents become enmeshed with constraints of structure and learn to reconstruct their interests and identity under the tutelage of the Commission, *while remaining agents with the choice to do otherwise.* Where the process is successful, the new identity and interests are not perceived as the sacrifice of self in favour of others, but as the realization of a different and superior conception of the national self and the national interest. Where the process is resisted – as in the case of unionists in Northern Ireland and Britain in the EU – the prospect on offer with integration is deemed to entail the denial of self.

The processual character of seduction or enmeshment into an integrated community draws attention to its temporal dimension as a social project – and recalls the depiction of identity, similarly, as project. This should be understood as a continuous flow of action on the part of human agents – as individuals and as state leaders – initiated and managed by an elite or institutional body, but accomplished by actors who may not intend, or be fully aware of, the consequences of their actions. The reconstruction of an *individual's* identity is conceivably an intended outcome of his or her agency. It is inconceivable that *collective* identity be reformed on the basis of intended action alone. The 'imagined community' which directs British interests in the European Union, and the quite different identity which guides Germany, are neither the intended action of their respective populations, nor are they the imposition of a determinative structure or political elite. They are the accomplishment of both. A security community could never be accomplished without the enmeshing of individuals' *choices* in a project consciously managed by a leadership elite.

The revised concept of spillover, secondly, offers insight into the relation of identity and interests, which can enrich the sociological, or 'social constructionist' approach to international politics. If we understand identity as a structure, and interests as the action element within the framework of this structure, then the idea that interests are formed as the consequence of identity suggests a structural determinism at odds with the social theory outlined in the previous chapter. It is also at variance with the strong emphasis on the causal role of interests in neofunctionalism, and with an intuitively plausible view of how identities – individual, as well as collective – come to be formed and changed in practice. The apparent fact that national identities are formed and reformed as the consequence and instrument of the pursuit of elite interests is supported in the social constructionist literature on nationalism and national identity.[30] Likewise in neofunctionalism, the shift in loyalties and attitudes

---

[30] Ernest Gellner, *Nations and Nationalism*, Blackwell, Oxford, 1983; E. J. Hobsbawm, *Nations and Nationalism since 1780*, Cambridge University Press, Cambridge, 1993; Benedict Anderson, *Imagined Communities: Reflections on the Origins and Spread of Nationalism*, Verso Press, London, 1989.

(identities) is mainly seen as the *result* of the upgrading of interests, while allowing that the relationship is a dialectic one in practice.

Identity and interests cause each other. A seduction model of integration points to a dynamic of identity and interest, which locates the source of identity- and interest-formation in the learning process of interstate cooperation – in the 'coordination reflex' which integration literature attributes to individual officials who are professionally engaged in the process; and it locates the source of identity construction in the pursuit of interests, or wants. Such a conception of the dynamic is consistent with a more adequate theory of social action, which restores human agency and the element of choice in the formation of individual and collective identity. We are who we want to be.

How we should understand this human freedom and creativity in the face of the widespread perception of professional and lay analysts to the contrary, and in the light of the constraints of structure outlined in the previous chapter, will be addressed in the concluding chapter. How collectivities in practice seduce and are seduced into – or out of – an integrated security process according to the model outlined is the subject of the next chapter.

Part III
Practising security

10   Doing security by stealth

From the early 1990s until the Belfast Agreement of April 1998, a new relationship between the actors at the centre of the Northern Ireland conflict was negotiated, formalized and agreed, to institutionalize the conditions of an historic accord. What happened is, in considerable part, a matter of interpretation and the selection of facts to support it. And how we interpret it depends on the theoretical premises and philosophical assumptions which we bring to bear on this – as on any – empirical event which we seek to explain and understand.

In roughly the same period of the 1990s, something happened in regard to American foreign policy and its impact on European security. The decade began with the bipolar relationship still in place, though immeasurably warmer and more cooperative than it had ever been during the Cold War. From early in 1994 until the NATO summit meeting in Madrid in 1997, the conditions were laid for an agreement between the sixteen member-states to expand the Alliance eastwards. Again, where we look for the facts and the reasons to explain this decision, and how we interpret its likely impact on security in Europe, depend on prior theoretical ideas about the unit actors and the nature of the constraints which influence them, about our capacity to explain human events in scientific terms; in short, about what kind of world we think we are living in.

Overlapping with these events, a third period from 1991 to the decision to intensify European integration through a monetary union and the integrative measures announced in the Amsterdam Treaty of 1997 raises a different puzzle. The end of the Cold War confrontation between West and East marked the end also to a factor which had lent some degree of solidarity to the West and contributed to its capacity to integrate. That the West's liberation from a common enemy should signal the unravelling of its integrated institutions seemed to be borne out in the extraordinary expression of public disenchantment with the EU indicated in the debates and ratification process on the Maastricht Treaty in 1992. The decision to deepen integration, therefore, runs counter to an intuitive assumption – shared by a sizeable body of theory – about the nature of the integration process over the previous forty-five years.[1]

Two ways of practising, or 'doing', security have been discussed in this book. One is the traditional up-front approach centred on the perception of external threat and the organization of material resources to remedy the vulnerabilities exposed to the perceived aggression. That such practices are, in some degree, always prudent and on occasion may constitute the only sensible strategy of security immediately available to a state is acknowledged. Security in this sense is military defence; it represents that dimension of security which traditional practices and ideas have made the defining boundaries of the concept itself.

It has been argued at length, however, that military defence is only one aspect of a security policy responsive to the everyday needs of the individuals who are its subject. Furthermore the practices involved in doing security exclusively on this narrow dimension carry the risk of exacerbating or creating the problem of external threat which they are intended to resolve.

The second way of doing security does not exclude the essentially material orientation of the first, nor does it address the cognitive factor of identity and intention to the exclusion of the material. It focuses primarily on addressing the long-term security problem of regional relationships in terms of the management of identity and interests: in other words, the problem which arises from the *normal* conditions which generate the human need for security.

Abnormal conditions of threat to the territorial survival of a state and the physical survival of its people can arise from factors *external* to it and to its institutions of state. Belgium in World War I and other small neutrals in World War II were hardly complicit in constructing the threat and invasion which ended their autonomy and statehood. It is at least questionable, however, to view the threat of the Soviet

---

[1] Kenneth Waltz, *Theory of International Politics*, Addison-Wesley, Reading MA, 1979 pp. 70/71 is echoed in Anthony Hartley's view of the Cold War origins of the EU in *The World Today*, January 1994, pp. 19–20.

Union to the people of Western Europe in a similar light. Political elites in the West played their part in transforming the security concerns of their own people from normal, human needs to the abnormal fear for survival.

Another example of such a transformation can be found in the post-Cold War escalation of tension between India and Pakistan. Without straining the comparison and ignoring the significant differences between the two regions, the Indian subcontinent and the Northern Ireland situation can be used to sharpen the contrast between the two conceptions of security policy.

The sudden escalation of military tension between India and Pakistan in May 1998 exemplifies the absurdity of pursuing the logic of national security.[2] Within two weeks following the Indian tests on 11 and 13 May, the smouldering antagonism of a nationalism which the Cold War had not contained, but which the end of the Cold War intensified, was inflamed with Pakistan's tit-for-tat demonstrations of nuclear capability. Within those two weeks, the security concerns of the vast population of this subcontinent were reconstructed by political elites from normal basic needs to the special needs of survival in what could now be seen as the 'real' world of the realist jungle. Even as urban crowds in India danced to the tune of their politicians, their elite counterparts in Pakistan were getting ready to drop the other shoe. While urban Pakistanis celebrated their counter-attack, the mass of the people in whose name this military response was made found themselves living in a state of emergency and the suspension of human rights. Promising them an austerity progamme and yet higher levels of economic hardship to pay for it, Prime Minister Nawaz Sharif announced his security policy on 'this auspicious day of historic importance': 'We have evened the account with India.'[3]

The primary justification on both sides of the Indo-Pakistan conflict is the existence of external threat to national sovereignty. Both parties have dismissed the condemnations of the official five nuclear powers on the grounds – not wholly fanciful – that they cannot expect non-proliferation and demand the right to monopolize nuclear weapons at

---

[2] See Marshall M. Bouton, 'India's problem is not politics', *Foreign Affairs*, 77/3, 1998; James Manor and Gerald Segal, 'Taking India seriously', *Survival*, 40/2, 1998; William Walker, 'International nuclear relations after the Indian and Pakistani test explosions', *International Affairs*, 74/3, 1998.

[3] *The Irish Times*, 29 May 1998.

the same time. If nuclear deterrence is as good as the five always claimed, then it must be good for others who perceive military threats to their security. That the security of the people of Japan and Germany has been enhanced by their development of non-military, economic instruments is not seen as relevant to 'security' by those who make policy in the region.

In the same two weeks, the people of Ireland rejected the option to restore the normality of three centuries of no-surrender politics, and to elevate 'compromise' from its grubby retreat in political practice to a moral principle of public discourse.[4] Political elites had also played an indispensable role in managing the process of reconstruction which made this security policy possible. It was embarked upon and sustained in the face of pressure to restore and strengthen the traditional policies of security which had not succeeded in realizing the goal of military defeat of the IRA. A campaign of no-compromise with the opponents of 'democracy' was fought by religious and political fundamentalists on the unionist side, while IRA and Sinn Fein splinter groups mounted a mirror-image version against the opponents of 'self-determination' in support of their nationalist aim of a united Ireland and its expression in the Irish Constitution.[5] The Belfast Agreement expressed the public desire for a censure, if not yet a plague, on both their houses.

Northern Ireland is different, of course. The partition question displays only a superficial similarity with the dispute in South Asia, which is a creature of its geographical and geopolitical context. But all international disputes are different; all marital disputes are different for the same fundamental reason. We may be persuaded by a comparative politics which discovers similarities, just as we are easily persuaded by a realist politics which defines regularities, but the devil is in the philosophy, in the explanatory model and causal inference used to make sense of the facts.

The model of understanding security outlined in the last chapter is not inimical to generalizations about human behaviour drawn from

---

[4] Seventy-one per cent of the people of Northern Ireland and 94 per cent of the electorate in the South voted on 22 May 1998 to support the Belfast Agreement. See Richard Sinnott, 'The Belfast Agreement Referendums', *The Irish Times*, 25th May 1998.
[5] Political fundamentalism in Protestant mode is represented by the Democratic Unionist Party led by Ian Paisley, with more secular support from the minority United Kingdom Unionist Party.

the observation of similarity and regularity. It excludes only those which are offered as universal laws, and which ignore the fact that all social generalization is dependent on the affirmation of the subject and is vulnerable to contradiction by the same subject. As collective actors, Pakistan and India display the part of affirmation and vulnerability in respect of generalizations about international affairs; they are not the passive objects of systemic laws. That they had an option to act otherwise in May 1998 is obvious to everyone outside the political ideologues in both countries. Their innocence of freedom in the matter does not undermine the point being made. Whether they have an option to move, like France and Germany in 1952, like Northern Ireland later, in the direction of a more comprehensive security relationship in the future cannot be ruled out by the uniqueness of the structure and scale of their conflict in the past. Further observations in that regard will be made after discussion of other cases illustrating the argument for a broader conception of security.

The theoretical formulation presented in the last chapter is intended to provide a framework for the understanding of security and security policy in this broader sense, and of its related concepts. Here we look at some of the practical implications of that theory in the context of particular security policies applied to contemporary problems. The facts of these cases do not easily fit the assumptions of traditional security studies.

Doing identity and interests

Identity and interests are analytically separate elements of all collective action. Logically, we pursue interests in relation to who we are, to the kind of entity for which such interests are appropriate. But we cannot know who we are in a vacuum of interests or wants, as Marx was aware; we become identified with an individual or collective self through the pursuit of these rather than other preferences.

In practice, collective identities can exercise a considerable degree of constraint over the options to redefine our interests and to reconstruct our identity. In certain circumstances a sense of collective identity can exist in relative detachment from material interests, just as in other conditions material benefits – or threats – encourage the reassessment of who we are and who we want to be. The dynamics of identity and interest can be explored in relation to the peace process in Northern Ireland.

The Northern Ireland peace process offers, on the face of it, a clear illustration of the salience of collective identity as the relatively independent variable in the genesis of conflict and in its transcending. A people divided for centuries by religion, political allegiance, cultural adherence and myth has reflected on its divisions and re-examined its ideological roots to find space to compromise in favour of the other, and of a common sense of belonging. As one prominent journalist put it in the euphoria of the Belfast Agreement: 'it is people who identify themselves, not governments or tribes who tell them who they are'.[6]

Concessions central to the ideology of both sides of the Northern Ireland conflict have now been enshrined in a legal agreement. The IRA has conceded what was once seen as the cornerstone of the nationalist sense of itself: the territorial claim to the unity of the island and the political unity of the people living on it, expressed in the famous Articles 2 and 3 of the Irish Constitution. This concession in the Belfast Agreement reflects what has been a fact of life since partition in 1922, but that fact has only focused the nationalist aspiration all the more narrowly into a collective vision which inspired its extreme elements to overturn it by force.

Moreover, it is not now the people of Ireland who are given the right to change this fact of life, but only the electorate of Northern Ireland itself. Since the traditional supporters of maintaining the union with Britain are in a majority of 2:1 over the nationalists, in effect the IRA has conceded a unionist veto over future constitutional change. The constitutional claim to jurisdiction over the territory and people of Northern Ireland must be replaced by a non-juridical aspiration.

On the unionist side, therefore, the Belfast Agreement guarantees their identity as British – through the union with Westminster – as long as this is the will of the majority. But this is not an advance on the status quo, since the Government of Ireland Act of 1920 gave them the same guarantee. Unionists too have signed up to significant compromise. New institutions and a specially devised voting system will give the minority nationalist parties a role in the government of the

---

[6] Fintan O'Toole, *The Irish Times*, 13 April 1998.

province and will give some elected representatives in the Dublin government an executive voice in the internal affairs of Northern Ireland.

Who wins in this clever compromise depends upon how we understand the game being played and the prize on offer. Like all intercommunity conflicts, this one is certainly a game or conflict about identity. And in some respects at least, identity can be seen as a salient issue – never wholly detached from interests, but exercising a predominance over the questions under negotiation which cannot be translated without residue into material interests. The nub of the historic problem dividing the people of Northern Ireland since 1922 has been the identity question and the political means of expressing it: are we Irish and Catholic, like the South, or British and not Catholic, like the mainland? The material interests introducing complexity into this simple dilemma played differently and more or less heavily on one or other side of the dispute at different times.

In 1983, after fourteen years of apparently intractable violence, the government of the Republic of Ireland initiated a process of examining what it meant to be Irish, with clear reference to the need to reconcile ancient perceptions of antagonism between the unionist and the nationalist traditions on the island. The New Ireland Forum in 1983 was an attempt to rethink nationalist attitudes in the light of unionist concerns, and to develop a more pluralist agenda for all-party negotiation on the basis of alternative resolutions of the problem, rather than the unitary state hallowed by the irredentist republican tradition.[7] In particular, it was an attempt publicly to exorcise from public life any basis for the unionist claim that their identity and rights were incompatible with the Catholic influence on politics and culture in Southern Ireland and, therefore, with an all-Ireland solution to the problem.

Reconstructing national identity at home in the hope that this alone would persuade the British government to redefine its interests and Northern unionists to perceive their own identity as malleable would have been a naive exercise. Locating and cultivating influential international opinion in order to bring pressure to bear on other actors in the process to respond to the government initiative was a second strand in the strategy. Together with the Forum, a background diplomatic strategy was employed by the Irish government from the

---

[7] Report of the New Ireland Forum, Government Publications, Dublin, 1984.

mid 1980s, to focus the efforts of prominent Irish–American politicians away from IRA-linked support groups and directly on the White House.[8]

The success of this Forum in holding a mirror to the culture of church and politics in Ireland was undoubtedly aided by the continuing process of religious secularization which eroded the power of Catholicism and contributed to the redefinition of Irishness quite independently of the government's efforts. By the mid 1990s at least, Irish Catholicism was in fast retreat from the monolithic and homogeneous entity which Northern Protestants perceived as its eternal condition and as constituting the fundamental grounds for resisting any moves towards integration. In displaying for the first time the considerable disunity and disagreement of interest groups with the traditional theocratic tendency of the Catholic hierarchy, and in forcing the Catholic bishops publicly to address the role of Irish Catholicism in constructing and sustaining the unionist image of the Republic of Ireland, the Forum helped to advance a shift in Irish national identity which had been progressing slowly since the Second Vatican Council.[9]

Identity theorists might view the role of the Forum, as they tend to see the peace process as a whole, as confirmation of the causal efficacy of the cultural to the neglect of the material. As the journalist cited above put it, it is the people who choose their identity, not governments or elites who tell them who they are. If the particular phenomenon of the Forum seems to lend some plausibility to this approach, it should not deceive us into thinking that Irish society or the nationalist community in the North have changed their identity through a cognitive process of negotiation and reason. We are collectively who

---

[8] It is doubtful if the voting patterns of Irish-Americans – estimated at one quarter of the US population – plays the significant part in American politics which successive administrations have assumed. The question has never been adequately tested, but the belief has powerful resonance for White House strategists. On the US–Northern Ireland connection, see John Dumbrell, 'The US and the Northern Ireland conflict 1969–94: from indifference to intervention', *Irish Studies in International Affairs*, 6, 1995, pp. 107–125; Adrian Guelke, 'The United States, Irish Americans and the Northern Ireland peace process', *International Affairs*, 72/3, 1996, pp. 521–536.

[9] Immediately following the Downing Street Declaration, Irish Taoiseach Albert Reynolds announced the convening of a successor to the New Ireland Forum under the title of Forum for Peace and Reconciliation. This official examination of the political and religious culture demanded by the peace process differs from its 1983 predecessor in inviting submissions from Sinn Féin and the unionist paramilitaries.

we want to be, but the process of change has been conditioned in large part by the stick and carrot, the pressure and blandishments of material interests, as I shall argue.

A stronger case for the relative detachment of identity from interests may be seen from the other side of the conflict in unionist efforts to resist the seduction of the peace process. Particularly evident in the theologically fundamentalist wing of unionism led by Ian Paisley and his Democratic Unionist Party, this resistance to the peace process has so far shown itself impervious to material considerations. Paisley and his fellow-spokespersons for fundamentalism show a certain socio-logical sophistication in their insistent warnings to the unionist community not to be seduced by promise of material gain into a relationship with Dublin which will inevitably result in the erosion of Protestant principles. (In the fundamentalist creed, the first principle of Protestantism is the resolute conviction that Roman Catholicism is an unchangeable, imperialist power and the implacable enemy of most of the other principles of Protestantism.[10]) The union with Britain is the only guarantee of the liberty of Protestants in Northern Ireland, and the peace process threatens its destruction. In the past, this movement has been numerous and powerful enough to threaten the stability of British governments and to threaten the election to public office of any unionist showing a weakness on the union.[11]

This makes it difficult for unionism as a whole to accept the Belfast Agreement signed by David Trimble on behalf of the majority political grouping: the Ulster Unionist Party. The major difficulty is that union-ists have for so long perceived their political interests as being defined in terms of an historical/theological identity which is fundamentally incompatible with the British and Irish concerns reflected in the peace process. This is not to claim that support for the union today carries all the metaphysical baggage of post-Reformation theology. Still less does it mean that unionist interests *cannot* be reconstructed to embrace a measure of common cause with nationalists, in line with

[10] For an account of Protestant ideology in Northern Ireland, see Frank Wright, 'Protestant ideology and politics in Ulster', *European Journal of Sociology*, 14, 1973; Dennis Cooke, *Persecuting Zeal: A Portrait of Ian Paisley*, Brandon Books, Dingle, 1996; Brian Walker, *Dancing to History's Tune*, Institute of Irish Studies, Belfast, 1996.

[11] At the time of writing, it cannot threaten the comfortable majority of the Blair government in Westminster, but its deputy leader, Peter Robinson, announced that it would use its influence and resources to undermine unionist candidates who support the peace process in the forthcoming elections to the Assembly. See *The Irish Times*, 24 May 1998.

the economic and political opportunities envisaged in the peace process.

Rather, it is to claim that the obduracy of a history defined by a Calvinist understanding of Catholicism, and neatly mirrored by a fundamentalist form of Irish Catholicism south of the border, provided Northern Presbyterianism with an uncomplicated image of self and the other. This has made opposition to any involvement in their affairs by Dublin a primary principle of action in its own right, transcending any material interests which might compete with it. Irish Catholicism represents the antithesis of the core beliefs of the powerful Calvinist voice in unionist politics.[12] When 'Ulster Says No!' in this tradition, it hears the tocsin sounded against the prospect of government by Rome and against the proven treachery of a Westminster government which might contrive it.

In a 1995 study of religious belief in Northern Ireland this obduracy of history in Protestant perceptions of their political future is revealed. Over 80 per cent of Protestants were convinced that 'Northern Ireland should remain part of the United Kingdom, with the most common objection to Irish unity being 'the power the Roman Catholic Church would have in a united Ireland. Confirmation of the stronger attachment to doctrinal and moral beliefs among Protestants/unionists and of their resistance to secularizing trends elsewhere in the UK was unambiguous: the young – under 24 years-old – Protestant churchgoers are more traditional in their theological and moral beliefs than their parents and grandparents, while the reverse is true of Catholics.[13]

It is arguably also a fairly detached sense of identity which accounts for the fidelity of German pro-Europeanism on the one hand and the Euro-scepticism endemic in British politics, on the other. Germany chose to define its identity in terms of a Western democracy integrated within a security community, while Britain chose to define itself as a marginal European and to emphasize its transatlantic and Commonwealth links in opposition to integration. This marks the historic choice at the origin of the Community in 1952, and continues to

---

[12] An account of the role of theology is given in Bill McSweeney, 'The religious dimension of the troubles in Northern Ireland', in Paul Badham (ed.), *Religion, State and Society in Modern Britain*, Mellen Press, London, 1988.

[13] Frederick Boal, David Livingstone and Margaret Keane, *Them and Us?*, Northern Ireland Office Central Community Relations Unit, 1996.

structure their different relationship with the Community at the end of the 1990s. Like many other countries in Europe after World War II, they both faced the same problem which individuals and collectivities routinely address at critical junctures in their lives, but which now posed itself with unprecedented starkness: Who are we?

Britain chose to distance itself from the Community because its post-war governments saw the possibility of reconstructing its prewar identity in line with economic and strategic interests alien to the integration project.[14] While, again, one cannot separate out the material self-interest from the moral choice in respect of identity, the British case sharpens the focus on identity. The idea that Britain was in Europe, but not of it, and must disentangle itself from the legacy of wartime involvement with the European allies in order to reassert its role as a major world power, proved a powerful motive for rejecting the Schuman Plan for European integration. Arguably, the case for short-term material self-interest should have led Britain in 1952 to the same decision eventually made in 1961, when application was finally made for membership of the Community. But this appeared to the political leadership of the time to entail the surrender of a centuries-old tradition of imperialism and independence to the uncertain benefits of integration with the 'lesser' states of Europe.

Who are the Germans? The question they addressed in the immediate aftermath of the war continues to arouse debate at every level of German society today and in the societies of its European neighbours. It was essential for the legitimacy of Adenauer's post-war foreign policy that a formal, speedy resolution of the question be adopted. But the identity of a society committed to cooperation and integration with its democratic neighbours was not there for Adenauer or anyone else to *discover.* History had provided different packages from which to select an answer – the Germany of Kant, Nietzsche, Marx or Herder offered a range of options, a variety of recipes from which Adenauer and the German people could select appropriate ingredients.

This choice was not, and could not, be made in a vacuum of external pressures and competing domestic interests. While these factors

---

[14] See Alan Milward, *The Reconstruction of Western Europe 1945–1951,* Methuen London, 1984; Anne Deighton, *The Impossible Peace: Britain, the Division of Germany and the Origins of the Cold War,* Oxford University Press, Oxford, 1993; Stephen George, *An Awkward Partner: Britain in the European Community,* Oxford University Press, Oxford, 1990; Peter Hennessy, *Never Again: Britain 1945–1951,* Jonathan Cape, London, 1992.

limited the freedom of choice, they did not eliminate it. Both at that time, and increasingly throughout the post-war period, Germans struggled to find adequate and credible expression of the cooperative democracy which they chose, and to distance themselves from other options which history offered as candidates. In particular, their choice of self-containment within a West European identity was a voluntary strategy to restrict their freedom to choose, in the future, the Germany of Nazism and the Holocaust.[15]

In opting to subordinate the various nationalist identikits in favour of a European Germany, Adenauer and his successors were not abandoning national interest in a spirit of self-sacrifice for the good of others. They were choosing, from an array of competing German interests, that self-interest which served a new identity, which repudiated the romantic nationalism of their past, and which converged with the interest of European integration. The choice of an integrationist foreign policy was, in effect, a choice of a cooperative rather than a self-help identity. Were they in the future to choose, under the pressure of foreign stereotypes or native nostalgia, to re-identify themselves with past romanticism, a quite different set of policies would emerge to mark their new interests. But they are so identified in their Europeanism today, because of choices made in the past, that such a reversion would be perceived as being against their self-interests. Neither today nor in Adenauer's day are self-interest and national identity independent of moral choice.

The primacy of interests

If we follow the reasoning of identity theory, we might expect identity to be the salient factor also in relation to the American option to press for the enlargement of NATO and the Russian decision to oppose it. That the American decision emerged primarily as a consequence of domestic pressures rather than the external demands of candidate countries in Eastern Europe, or the vague spectre of threats from the so-called 'security vacuum' in the former Soviet Union, is hardly in doubt. David Campbell's thesis, however, would locate the source of the decision in the internal *cultural* response to the moment of crisis at

---

[15] On German self-containment, see Wolfram Hanrieder, *Germany, America, Europe: 40 Years of German Foreign Policy*, Yale University Press, Newhaven, 1989; Alfred Grosser, *The Western Alliance: European–American Relations Since 1945*, Macmillan, London, 1980; Deighton, *The Impossible Peace*.

the end of the Cold War and the sudden departure of the historic enemy which had occasioned it.

It was clearly not the contemplation of the collective self which played the major role in triggering the decision in Madrid in July 1997, but the mundane calculation of interests. The rhetoric of American identity certainly reappeared in all the religious overtones familiar to students of American moralism.[16] In the period following Clinton's election promise to a strongly East European constituency in Chicago – 'the question is no longer whether NATO will take on new members, but when and how'[17] – the cloak of morality has been used to shield the gaze of middle America from the glitter of profit and the prize of expanding the defence industries in tandem with the Alliance.[18] Nonetheless, the intonation of American exceptionalism, at this juncture of history as on others, seems to be a necessary condition for self-interested foreign policy to pass the test of public support and Senate ratification. In the rhetoric of NATO enlargement we see once again 'the flowering of a sweet-smelling but noxious illusion', in Mark Danner's acid comment on the myths which replace reason in public discourse on foreign policy.[19]

The stated aims of expanding the Alliance are that of promoting democracy, political stability, and the market economy in Eastern Europe. 'The long-term objective is the integration of the economies of North America and Europe . . .. [The aim is] an agenda for common economic and political action to expand democracy, prosperity and stability.'[20] This interpretation of the aims of NATO expansion by US Secretary of State Warren Christopher was echoed by his colleague, Strobe Talbott, in addressing the common challenges facing the United States and the European Union. NATO enlargement, he said, 'will contribute to the conditions for the enlargement of the EU of which we are not a member but in which we have such a profound –

---

[16] Arthur Schlesinger Jr, *The Cycles of American History*, Houghton Mifflin, 1987, chapter 1; Mark Danner, 'Marooned in the Cold War: America, the Alliance, and the quest for a vanished world', *World Policy Journal*, Fall, 1997, pp. 1–23.

[17] President Bill Clinton, to Press Conference with Visegrad Leaders, Prague, 12 January 1994, White House press release, 13 January 1994.

[18] Benjamin Schwarz, 'Why America thinks it has to run the world', *Atlantic Monthly*, June 1996, pp. 92–102, and 'Cold War continuities: US economic and security strategy towards Europe', in Ted Galen Carpenter (ed.), *The Future of NATO*, Frank Cass, London, 1995.

[19] Danner, 'Marooned in the Cold War', p. 10.

[20] Christopher Warren, Madrid 2 June 1995, USIA.

I'd even say vital – interest.' NATO would create the stable and peaceful environment required for EU expansion. 'EU governments and Western investors must also be confident about the long-term deep-seated security of the region and that's what NATO is all about'.[21]

Promoting democracy, projecting stability, and fostering the market economy are the three great virtues which have replaced the fight against communist expansion in the Cold War as the basis of a political strategy to advance the claims of NATO. But the strategic thinking underlying US post-Cold War foreign policy was couched in less altruistic terms in the Pentagon's 'Defence Planning Guidance'. The United States, it claimed, must continue to dominate the international system; it must 'discourage' the 'advanced industrial nations from challenging our leadership or . . . even aspiring to a larger regional or global role'.[22]

Like David Campbell, Benjamin Schwarz, a Rand Corporation analyst, argues that it is an error to assume that American foreign policy is a response to the pressures of other states. By contrast with Campbell's identity theory, however, Schwarz emphasizes the causal significance of material interests. He views US security policy as having been 'primarily determined not by external threats but by the apparent demands of America's economy'.[23] He sees US policy during the Cold War as having less to do with the Soviet threat than with the aspirations outlined in the National Security Council's famous NSC-68, which defined policy in 1950. It was 'to foster a world environment in which the American system can survive and flourish . . . a policy which we would probably pursue even if there was no Soviet threat'.[24] Schwarz cites Anthony Lake, Clinton's National Security Advisor in his 1993 address 'From Containment to Enlargement' announcing the administration's new foreign policy doctrine: 'the expansion of market-based economies abroad helps expand our exports and create American jobs'.[25]

---

[21] Strobe Talbott, 'The US the EU and our common challenges', remarks at the transatlantic conference 6 May 1997, USIA.

[22] Leaked to *The New York Times* in 1992 and cited in Benjamin Schwarz, 'Why America thinks'.

[23] Schwarz, 'Cold War continuities'.

[24] *Ibid.*, p. 88; see also Fred Kaplan, *The Wizards of Armageddon*, Simon and Schuster, New York, 1983, chapters 8 and 9.

[25] Schwarz, 'Cold War continuities', p. 89.

If Schwarz is correct, the political analyst trying to infer and rank the competing goals of American foreign and domestic policy, must look behind the moralizing and externalizing of US foreign policy, and beyond the angst which reconstructs the national identity on the back of external events. A different theoretical perspective suggests a different rule of thumb to guide the selection and interpretation of evidence: the Clinton maxim of his first term of office – 'It's the economy, stupid!'

Russian concerns with national identity were also driven by interests after the end of the Cold War. Granted the complexity of the concept of the Cold War and its termination, and the multiple factors which must be weighed in any attempt to explain it, there can be little doubt that the judgment of rapidly declining economic interests and incapacity to sustain the arms race on the part of Gorbachev and the Soviet leadership played a substantial part in the redefinition of national identity which constitutes the end of the superpower confrontation.[26] Russia took its place among the democracies of the world because its interests were redefined in the learning process of long negotiation with Western democracies since the beginnings of détente in the early 1970s. Self-interest might have presented itself differently to leaders other than Gorbachev. His perception of it was expanded to reject the narrower calculation of political survival and ideological collapse which would certainly have inhibited his predecessors in following his example. But his calculation of interest clearly depended on Russian expectations of Western behaviour, particularly with regard to the vulnerability of Soviet borders to any revision of NATO strategy which might exploit the new situation.[27]

As in NATO expansion, so in the application of British security policy in Northern Ireland, identity does not always play the causal role assigned to it in identity theory. While Northern Ireland exemplifies the significant place of collective identity in generating and sustaining

---

[26] Fred Halliday, *Rethinking International Relations*, Macmillan, London, 1994, chapters 8, 9; Michael Cox, 'Rethinking the end of the Cold War', *Review of International Studies*, 20/2, 1994, pp. 187–200; John Lewis Gaddis, *The United States and the End of the Cold War*, Oxford University Press, Oxford, 1994; John Lewis Gaddis, 'International relations theory and the end of the Cold War', *International Security*, 17/3, 1992/3, pp. 5–58; Michael J. Hogan, *The End of the Cold War: its Meaning and Implications*, Cambridge University Press, Cambridge, 1992.

[27] Danner, 'Marooned in the Cold War', p. 5.

conflict, it is also Northern Ireland which illustrates powerfully the inseparable relation of interests to identity and, in some periods and for some actors, the primacy of interests.

The Belfast Agreement, and the accompanying measures announced by the British, Irish and American governments to entice the parties and people to accept it, is a neat example of the application of a comprehensive concept of security, of its intricate link with the question of collective identity, and of the dynamic relation of identity and interests in the concrete implementation of security policy. In place of the failed policies of the British government over the period of violent conflict since 1969, and sporadic conflict since the partitioning of Ireland in 1922, Britain's conversion to a model of security more closely associated with European integration is ironic in the light of its antagonism to that model elsewhere, but not surprising in the context of changing interests in relation to Northern Ireland since the end of World War II.

The signing of the Belfast Agreement on 10 April 1998 by leaders of all the political parties in Northern Ireland – including those nationalist and unionist parties which are closely linked to paramilitary organizations – has been internationally acclaimed as the culmination of the peace process and the beginnings of a new era of community in Northern Ireland. This Agreement, however, may not survive the efforts of splinter paramilitary groups to destroy it; it may not herald the victory of compromise over ideological principle which is widely anticipated. Like the IRA ceasefire of 1994, the consequences of the Belfast Agreement may yet challenge the optimism of the parties who signed it, and the faith in the peace process of the majority of people who supported it.[28] The Agreement does not determine the outcome it anticipates. That still depends on the choices to be made by the principal actors and by the public constituencies which they represent.

Like the IRA ceasefire, however, this Agreement is not the peace process, and the peace process in Northern Ireland is not resting on foundations as fragile as the goodwill of politicians and the convergence of public sentiment. It is constructed on a firmer base which

[28] For the whole island of Ireland, the percentage vote in support of the Agreement was 85 per cent, with 15 per cent against. Among traditional unionist supporters in Northern Ireland, however, it is calculated that only a slight majority voted in favour. Source: Richard Sinnott, 'The Belfast Agreement Referendums', *The Irish Times*, 25 May 1998.

is not as vulnerable to the unpredictable elements of the democratic process. That base is located primarily in the interests of the main actor, Britain, on whose perception of the problem and policies to deal with it the other actors must depend.

The Belfast Agreement proposes four major constitutional changes to the two jurisdictions in Ireland. An elected Assembly, or parliament, for Northern Ireland in which executive power must be shared by representatives of the main political parties; an executive role for the Dublin government in certain key areas of policy for the province; an effective veto by the majority of people in Northern Ireland over future constitutional change; the amendment of Articles 2 and 3 of the Irish Constitution claiming jurisdiction over the whole territory of the island.

Thus the first two can be interpreted as weighted in favour of nationalists, while the other provisions lean towards the unionist need to protect their identity. In addition, three important provisions in the Agreement address non-constitutional questions: the reform of the police force, the early release of political prisoners, and the process of decommissioning of weapons held by paramilitaries within two years of the election of the Assembly.

The enticements which accompany the agreed text are, politically, an integral part of the Agreement reached, even if this document, like the official accords which preceded it since the Anglo-Irish Agreement of 1985, excludes any suggestion that the British government would deviate from playing the role of neutral facilitator. One week before the referendum on the Agreement in Northern Ireland and the parallel referendum in the South, a £315m British programme for economic development of the province was announced by the Chancellor of the Exchequer, Gordon Brown. It was calculated to build on the peace process, though it was not made conditional on the acceptance of the Agreement in the referendum seven days later. 'Having created a framework for peace', he explained, 'we can now create a framework for prosperity.'[29]

In direct response to the IRA ceasefire of August 1994, the EU Commission set up a Special Support Programme for Peace and Reconciliation at the request of its then-President Jacques Delors. Throughout the period of ceasefire and its later breakdown in February 1996, and the protracted negotiations and talks which ended

[29] See reports in *The Guardian* and *The Irish Times*, 13 May 1998.

with the Belfast Agreement, a five-year disbursement of £400m made directly to cross-community cooperative projects has provided a powerful incentive to create the material conditions for peace. Deliberately calculated by the Commission to bypass government and party channels, the project has involved an estimated quarter of a million people in cooperative tasks.[30]

From the United States, Australia, New Zealand and Canada, investment and aid have been targeted on Northern Ireland projects designed to advance the prosperity of the region as a whole and to strengthen support for the peace process. The injection of money into the long-term viability of the economy of Northern Ireland has thus been an ongoing commitment on the part of multiple international donors since the IRA ceasefire of 1994. It represents a kind of peace dividend, since the annual expenditure involved is probably no greater than the added cost of traditional security measures to the British exchequer during periods of tension in the early 1970s. There are material benefits for the major donors of course – notably the political gains on offer to Britain and to the Blair government as well as the US Administration. There are, in addition, the financial rewards to private investors – mostly American – of creating a stable climate for profit in a favourable tax environment.[31]

But this is a peace dividend with an inbuilt purpose, even if all the donors have carefully avoided making an explicit link between material benefit and support for the Agreement. If we see the Belfast Agreement as a blueprint for transforming the relationship between the conflicting communities in the North, the change in identity which this logically and practically entails must be seen, not as the direct outcome of moral choice on the part of the major participants, but as the indirect consequence of a transformation of self-interest. This makes the peace process no less a choice and no less moral for being grounded in the interests of the parties directly concerned. Seduction is not coercion, as the powerful Paisley campaign to protect the Protestant identity against the blandishments of the peace process

---

[30] See the report by Patrick Smyth, *The Irish Times*, 14 April 1998.
[31] The potential of this type of corporate investment is considerable, though it is also most vulnerable to any breakdown in the peace process. A total of 14,000 employees in 51 US companies operate in Northern Ireland, compared with 60,000 in 430 companies in the Republic of Ireland. See Roger MacGinty, 'American influences on the Northern Ireland peace process', *Journal of Conflict Studies*, 17/2, 1997, p. 43.

demonstrated.[32] The moral choice embodied in the Agreement must be seen as the option for a broader definition of interests than that locked historically into the zero sum of sectarianism – interests designed to lead progressively to an inclusive sense of collective identity in place of the exclusive versions historically cultivated and transmitted through generations.[33]

From the standpoint of Westminster, it is clear that British interests cannot be neutral in regard to the outcome of the negotiation process. The declaration that Britain has 'no selfish strategic or economic interests' in the constitutional future of Northern Ireland[34] cannot disguise the fact that important 'selfish' interests in detaching Northern Ireland from the British identity map have been developing for decades. Since the partititioning of Ireland in 1921, the province was always an ambiguous offshore element in the wider collectivity of the United Kingdom. Behind the rhetoric of playing neutral facilitator to the peace process, the British government, with the cooperation of Dublin, has played the role of active persuader. The concessions and side-bargaining described above were planned to ensure that any Agreement reached in Belfast was not left to the lottery of conflicting opinion and the normal workings of majoritarian democracy. It needed to establish an agenda designed to promote British interests in the process of gradual devolution and, in effect, to weaken support for the union within Northern Ireland.

Several factors contributed to persuading the government of John Major that it was time for a decisive break with the security policy of the past. The declining strategic importance of Northern Ireland since the end of World War II; the escalating costs of the Westminster subvention required to support the Northern Ireland economy and

---

[32] Paisley fundamentalism cannot threaten the comfortable majority of the Blair government in Westminster, but its deputy leader, Peter Robinson, made it clear that it would use its influence and resources in a continuing campaign to undermine the peace process. See *The Irish Times*, 24 May 1998.

[33] There is nothing inevitable in the 'social engineering' underlying the Belfast Agreement – or in any attempt to transform and manage collective relations. Prior to the two referenda on the Agreement, it was far from certain whether the choices made north and south of the border would herald the success of the design or the return to sectarianism.

[34] First announced by Northern Ireland Secretary of State, Peter Brooke, 9 November 1990 and formally repeated in the London Declaration of December 1993, a joint Anglo-Irish statement widely considered to have opened the door to the IRA ceasefire the following August.

security apparatus; the increasing export of IRA violence to the British mainland since the early 1980s, in particular the shift from civilian targets to political and financial; growing support of British public opinion for withdrawal from the province and detachment from the British mainland; the evidence of a new political culture in the Republic of Ireland, more amenable to negotiation on the terms of a workable peace process; the pressure of successive US governments and, particularly, the aggressive involvement of the Clinton Administration to settle the Irish question in favour of what is perceived to be Irish–American nationalist opinion.[35]

British public support for devolution in Northern Ireland reflects the ambiguity of the province in terms of national identity. If it is problematic to make sense of a 'British' identity today, as distinct from an English one, it has always required some mental agility to extend national identity to the whole of the United Kingdom. Opinion polls in the past few years make depressing reading for any unionists still inclined to believe the rhetoric of the union. While 72 per cent of the people of Northern Ireland preferred to remain part of the UK in 1992, only 30 per cent of the British people saw the identity of Northern Ireland in the same light. In a different poll two years later, 70 per cent of the British people opted for some form of detachment of Northern Ireland from Britain, either through independence or unity with the Republic of Ireland, while British support for the union remained at 30 per cent.[36] These polls reflect the political reality of an offshore region, geographically and constitutionally set apart from the core nation since its inception, with its identification with the crown thus exposed to the test of its performance on economic, political and strategic indicators in a manner which would be unthinkable for Somerset or Cornwall.

Questions of material interest have made the peace process more attractive in the Republic of Ireland also, and helped to remove some of the obstacles to compromise and cooperation which Ireland cultivated in the past. The rapidity with which Ireland is breaking with its monoculturalist past, allowing it to seize the political advantages

---

[35] See Dumbrell, 'The US and Northern Ireland'; Guelke 'The United States'; MacGinty, 'American influences'.

[36] Sources: The 1992 British Election Study, ESRC Data Archive, University of Essex; Gallup Political Index 1979–1994, cited in Bernadette Hayes and Ian McAllister, 'British and Irish public opinion towards the Northern Ireland problem', unpublished paper, IPSA conference, Drogheda, October 1995.

offered by the convergence of interest on the part of the other main actors in the peace process, is matched by the speed of economic growth which the country has enjoyed in the same period. Since 1994, the economy has grown at the extraordinary rate of 7 per cent, leaving Ireland in 1998 with a predicted annual growth rate of 5 per cent or more for several years.[37] It is difficult to sustain this level of growth in an export-driven economy and, at the same time, to sustain the exclusivist Catholic ethos which was a defining characteristic of national identity in the past, and which presented an insuperable barrier to closer integration with Northern Protestants. Ireland's new wealth, moreover, is a function of its membership of a community of secular states in Europe.

This is not to imply that the EU has set the price and the Irish have sold their identity. The EU is not the only source of growth in the Irish economy, and factors other than wealth have also eroded Ireland's attachment to traditional Catholicism. The conflict in Northern Ireland is not just about economics, and the entrenched identities are not commodities easily bartered for material interests, as Paisley's fundamentalists have shown. Wealth can be an irritant or an ointment; its distribution can be a source of sectarian rivalry as well as a means of integration. The Belfast Agreement is a plan for integration, designed to ensure that material interest will work as a balm to the reconstruction of identity. Its accompanying incentives are essential instruments to that end.

It should be clear that the strategy employed in the Northern Ireland peace process was not the invention of civil servants in Dublin or Westminster, still less of the political leaders who signed up to it in Northern Ireland. It is an application of the neofunctionalist model of integration applied to the construction of the European Union. In this model, it will be recalled, identities and interests are viewed as inseparably linked and mutually constituting properties, although the management of their reconstruction in the case of the EU was flawed in making unwarranted assumptions about the automatic spillover of political allegiance – identity – from interests.

Classical neofunctionalism is at the other extreme to identity theory in emphasizing the material factors to the exclusion of the cognitive, exaggerating the causal potential of *interests* in relative detachment from identity. The history of European integration is one of step-by-

---

[37] 'Ireland shines', Special Report, *The Economist*, 17 May 1997.

step expansion of common interests driving the legal and political train of common identity. With the notable exception of the United Kingdom, political elites, national bureaucracies and interest groups across the Community were successfully enmeshed in the cooperation process and drawn into a community allegiance which encouraged a sense of the collective good. The crisis following Maastricht in 1992, however, revealed the extent to which continued support for European integration depends on *public* allegiance, not just that of the bureaucratic and business elites who served as the principal point of reference for the neofunctionalist calculation and upgrading of interests.

A sense of the common good and of their longer-term interests on the part of India and Pakistan may require an external persuader for South Asia – as it did for the EU and Northern Ireland – to emancipate itself from the constraints of its past. The freedom of India and Pakistan to choose a different conception of security to structure their relationship must be affirmed, however. The Franco-German relationship today is a product of choices made at the end of World War II, when its conflictual character made it structurally similar to that of India and Pakistan. It is easy to point to unique features of the time and the fortuitous convergence of interests to account for the transformation of identity in France and Germany over the next decades. One could make the same point against generalizing about Northern Ireland as a model for the Basque Country[38] or, indeed, for South Asia.

One generalization emerges from the analysis of this book, however, relevant to the resolution of conflictual structures like those of South Asia and the Basque Country: that human agency is complicit in the structures which constitute it. To put it more plainly: we choose who we are and who we want to be. We are no more determined by universal laws of anarchic social structure to act out the roles assigned to states in conflictual association by orthodox political science, than we are to act out the cooperative roles structured for us by a comprehensive security policy or peace process. As noted above, the Belfast Agreement does not determine the outcome it

---

[38] Spokespersons for Herri Batasuna, the political organ of the Basque separatist movement, called on the Spanish government to apply the model of the Belfast Agreement to the settlement of the Spanish dispute. The appeal was rejected on grounds of the unique circumstances of the two situations. *The Irish Times*, 23 May 1998.

anticipates. France and Germany had a choice in 1952 to construct a different world, as they have a choice today to return to the old one.

Brazil and Argentina also had a choice between alternative worlds when they faced the possibility of a nuclear arms race in the 1980s, when both were pursuing a policy of traditional national security. Had they not chosen then to abandon nuclear deterrence in favour of the pursuit of common interests,[39] Latin America might now be facing the same insecurity as the people of the Indian subcontinent.

Identity and interests, it has been argued, are analytically distinct and dynamically interrelated dimensions of all stages in the formulation of security policy in its comprehensive sense. Whether security policy is oriented to the construction of a security community – or 'peace process' – as in the case of European integration and Northern Ireland, or a military alliance with negative implications for security in the broader sense, as with NATO expansion, the place of interests and identity is central. We choose the friend as we choose the enemy, and the process of interaction with both is the school in which we learn how to define the national interest and the collective identity which it logically presumes.

Like the major treaties of the European Union, the Belfast Agreement in Northern Ireland may be considered the foundation of a new school of learning. It is a school already chosen under differing constraints by the participating parties, and designed to deepen the structures of cooperation which will entice, enmesh and seduce a wide range of actors into an integrated security community. The cooperation habit – or 'coordination reflex' in Eurospeak – is a concept preferable in this context to 'structures', though it relates to the same idea understood reflexively to capture the interplay of choice and constraint in the unfolding of social action.

---

[39] Brazil and Argentina signed the Bilateral Agreement for the Exclusively Peaceful Uses of Nuclear Energy in Guadalajara, Mexico, in July 1991. This agreement was ratified and came into force in December the same year.

11 Conclusion: Security and moral choice

The principal focus of attention throughout this book has been the problem of security in the international order – how we define it, how we understand it in relation to everyday concerns, and how we define the threats and policies consequent upon a particular understanding of it. What began as an attempt to clarify and develop this concept in the relatively clear waters of the security studies mainstream, has ended in murkier currents. What started under the stimulus of Buzan's contribution to that tradition, has emerged along a deviant path into the tradition of sociology which he rejected. Identity, interests and moral choice – these are the sub-themes which came together in the course of the discussion and which, in the end, appear to be inseparably linked in any adequate account of security and security policy, whether at the academic or the policy-making level.

In addition, the problem had to be addressed of including a wider range of human needs under the heading of a concept traditionally defined in narrow, operational terms, without losing analytical control of the security needs of collectivities, including states.

If these are seen as underlying topics of the general concern with security, an overarching thesis was identified early in the discussion, gradually emerging as the condition for handling the interrelation of the sub-themes and, at the same time, the outcome of identifying them as such. This relates to the question of what kind of world it is in which the idea of security and security policy arises. What is the international order from which some scholars derive an understanding of security as an objective reality, measurable and manipulable according to the same tenets which apply to nature, while others view it in radical disjunction from the natural?

The historical analysis of the attempts by scholars to capture the subject of security as it relates to international affairs shows the complexity of the topic. Security is a slippery term indeed, rooted in a fundamental human emotion which takes on different forms and emphases as it expresses itself at different levels of community.

Since the end of World War I, when intellectuals began to formalize the attempt to understand and explain the great issues of war and peace, the debate about security and about the appropriate methods of studying it has never been finally resolved in favour of one school or its rivals. The philosophical and interdisciplinary approach of the early 'political theory' period was never entirely vanquished by its successors in 'political science'. The idea that security in the international realm must be rooted in the meaning which the term has for individuals, and must have its primary reference in the needs of individuals, was never banished from the debate, even in its so-called 'golden age'.

Neither did security lose its power to evoke the positive as well as the negative aspect. The analogy with health was drawn to clarify the notion of a positive dimension of security based on a moral conception of human needs. This was shown to expose the normative quality of *any* conception of health or security. State security within the traditional school of security studies rests on a conception of human needs, it was argued. It is a moral judgment about human needs, disguised as an objective discovery or an axiom of common sense, which grounds state security in the primacy of the survival of the state. Without reference to evidential criteria or philosophical justification, human individuals in general are assumed to be the bearers of a hierarchy of interests or needs which places physical survival at the apex and implies a correlative need for the power of the state to be mobilized as an instrument in its defence.

Notwithstanding the current of humanistic ideas about security which survived the influence of the political science tradition, this influence has been, and remains, a significant factor in divorcing the conception of security applicable to international affairs from the concern expressed in everyday life by individuals. The elaboration of a scientific procedure in the school of structural realism, based on the belief that the international order constitutes an object of inquiry separate from the social order and susceptible to the quantitative methods required for a cumulative science, played a major part in achieving this divorce.

Various assumptions helped to legitimize this separation. The idea that nothing coherent can be said about the international order if the level of inquiry is reduced to that of the individuals who comprise it was supported by evoking the intellectual sin of 'methodological individualism'. Correctly understood, methodological individualism is indeed a fallacious doctrine, consigning the collective actor of the family or state to the residual category of an aggregation of individuals, and ignoring the unconscious element of structure in the conditioning of individual behaviour.

The view that security is 'essentially contested' is another assumption employed to warrant the separation of the collectivity from the individual. It conveys the idea that there is something peculiar about a class of social concepts which bear a heavy subjective weight – like peace, justice, security – and which sets them apart from others not so contested. The cultivation of this myth in the field of security studies, it was argued, functions to justify the avoidance of the problem of definition – how can one set boundaries to an idea which is 'essentially' disputed? But at the same time it permits the smuggling of an implicit, operational definition in terms which disregard the unruly contestation at the individual level in favour of the objective facts of the 'state', its capabilities and its vulnerabilities. As discussed in chapter 5, it is not incorrect to view security as essentially contested; the error lies in the presumption that other social concepts in general – like the state – are any more stable, any less prone to the slippage of meaning which is a condition of the social.

In the scientific tradition of neorealism, the state became the irreducible actor within a *sui generis* world of the international system. Not only were individuals' understanding of the central concepts which directed its behaviour ignored, but states were cast in a uniform mould as undifferentiated entities responding to the stimulus of their external environment. As actors trapped within an unchanging structure of anarchy, they were defined irredeemably in their character or identity, and in the interests which impelled them to interact. This is the realists' 'real' world, where the appearance of change in the identity of the state disguises the immutable condition of nature, only to be revealed as illusory by the inexorable laws of the international order.

States go to war, make peace, balance against each other or cooperate with each other. But we delude ourselves, according to realism, if we believe that the change of behaviour indicates anything more fundamental or permanent than a change of strategy. To expect states to change the fundamentals of their character, for Waltz, Mearsheimer and their realist colleagues, is to expect the geopolitical equivalent of transubstantiation. As boys will be boys, states will be states. Chronic insecurity is the environmental condition and egoism is the nature of the actors born into it. In this tradition, states can cooperate but they cannot become cooperative, and the structure which constrains them is, in turn, determined by the self-seeking character of its unit actors.

The science of the international has been under sustained attack since the middle of the 1980s – not simply by peaceniks and utopians on ethical grounds alone, but by scholars rigorously examining the assumptions and claims of the neorealists and exposing their inadequacy. Under various labels, a growing anti-positivist literature in international relations theory has been attempting to apply the deconstructionist impulse of contemporary sociology to the central concepts of international relations. In part II of the book, this developing body of sociological theory was opened up for examination as to its potential for the study of international security.

This brought to the forefront of analysis the meta-theme which transcends the issue of security and which has been a major concern of the book as a whole. Understanding better what kind of world we live in, it was argued, is the condition of recovering the human and moral dimension of security and security policy. It is not just security, as understood within the dominant school of security studies, which fails the test of its own criteria of scientific evaluation, but the approach to the meta-question which informs this school and the study of international relations in general. The theoretical argument of part II is thus as much concerned with arguing a theory of international relations which provides an alternative perspective on security as with the specific topic of security.

What remains to be done in this final chapter is to draw together these two lines of argument concerning the nature of the social order and the topic of security, and to offer a plausible alternative understanding of both to that which is provided in mainstream international studies.

Different worlds, different security

It is the contrast between two different views of structure and causality which gives rise to the different worlds from which we construct our accounts of international security. One approach views the natural and the social as a unity, both constructed of objective elements independent of our attempts to understand them, and susceptible to the same method of observation and explanation. The other sees a social world composed of human volition and habits – basic elements of agency and structure – which do not coalesce into a stable regularity which can be objectively measured and scientifically analysed.

What was termed the social constructionist approach to this distinctive reality sees the international order as part of the social, and the social as comprising an ontologically different reality from the natural. In the most pervasive application of this approach, drawing on the Durkheimian school of sociology, the basic stuff of social structure is cognitive. We project a world of norms, rules and institutions, and they thereby acquire a facticity which we perceive as the objective constraint on our thinking and behaviour. But this is still 'a humanly produced, constructed objectivity' according to Berger and Luckmann who have contributed considerably to the popularization of this approach. Institutions are the product of human practices.

As argued, however, the world of their theorizing turns out to be no more hospitable to human volition and creativity than the world of nature which they thought to supplant. Tracing its source to human ideas, values and practices helps us to see society as a human product in the sense that Durkheim saw the fundamental categories of space and time and the religious impulse as the product of social needs and constraints. It does not rescue human individuals from the constraints imposed by the conception of structure which Berger and Luckmann's work promised to overcome. If structure is seen as a constraint on action independent of the agent, *it matters little whether it is also seen as a cognitive rather than a material entity.* The view that structure and human agency are independent entities opens the social world to the search for causal generalizations of the same law-like character as those which can be inferred in the natural. Berger and Luckmann conjured a closed system no more capable of accounting for the obvious fact that institutions change – at times dramatically – than the Parsonian grand theory which they claimed to oppose. They understood correctly that human creativity is the only key to explaining this phenomenon, but could not devise a general theory which would allow for this and, at the same time, function as the explanatory model of social action to which they aspired.

Social constructionism and neo-liberal constructivism

Drawing on the tradition of social constructionism, a perspective which promised a radical reconceptualization of structure and causality in the social sciences was introduced to international relations theory at the end of the 1980s under the label 'constructivism'. As different scholars practising different shades of rationalist inquiry soon realized, however, constructivism does not necessarily pose a challenge to the methodological principles and epistemological assumptions of the mainstream approach to explaining the international order. Proponents of this predominantly American school saw in the application of the work of Durkheim and the Durkheimians a progressive turn to sociology rather than a step back to its discredited past, and one which did not force them to push their critique of Waltzian neorealism beyond the exchange of a material for a cognitive definition of structure.

Alexander Wendt is not only the principal figure in the emergence of this school but represents in his writings a common position on the metatheoretical principles of constructivism in contemporary international relations scholarship. His view of causality and structure in the social order is essentially in line with that of Ruggie, Adler, Finnemore and others,[1] and with a growing consensus among constructivists that theirs is an eirenic endeavour capable of bringing intellectual harmony to a discipline threatened by dissident critics of its positivist mainstream.

There has been a notable effort on the part of international relations scholars in the past few years to check the growth of factions within the discipline and to reconcile the main schools of theory and metatheory identified by Robert Keohane as the 'rationalistic' and the 'reflective'. The theme of the 1999 ISA Washington Convention, 'One Field, Many Perspectives', the 1998 ISA Presidential Address, and a flush of articles in the journals, attest to a concern – widespread in the

---

[1] John Gerard Ruggie, 'What makes the world hang together? Neo-utilitarianism and the social constructivist challenge', *Constructing the World Polity: Essays on International Institutionalization*, Routledge, 1998, Introduction; Emanuel Adler, 'Seizing the middle ground: Constructivism in world politics', *European Journal of International Relations*, 3/3, 1997, pp. 319–363; Martha Finnemore, *National Interests in International Society*, Cornell University Press, Ithaca, 1996.

United States, scarcely felt in European circles – to resolve Keohane's problems.[2]

The ambiguity noted in chapter 6 in relation to Wendt's avowed radicalism is somewhat clarified in his more recent account of the metatheoretical basis of constructivism, and merits further analysis here in light of the theoretical discussion of the preceding chapters.[3] He makes it clearer than before that he sees 'no fundamental epistemological difference between the natural and social sciences', and he repeats his explicit commitment to constructivism as a bridge between the rationalist and the reflectivist approaches to explaining the international order. Taking issue with the views of Hollis and Smith, who see the causal mode of analysis in natural science as opposed to the interpretative one appropriate to the social order, he states that 'the intellectual activities associated with Explanation and Understanding *both*, are, and should be, practised in *both* domains'.[4]

For Wendt, the important distinction relevant to our knowledge of the natural and social worlds is the distinction between different kinds of explanation – 'between explanations that answer different kinds of question, causal and constitutive'.[5] A causal relationship must satisfy the three conditions: that the cause is antecedent to the effect, that it is independent of it, and that the effect could not have occurred without it. A constitutive relationship exists where only the third condition applies – it defines the properties of an entity without which the thing itself would not exist. It gives the identity of the thing observed. It tells us, for example, what it means to speak of a 'Cold War': 'The relationship between the factors constituting . . . a Cold War is one of *identity*, in the sense that those factors define what a Cold War *is*, not one of causal determination.'[6]

---

[2] Robert O. Keohane, 'International institutions: two approaches', *International Institutions and State Power: Essays in International Relations Theory*, Westview, Boulder, 1989; Margaret G. Hermann, 'One field, many perspectives: building the foundations for dialogue', ISA Presidential Address, *International Studies Quarterly*, 42/4, 1998, pp. 605–624.

[3] Alexander Wendt, 'On constitution and causation in international relations', *Review of International Studies*, 1998, pp. 101–117; see also his *Social Theory of International Politics*, Cambridge University Press, Cambridge, forthcoming 1999.

[4] Wendt, 'On constitution', p. 102. For his earlier commitment see Alexander Wendt, 'Anarchy is what states make of it: the social construction of power politics', *International Organization*, 46/2, 1992, p. 394; Martin Hollis and Steve Smith, *Explaining and Understanding International Relations*, Clarendon Press, Oxford, 1991.

[5] Wendt, 'On constitution', pp. 103/4.

[6] Wendt, 'On constitution', p. 106.

This does not mean that he restricts causal accounts to the natural order and allocates the 'constitutive' ones to the social. On the contrary, he stresses that both are relevant to the proper understanding of the natural and social sciences. Ideas can have causal effects as well as constitutive. For example, the shared understandings which *constitute* the identities of masters and slaves also have *causal* effect on their behaviour – 'functioning as independently existing and temporally prior mechanisms motivating and generating their behaviour'.[7]

The influence of Durkheimian determinism could hardly be clearer, lending objectivity and independence to the collective conscience (shared meanings) in the same disregard of the reflexive character of social action and of what Giddens terms the 'double hermeneutic' of the social order. As with Durkheim's social constructionism so with Wendt's constructivism, the insight that humans construct the social and international order is rendered vacuous for the agency of individual actors by the theoretical framework in which human agency is rediscovered as an object – an effect of external, antecedent causal factors no less determined by explanatory 'laws' than the material world of Waltz.

Wendt rests his case on a questionable distinction between the constitutive and the causal (confusingly referred to as 'how' questions and 'why' questions),[8] and on the view that both types of question are applicable to the ideas of the social and the material stuff of the natural order. In this he echoes the more familiar, misplaced distinction between constitutive and regulative rules on which Ruggie has built his constructivism – independently of Wendt, but on the same foundations of Durkheim and the causal explanation of ideas.[9] Contrary to Ruggie, all rules have a constitutive and regulative character, depending on the context in which we choose to focus on them.

Contrary to Wendt, to ask what is the structure of a physical entity such as a living body is only superficially to ask for a constitutive *as distinct from* a causal understanding. All understanding of the natural order, which is not reducible to empirical description or analytic definition, seeks causal explanation. We can describe the parts which biologically make up a human being in constitutive language – heart,

---

[7] Wendt, 'On constitution', p. 107.
[8] Wendt, 'On constitution', pp. 104/5.
[9] Ruggie, 'What makes the world'.

brain, etc. – but this assumes that we understand their causal function. The human brain is an organ antecedent to, and independent of, its behavioural effects. To say that it is a constituent of being human is merely an analytically distinct form of the same causal expression – a human being is constituted by having a brain which functions in a particular causal way.

Conversely, we can frame an antecedent causal account of social action, but only by freezing it analytically out of the temporal context in which it derives its meaning and by ignoring or bracketing the agent's side of the co-constitution of action. In the example given by Wendt,[10] the question 'Why did Gorbachev move to end the Cold War?' is framed to elicit such a causal response, inviting analysis which points to antecedent and independent factors such as 'domestic financial crisis' and 'American technological superiority'. This is the conventional approach to understanding the social order and it is useful in exploring the empirical evidence and the logic of inquiry. But it is a fiction, and an obstacle to uncovering the event under investigation, unless we bear in mind that Gorbachev's move is part of a temporal process which must be unravelled, deconstructed, in order to understand it. It is to cast 'superiority', 'crisis', and 'Cold War' as fixed things rather than fluid meanings. We cannot know how far American technology was constructed as 'superior', and domestic finances projected and fed into popular opinion as 'crisis', by Gorbachev and others contributing to his decisive move, without interpretative inquiry. To assume that Gorbachev discovered 'crisis' and 'superiority' out there in the Soviet ether and moved in response to it is unwarranted without rigorous investigation of the meanings which entered into the social practices constituting the Soviet political culture of the Cold War.

A 'constitutive' account of the social is one which uncovers the practices which enter recursively into the construction of an event or social concept, and which respects the dual influence of agent and structure in the co-constitution, or *co-causing*, of social action. If we follow the logic of the reflexive sociology on which Wendt originally claimed to base his quest for a radical alternative to Waltzian theory, all understanding of the social order is and must be constitutive in the sense explained. We can rephrase Wendt's question. 'What enabled Gorbachev's move to end the Cold War?' more obviously highlights

[10] Wendt, 'On constitution', p. 104.

the temporal, processual, character of social action and serves to elicit the same facts but not to imply the same kind of causal relationship between them.

We can further illustrate the difference between asking causal questions in the search for antecedent causes and asking social ('constitutive') questions which require the contextual analysis of process, by drawing on a more common and familiar problem of human relations. 'Why did Helen initiate divorce proceedings?' The answer might be given: 'Because John had an affair'. (For Helen and 'affair' read Gorbachev and crisis.) But we are too well-versed in the nuances of social relations at this level to accept at face value that John's affair can stand as a cause antecedent to, and independent of, Helen's action. What the purportedly 'causal' question invites is an account of the development of the relationship which makes sense of the end-point on which it focuses.

The difference of analysis explored also helps to illustrate how the rationalist and the reflexive approaches to the social and international order cannot be mediated by one which merely replaces the material structure of the one with the ideational structure of the other, within the same framework of causal explanation. The gap between the two approaches derives from seeing a different world – one which is explicable by causal inference, on the one hand; on the other, one which is constituted by the knowledgeability and skill of individuals monitoring and managing structures of meaning which enable them to communicate and which constrain their options in so doing, and which cannot be known except by exploring what the actors know. In both worlds we need to infer structure and causality. But the meaning of these terms and their interrelationship in the constitution of the social order are so different as to warrant the claim that there is no ecumenical epistemology which can bridge the gap.

Wendt appears to have abandoned the recursiveness of the agent–structure relationship which earlier characterized his break with the mainstream approach, in favour of a social constructionist one permitting causal explanation of social events according to the model of natural science. 'Neo-liberal constructivism' is a more accurate label for a school which has far more in common with the liberal-rationalist emphasis on transnational cooperation, institutions and norms, and on the unproblematic primacy of the state, than with a research agenda based on reflexivist principles of the continuity of the collective and individual actor and of the co-constitution of agency and structure.

A reflexive model of social order

Security only makes sense if individual human beings are seen as its primary referent, or subject. If we allow the assumption that physical survival from external threat is the primary human need which must be secured by the state, traditional state-oriented security policy follows. But human needs in general are not objectively classified according to such a hierarchy. Which need is primary for the purpose of organizing security policy is not just a matter of empirical observation, but of philosophical and moral judgment.

The basic need for security, it was argued, is that which expresses itself as such in everyday life and in all social action. It is the security of social relations, experienced in confidence in our capacity to understand, monitor and manage them in day-to-day activities. It is from this elemental experience, by definition common to all individuals, that we derive the social order as the general condition of ontological security and the structural focus of security policy. A human security policy, then, cannot be derived by aggregating individual needs, on the one hand, or by attributing such needs to the state *a priori*, on the other. Neither should it be conceived in terms of the maintenance of social control, of law and order. This is not to deny that social order in that sense is a necessary consideration for the management of social order in the more basic sense discussed here. When agents of the state move to reduce the level of burglaries in an urban area, mount covert operations against groups suspected of threatening military installations, or attack villages suspected of harbouring terrorists, each of these actions is directed towards the maintenance of order in the sense of social control. Whether they also contribute to sustaining the social order in the basic sense of the conditions for social action cannot be assumed. But if a security policy is to serve human needs, then it must serve the purpose of managing this social order and not only the conditions for social control.

Social order is the fundamental security question in the light of which policies of social control must be judged. It relates to the conditions which facilitate confidence in the predictability and routine of everyday social life. Such conditions are clearly threatened by factors which are traditionally counted as threats against the state, but they may equally be threatened by policies of the state legitimized in the name of a security policy which has only negative relevance to social order. The secret policing of society in most countries of Eastern

Europe during the Cold War, for example, was calculated to *disrupt* the social order so as to increase social control by the state. The surveillance work of the Stasi in the former German Democratic Republic systematically undermined the routine and normality of life for most of the population to much the same effect as the experiments of Garfinkel described in chapter 8. The exposure of the weakness of the state at the end of the Cold War in its incapacity to mobilize its citizens in its support and to resist the mass exodus which followed can doubtlessly be traced in part to its state security policy. Not to see such a state security policy as the major security problem for the society of East Germany is one of the absurdities which follow from the state-centred approach of security studies.

The security of the social order is inseparably linked to the identity of the collectivity which is its subject. This follows from consideration of the relational character of ontological security as we experience it in interpersonal social action. Social action is fraught with the question of the security of the actor in respect of shared knowledge, norms and practices and the skill to manage them. The confidence which is a condition of such mutual knowledge is based on confidence in a shared identity – fundamentally a common identity as human, over-laid with other identities which may add to, or detract from, the confidence of actors in their practical skills to interact and to sustain order or routine. It is when this confidence in the social order is threatened or disrupted that we can speak of a breach of identity and a security problem. Nationalist elites, when they contrive to fracture collective identities or to construct a new solidarity across old divisions, are reproducing at the collective level the same logic inherent in social action at the level of the individual. The security policies embodied in NATO expansion and in the Northern Ireland peace process are practices in the reconstruction of social order as well as practices of social control.

We misunderstand both ontological security and security at the collective level if we restrict analysis to the cognitive, cultural dimension, however. Material resources play a central role in both. Just as interpersonal relations cannot be analysed as the negotiation of meaning through the practical exercise of communication skills alone, without regard for the imbalance of power arising from unequal command over resources, so with the construction and management of collective identity. Material interests interact with cognitive options to influence the choice of identity.

Identity theory exaggerates the causal role of identity and fails to account for the evidence of its manipulation by interest groups and the role of interests in constituting the process by which actors learn to shift to a new position on the continuum of anarchy. (The fundamental properties of states in the neorealist approach are, after all, identity *and* interests.) Both are subject to revision in terms of their malleability in the context of state interaction. Without factoring the dimension of interests into the learning process, it is impossible to explain how a change of identity could occur. It is idealistic to imagine that individuals or collectivities, socialized by habit and history into a particular sense of self, will choose to change without the incentive or pressure of self-interest. The dynamic of identity and interests was sharpened by looking at the opposite error to that of identity theory – the neofunctionalist theory which exaggerated the causal role of interests by subordinating the choice of collective identity to the choice of interests.

The conception of the social world which generates the analysis of security presented in the foregoing chapters is a reflexive one. What is entailed in a reflexive model of the social order can be summarized as follows in propositional form. Identity and interests are mutually constituted by knowledgeable agents, monitoring, managing, and manipulating the narrative of one in respect of the other. To say that both are chosen by human individuals is, firstly, to make a claim – with constructivism, but against neorealism – that the behaviour of states is an effect of cognitive *and* material structures, of the distribution of power informed by ideas. Secondly, the choice is made in the context of interaction with other states in the international arena, and with sub-state groups within the domestic. Thirdly – and against constructivism – state choices are not only constrained by structure; they effect the progressive transformation of structure within a reflexive structure–agent relationship which can never be dissolved in favour of the determinative role of the actor or of the structure of action. This implies, fourthly, that the concept of structure and the conception of causality in the social sciences must be radically distinguished from the ideas applicable to our understanding of the natural order. To affirm the co-constitution of behaviour by agent and structure is to affirm causality in the social order, but it is not to affirm what we mean by 'cause' in respect of the natural order. In the real world, in contrast to that conjured as such by mainstream security analysts, there is no objective structural entity which can function as an independent cause of social relations. There is nothing out there in social behaviour which can stand as an effect of events or conditions which are independent of the human agent. This is simply a different kind of world.

It follows, finally, that our capacity to explain the behaviour of states or other actors in terms of generalizations drawn from observation of regularity and pattern is strictly limited by the nature of the social world itself – not by its empirical complexity or our limited intelligence which time and technology, in principle, can surmount. That we can observe regularities and draw upon them to construct an account of behaviour which is not restricted to the experience of the actors is a philosophical position argued here against a radical postmodernism. Meta-narrative is thus affirmed; some accounts of social reality are superior to others. The evidence allows us to judge, for instance, that structural factors inhibit the capacity of agents in a Indian subcontinent to choose in favour of common interests and a transformed Indian or Pakistani identity which might result, or that the constituents of identity among Serbs or Irish are not given by nature or fixed by history or casually malleable by the sovereign will of their incumbents.

To affirm the possibility of generalizations about human behaviour is to state the obvious. We could not speak without the generalized meanings given in language; human beings could not communicate at all except in the context of common meanings and practices structured by repetitive action and routinely reaffirmed norms and rules. But *generalizations are not laws*; they are resources which actors draw upon to make action possible, to give reasons for action, and thus to appropriate as an element of action itself. Generalizations circulate through the framework of the social order, from observer to agent, from agent-as-observer to behaviour, making it impossible to conceive of a social law which functions for social action like the law of gravity. The regularities of the social order, which constitute the objective basis of all attempts to construct a science of the social, are always in some part the accomplishment of individual actors, never merely the effect of external constraint. Social pattern and regularity are like shadows in Plato's cave: they are indeed real but they are not the kind of entities which our perceptual habits have accustomed us to see.

There cannot be an *explanatory* model of social behaviour which, at the same time, accounts for the capacity of the individual to escape the constraints of structure and to promote its transformation. If we want laws of social action, we have to construct measurable descriptions of it which accurately reflect the regularities observed and which relate them to causal properties of structure which are independent of the knowledgeability and skill of the actor to embody them in the action itself. If we reject the possibility of such models, it is not just because of the failure of the social sciences to build the body of cumulative knowledge which one would expect if human behaviour were amenable to scientific explanation. It is because social action and social order are not the kind of thing that lends itself to such treatment. Faced with the evidence of human creativity and social change, on the one hand, and the pattern and non-randomness of behaviour, on the other, an alternative account of agency and structure is required to that which resolves the tension in favour of one or the other. This entails the fundamentally different conception of structure and causality of a reflexive sociology.

We can predict some human behaviour, individual and collective, with statistical accuracy, resulting in increased insurance premiums for certain classes of car drivers, higher educational attainment for children of specifiable social backgrounds, or escalation of defence measures in conditions of interstate tension. But such predictions are unstable for reasons which cannot apply to physics or microbiology. They are always vulnerable to slippage from the arena of the observer to that of the behaviour, allowing the knowledge of the prediction to become part of the grounds for its fulfilment or a significant factor in its falsification. Thus it is never clear to the detached observer whether or how the prediction of low educational attainment is being monitored by the students for the purpose of fulfilling it or undermining it. It is only through analysis which is sensitive to the reflexivity and temporality of action that social prophecy can be unravelled as self-fulfilling or self-negating.

How different this world is from that of a positivist approach to social science can be gauged by contrasting the different perspective it yields on common issues of theoretical concern. Social change is not something that happens sporadically to the social order requiring special tools of investigation to understand the break with stability which is implied. It *is* the social order – essentially unstable, fluid and contested of its nature. Normative principles are not a factor which intrude on international affairs at the margins; they are the stuff of social action, furnishing the standards and norms which legitimize it as conforming or breaking with a notion of the routine, the normal, or stable. Time and history are not added dimensions to the research process, which can be left to a specialist sub-group of scholars concerned with that sort of thing. Time is part of the constitution of social action; it is only to the degree that we can grasp its temporal development that we can understand what it means to describe an event as an arms-race, a nuclear threat, or a personal bereavement.

Reflexivity as seduction

A reflexive sociology of international relations sees the social order as a fluid, unstable, reality constituted by humans relating through the medium of habits – through social practices which draw on habits to make behaviour meaningful, and constitute themselves as habitual at the same time. (Bourdieu's term 'habit' in place of 'structure', 'norms', 'rules' is useful to draw attention to the embeddedness of structure in human practices, to the taken-for-granted or non-*reflective* character of the reflexive monitoring of habit or routine – a phrase which can stand here as a definition of the social order.[11])

Such a world is held together and made coherent by concepts likewise fluid, unstable, and embedded in human practices, by sharp contrast with the understanding of social concepts in the objectivist tradition of political science. Habits have a seductive property. They offer an easy way to comprehension and community – to comprehension on the obvious analogy with language; to community in the sense that our identification with others (and against others) at every level of community relies on unreflective acceptance of common practices and norms signalled by common identity-markers such as religion, place of birth, colour of skin etc.

There is no persuasive explanation of why we should develop and change some habits of community as distinct from others unless self-interest is included as habit, dynamically interacting with the cognitive dimension of identity. As stated in relation to unionist fundamentalism in Northern Ireland, even habits of community which appear to transcend interests must be understood historically in terms of the duality of identity and interests.

What was called a seduction model of security in chapter 9 captures the fluidity and uncertainty and the embeddedness in human practices and interests which flow from this framework of international relations. Both parties to the Northern Ireland conflict are being

---

[11] Pierre Bourdieu, *The Logic of Practice*, Polity Press, Cambridge, 1990, chapter 3.

seduced into a new set of practices and a new habit of identity, in the sense that both must weigh the advantages and perils of a reconstructed narrative, compatible with new interests, against the old one – which was no less a product of elite management of material and cultural factors than the one on offer today. Unionists appear to have farther to travel and more to sacrifice in accepting the new project than their nationalist counterparts. This is an illusion born of freezing the description of their identity in the timeless conditions of the Belfast Agreement and its immediate context of a thirty-year conflict. In interpreting and describing social facts – and unionist identity among them – time is of the essence. Unionism was always a social project in which a particular British identity was contrived to serve the material and political interests of one section of the population against the threat posed by the other. Over time, the political success of this project has made the identification of unionism habitual and easier to divorce from the interests at stake.

Like political underdogs everywhere, nationalists in the past thirty years have always had a keener sociological nose for the reflexive character of this unionist project. When their rivals marched to the drumbeat of 'liberty' and 'No Popery!', displaying the symbols of Protestant identity under siege, nationalists caught the whiff of power. Now that power and identity are together under reconstruction, it is not surprising if unionists see the British role in the process in a clearer and more sceptical light as 'a cunningly contrived snare to enmesh the Ulster people into acquiescing and indeed accelerating the end of the Union and their British identity.'[12]

Security as moral choice

It has been argued that security depends on how we choose our identity and interests. The stress on choice throughout the book underlines its opposition to deterministic theories of international relations. If states live in a jungle, it is in part because they construct it thus; by ignoring its social construction in the search for laws of international politics, academics conspire in its reification and distort the objective world they purport to explain.

---

[12] Official response of the Ulster Unionist Party to the Anglo-Irish proposal, 'Frameworks for the future', on all-party talks on the future of Northern Ireland, 15 December 1995. See *The Irish Times*, 16 December 1995.

But the claim that we are who we want to be and the corollary that our interests are not bestowed by nature but by human choice suggest a distinctly voluntaristic view of social action. To return to the example of language: if language is clearly a social construction, how should we understand the freedom and creativity of the individual members of a language community? Surely they experience language as a constraint, not as a kind of template on which to write their own terms and rules? Religion and national identity are also the products of human activity, and therefore must be understood as the contingent products of human choice. But those born and living in a Muslim fundamentalist environment, or in parts of the American mid-west, are not likely to be aware of the options available, or to feel free to choose differently if they are.

Being male or female, egoistic or cooperative, is a human choice in some sense. But in practice even those who are consciously aware of the malleability of gender or political identity are not as free to choose either as the term 'choice' implies. Margaret Thatcher was as free to resist the temptation to retaliate militarily against Argentina over the Falklands issue in 1982 as Anthony Eden was to choose a different strategy other than the invasion of Suez in 1956. They had other options. But the cost–benefit equation for Thatcher in the domestic arena gave her an overwhelming incentive to play the game of national interest in the real world where it applies. One could make the same observation about the conduct of their relationship on the part of India and Pakistan in their competitive nuclear explosions in May 1998.

The fact and the knowledge that our situation arose from human choice once upon a time, and could have been different, do not emancipate us from its constraints. Contrary to the social construc-tionist perspective and to its inheritors in the constructivist school of international relations, the knowledge that the social order and its concepts are human products does not liberate actors from the determinism of structure and thereby open structural explanation to the creative dimension required to account for social change. To repeat, the difference Durkheim makes to the natural order of cause and effect is only to replace the material elements with the cultural.

We cannot consistently make the empirical concession that some choice survives the determinacy of structure within a conception of agency and structure that eliminates it. Waltz's well-known concession to agency, in his modification of the determinism in his *Theory of International Politics* to a 'shaping and shoving' in later writings, is no concession at all.[13] It constitutes no more than the recognition of the obvious fact that theories of international politics have not produced the tight causal explanation to which they aspire, and which is implied in the logic of the explanatory model which Waltz still defends. His idea of structure as an independent factor which sometimes forces agents to act or to refrain from acting, and sometimes constrains in more gentle fashion, is merely a less confident assertion of the original position; the logic is still deterministic, in that it postulates a bifurcation of opposition between structure and agency, rather than a dynamic relation of elements of a single moment of action.

The conception of agency and structure argued in chapter 8 implies the freedom of the agent to choose to act otherwise. Implicit in the assertion that we choose our identity is the qualification first noted by Marx: but not in conditions of our own choosing. The freedom of the agent to choose differently is a logically necessary implication of a theory of the duality of structure and agency as presented here. This implies that there can never be an instance of social action in which the agent has no options from which to choose.[14] But this tells us nothing more about the concrete conditions which are not of the agent's choosing, and about the degree of freedom of particular agents to resist their particular constraints, than the fact that agents have options. In the abstract, the claim that we choose our identity and interests – and with them our security environment – does not deny the severe constraints which are placed upon choice by history, ignorance and the imbalance of power. It denies the implication of determinist models of explanation, both in sociology and political science – that agents have no options which can alter the fundamental structure which causes their behaviour. Even the severe limitation on agents' freedom of choice evident in conditions of labour exploitation still requires that any account of their behaviour take into consideration the basic options between which they may choose to conform with, or resist, the constraint of structure.[15]

---

13 Kenneth Waltz, 'Response to my critics', in Robert O. Keohane (ed.), *Neorealism and its Critics*, New York, Columbia University Press, 1986, p. 343.
14 Anthony Giddens, *A Contemporary Critique of Historical Materialism*, 2nd edition, Macmillan, London, 1995, p. 63.
15 Anthony Giddens, 'A reply to my critics', in David Held and John B. Thompson (eds.), *Social Theory of Modern Societies: Anthony Giddens and his Critics*, Cambridge University Press, Cambridge, 1989, p. 258; *The Constitution of Society, Outline of the Theory of Structuration*, Polity Press, Cambridge, 1984, pp. 174ff.

The place of human choice in the construction of the international order can be disguised as necessity by the agent, making it easier to be asserted as such by the theorist. This was discussed in the context of the concept of the 'double hermeneutic', and it bears restatement here for its relevance to the question of choice and constraint. International relations theory has entered reflexively into the world it aspires to understand. The concepts of sovereignty, state, anarchy, deterrence, national interest, national security – all emerged from a dynamic interplay between 'first-order' theories of the social order by lay members of society and the 'second-order' accounts by professional theorists. The mutual spillage between the two levels of meaning places an irremediable instability at the heart of the object of inquiry for international relations scholars, and introduces the self-fulfilling prophecy as an inherent feature of social reality.

The assimilation into lay usage of technical concepts coined by experts to conceptualize regularities and causal relationships in human behaviour has long been familiar. For example, professional theories of racial superiority are taken up into lay modes of constructing social reality and organizing economic and social behaviour which then, in turn, present themselves as the real world, as the 'objective' evidence in support of the professional theories. It is a condition of conceptual spillage from the technical to the lay level of meaning that actors are not puppets, but knowledgeable agents adapting professional ideas to their own purposes. As with structure in general, we draw upon and *use* second-order ideas *to fulfil purposes which we already understand* – otherwise we would be as indifferent to racist theories as most of us are to macro-economics. Racist theorists are not wholly responsible for racist practices. The double hermeneutic of action and theorists' attempts to understand it underlines the *mutual* dependence of experts' and lay agents' theories on each other; it undermines the subjectivist view of the autonomy of the agent, and the objectivist view of the independence of structure.

The self-fulfilling prophecy analysed in terms of the double hermeneutic is accomplished as 'self-fulfilling' by actors and fed back as 'facts' into technical discourse. Thus, the observation that structure causes actors to behave in terms of a regular pattern implies – in the logic of the double hermeneutic – that actors in some measure employ that observation to accomplish the regularity observed.

Waltz does not investigate the interests and intentions of state decision-makers at the level required to expose this slippage of

217

meaning – having ruled them irrelevant *a priori*. We have to ask, therefore: How does he know that the causal principle of anarchy, which he identifies as an independent structural variable inferred from observation of state behaviour, is not simply the 'causal principle' formulated by state actors to justify, rationalize, and account theoretically for their behaviour as allowing for no alternative? Perhaps nowhere more than in the field of international relations is it likely that key human agents – the policy-makers of the state – should assimilate what Garfinkel called the second-order concepts of professional theorists and use them strategically for purposes which they understand as agents.[16]

The play of freedom and constraint within a reflexive model of social order can be illustrated further in relation to security and to the seduction entailed in managing identities and interests in the cause of security. Recalling the discussion of Northern Ireland and the European Union, it was noted that the process of transformation of the collective identities involved was facilitated by the conscious manipulation of interests. Like seduction in the everyday sense, this created the dilemma for actors who knew what was going on and experienced differently the pressure of interests against the need to sustain the narrative of identity. It would be quite erroneous to claim, however, that their freedom to choose was thereby negated, as some unionists claimed in Northern Ireland. The denial of freedom in such cases of seduction is strategic, since actors' knowledge of what is going on includes the knowledge that they have options. Such a denial in respect of collective seduction has interesting affinity with Sartre's concept of 'bad faith' in regard to seduction at the individual level.

To what extent the weight of history, habit, or imbalance of power constrains our capacity to choose who we want to be (and who we want to be against) or what material interests we want to pursue can only be inferred imprecisely through interpretative analysis of empirical evidence. In all cases, however, it follows from the analysis of social action presented in this book that identity and interests, and the security implications which follow from them, are human choices situated in historic conditions, not the product of laws or structures

---

[16] In their appeals to 'national interest' or to the fact that 'there is no alternative', state leaders like Nixon or Thatcher exemplify this reflexive skill of actors in projecting necessity in conditions of contingency. Such practices in the international arena contribute to the objectification of anarchy, leading observers mistakenly to infer an objective structure independently causing the practices in the first place.

external to the agent. In the early 1920s, women in general, and not just the self-reflective feminists, knew what they were doing in assimilating natural-law theories of gender difference into their daily lives. They knew this in the practical sense that they had options to conform to the world, or to reject it – and face the consequences – or to adapt the theory of gender to particular circumstances and interests. The difference between the two groups was that the feminists could articulate this practical knowledge in a counter-theory. Their options were still severely limited by the penalties which they faced but their freedom was enhanced by the knowledge that gender theory was a social construct susceptible to change which depended on agents' affirmation and reproduction for its causal effect.

In this sense, knowledge makes a significant difference to agency; not just the knowledge that our world is socially constructed in the Durkheimian sense, but that it is susceptible to human agency to reconstruct it. It is a necessary condition of our ability to exercise choice that we know that we have options. Knowledge is made politically available to the cause of social change to the extent that it is discursive and capable of being theoretically articulated. For this reason, a reflexive theory of the social order can support the moral and emancipatory impulse of a critical theory of international relations which aims to expose the contingency of all social arrangements, and the human choice and interests which gave rise to them, thereby advancing the possibility of constructing alternatives to the international order and to the organization of international security.

Bibliography

Adler, Emanuel, 'Seizing the middle ground: constructivism in world politics', *European Journal of International Relations*, 3/3, 1997, pp. 319–363.

Allison, Graham and Treverton, Gregory F. (eds.), *Rethinking America's Security: Beyond Cold War to the New World Order*, Norton, New York, 1992.

Anderson, Benedict, *Imagined Communities: Reflections on the Origins and Spread of Nationalism*, Verso Press, London, 1989.

Angell, Normann, *The Great Illusion: A Study of the Relation of Military Power in Nations to their Economic and Social Advantage*, Heinemann, London, 1910.

Arbatov, Alexei, 'NATO and Russia', *Security Dialogue*, 26/2, 1995, pp. 135–146.

Archer, Margaret S., *Culture and Agency: The Place of Culture in Social Theory*, University of Cambridge Press, Cambridge, 1989.

Asmus Ronald D. and F. Stephen Larrabee, 'NATO and the have-nots: reassurance after enlargement', *Foreign Affairs*, 75/6, 1996, pp. 13–20.

Asmus, Ronald, Richard Kugler and Stephen Larrabee, 'NATO expansion: the next steps', *Survival*, 37/1, 1995, pp. 7–33.

Ayoob, M. 'Security in the Third World; the worm about to turn?', *International Affairs*, 60/1, Winter 1983/1984.

'Defining security: a subaltern realist perspective', in Keith Krause and Michael C. Williams (eds.), *Critical Security Studies: Concepts and Cases*, UCL Press, London, 1997.

Baldwin, David A., 'Security studies and the end of the Cold War', *World Politics*, 48, October 1995, pp. 117–141.

Banks, Michael, 'The inter-paradigm debate', in M. Light and A.J.R. Groom (eds.), *International Relations: A Handbook of Current Theory*, Pinter, London, 1985.

Banton, Michael, *Racial and Ethnic Competition*, Cambridge University Press, Cambridge, 1983.

Barry, Charles, 'NATO's Combined Joint Task Forces in theory and practice', *Survival*, 38/1, 1996, pp. 81–97, p. 84.

Bauman Zymunt, 'Hermeneutics and modern social theory', in David Held and John B. Thompson, *Social Theory of Modern Societies: Anthony Giddens and his Critics*, Cambridge University Press, 1989.

Beck, Ulrich, 'The reinvention of politics: towards a theory of reflexive modernization', in Ulrich Beck *et al.*, *Reflexive Modernization: Politics, Tradition and Aesthetics in the Modern Social Order*, Polity Press, Cambridge, 1994.

Bell David (ed.), *The Development of the European Idea Since the Middle Ages*, Dartmouth, Aldershot, 1995.

Berger, Peter L. and Thomas Luckmann, *The Social Construction of Reality*, Allen Lane, London, 1967.

Bhaskar, Roy, *The Possibility of Naturalism: A Philosophical Critique of Contemporary Human Science*, Harvester, Brighton, 1979.

Boal, Frederick, David Livingstone and Margaret Keane, *Them and Us?*, Northern Ireland Office Central Community Relations Unit, 1996.

Booth, Ken, *Strategy and Ethnocentrism*, Croom Helm, London, 1978.

'Security and emancipation', *Review of International Studies*, 17, 1991, pp. 313–326.

'Security in anarchy: utopian realism in theory and practice', *International Affairs*, 67/3, 1991, pp. 527–545.

'Security and self: reflections of a fallen realist' in Keith Krause and Michael C. Williams (eds.), *Critical Security Studies: Concepts and Cases*, UCL Press, London, 1997.

Booth Ken (ed.), *New Thinking About Strategy and International Security*, Harper Collins, London, 1991.

Booth, Ken and Eric Herring, *Keyguide to Information Sources in Strategic Studies*, Mansell, London, 1994.

Booth, Ken and Steve Smith (eds.), *International Relations Theory Today*, Polity Press, Cambridge, 1995.

Bourdieu, Pierre, *The Logic of Practice*, Polity Press, Cambridge, 1990.

Bouton, Marshall M., 'India's problem is not politics', *Foreign Affairs*, 77/3, 1998.

Boyle, Kevin and Tom Hadden, 'The peace process in Northern Ireland', *International Affairs*, 71/2, 1995.

Boyne, Roy, 'Power-knowledge and social theory: the systematic misrepresentation of contemporary French social theory in the work of Anthony Giddens', in Christopher Bryant and David Jary (eds.), *Giddens' Theory of Structuration: A Critical Appreciation*, Routledge, London, 1991.

Brandt Commission, *Common Crisis: North–South Co-operation for World Recovery*, MIT Press, Cambridge MA, 1985.

Brill Alida (ed.), *A Rising Public Voice: Women in Politics Worldwide*, Feminist Press at the City University of New York, New York, 1995.

Brodie, Bernard, 'Strategy as a science', *World Politics*, 1, July 1949.

Broude, Norma and Mary D. Garrard, 'Feminism and art history', in their edited *Feminism and Art History*, Harper Row, London, 1982.

Brown, Michael E., 'The flawed logic of NATO expansion', *Survival*, 37/1, 1995, pp. 34–52.

Brubaker, Rogers, *Citizenship and Nationhood in France and Germany,* Harvard University Press, Cambridge MA, 1992.

Nationalism Reframed: Nationhood and the National Question in the New Europe, Cambridge University Press, Cambridge, 1996.

Bryant Christopher and David Jary (eds.), *Giddens' Theory of Structuration: A Critical Appreciation,* Routledge, London, 1991.

Brzezinski, Zbigniew, 'The premature partnership', *Foreign Affairs,* 73/2, 1994, pp. 67–82.

'A plan for Europe', *Foreign Affairs,* 74/1, 1995, pp. 26–42.

Buzan, Barry, *People, States and Fear: The National Security Problem in International Relations,* Harvester Wheatsheaf, Hemel Hempstead, 1983; 2nd edition, 1991.

'Interdependence and Britain's external relations', in Laurence Freedman and Michael Clarke (eds.), *Britain in the World,* Cambridge University Press, Cambridge 1990, pp. 10–41.

An Introduction to Strategic Studies: Military Technology and Internal Relations, Macmillan, London, 1987, p. 13.

Buzan, Barry, Charles Jones and Richard Little, *The Logic of Anarchy: Neorealism to Structural Realism,* Columbia University Press, New York, 1993.

Buzan, Barry, Morten Kelstrup, Pierre Lemaitre, Elzbieta Tromer and Ole Waever, *The European Security Order Recast: Scenarios for the Post-Cold War Era,* Pinter, London, 1990.

Buzan, Barry and Ole Waever, 'Slippery, contradictory? Sociologically untenable? The Copenhagen School replies', *Review of International Studies,* 23/2, 1997, pp. 241–250.

Buzan, Barry, Ole Waever and Jaap de Wilde, *Security: A New Framework for Analysis,* Lynne Rienner, Boulder CO, 1998.

Cameron, David, 'British exit, German voice, and French loyalty: defection, domination and cooperation in the 1992–93 ERM crisis', European Community Studies Association paper, Washington, May 1993.

Campbell, David, *Writing Security: United States Foreign Policy and the Politics of Identity,* Manchester University Press, Manchester 1992.

Politics Without Principle: Sovereignty Ethics and the Narratives of the Gulf War, Lynne Rienner, London, 1993.

Campbell, David and Michael Dillon (eds.), *The Political Subject of Violence,* Manchester University Press, Manchester, 1993.

Campbell, Colin, *The Myth of Social Action,* Cambridge University Press, Cambridge, 1996.

Carlsnaes, Walter, 'Democracy and peace', *European Journal of International Relations,* Special Issue, 1995, pp. 1–427.

Carpenter, Ted Galen (ed.), *The Future of NATO,* Frank Cass, London, 1995.

Carr, E.H., *Nationalism and After,* Macmillan, London, 1945.

The Twenty Years Crisis 1919–1949: An Introduction to the Study of International Relations, Macmillan, London, 1966.

Chilton, Paul, 'Security and semantic change', unpublished ms, n.d.

222

Bibliography

Clark, Jon, Celia Modgil and Sohan Modgil (eds.), *Anthony Giddens: Consensus and Controversy*, Falmer Press, Brighton, 1990.

Clarke, Michael (ed.), *New Perspectives on Security*, Brasseys, London, 1993.

Cohen, Ira, *Structuration Theory: Anthony Giddens and the Constitution of Social Life*, Macmillan, London, 1989.

Cohen, Raymond, 'Pacific unions: a reappraisal of the theory that "democracies do not go to war with each other'*, Review of International Studies*, 20/ 3, 1994, pp. 207–223.

Colley, Linda, *Britons: Forging the Nation 1707–1837*, Pimlico, London, 1992.

Comblin, José, *The Church and the National Security State*, Orbis, Marknoll, 1979.

Cooke, Dennis, *Persecuting Zeal: A Portrait of Ian Paisley*, Brandon Books, Dingle, 1996.

Cooper, Richard N., *The Economics of Interdependence: Economic Policy in the Atlantic Community*, McGraw-Hill, New York, 1968.

Cornish, Paul, 'European security: the end of architecture and the new NATO', *International Affairs*, 72/4, 1996, pp. 751–769.

Cox, Robert W. 'Social forces, states and world orders: beyond international relations theory', in Robert O. Keohane (ed.), *Neorealism and its Critics*, Columbia University Press, New York, 1986.

Cox, Michael, 'Rethinking the end of the Cold War', *Review of International Studies*, 20/2, 1994, pp. 187–200.

'Bringing in the "international": the IRA ceasefire and the end of the Cold War', *International Affairs*, 73/4, 1996, pp. 671–693.

Craib, Ian, *Anthony Giddens*, London, 1992.

Dalby, Simon, 'Contesting an essential concept: reading the dilemmas in contemporary security discourse', in Keith Krause and Michael C. Williams (eds.), *Critical Security Studies: Concepts and Cases*, UCL Press, London, 1997.

Danner, Mark, 'Marooned in the Cold War: America, the Alliance, and the quest for a vanished world', *World Policy Journal*, Fall, 1997, pp. 1–23.

Deighton, Anne, *The Impossible Peace: Britain, the division of Germany and the origins of the Cold War*, Oxford University Press, Oxford, 1993.

Delanty, Gerard, *Inventing Europe: Idea, Identity, Reality*, Macmillan, London, 1995.

'Negotiating the peace in Northern Ireland', *Journal of Peace Research*, 32/3, 1995.

Der Derian, James, 'The value of security: Hobbes, Marx, Nietzsche, and Baudrillard' in David Campbell and Michael Dillon (eds.), *The Political Subject of Violence*, Manchester University Press, Manchester, 1993.

Deudney, Daniel, 'The case against linking environmental degradation and national security', *Millenium*, 19/3, 1990.

Deutsch, Karl *et al.*, *Political Community and the North Atlantic Area*, Greenwood Press, Westport, 1955.

Dinan, Desmond, *Ever Closer Union? An Introduction to the European Community*, Macmillan Press, London, 1994.

LIVERPOOL 223
JOHN MOORES UNIVERSITY
AVRIL ROBARTS LRC
TITHEBARN STREET
LIVERPOOL L2 2ER
TEL. 0151 231 4022

Bibliography

Dorff, Robert, 'A commentary on *Security Studies for the 1990s* as a Model Core Curriculum', *International Studies Notes*, 19/3, 1994, pp. 5–27.

Dougherty, James E. *et al.*, *Ethics, Deterrence and National Security*, Pergamon Press, Washington, 1985.

Drakulic, Slavenka, *The Balkan Express: Fragments from the Other Side of War*, W.W. Norton, New York, 1993.

Drew, Paul and John Heritage (eds.), *Talk at Work: Interaction in Institutional Settings*, Cambridge University Press, Cambridge, 1992.

Dumbrell, John, 'The US and the Northern Ireland conflict 1969–94: from indifference to intervention', *Irish Studies in International Affairs*, 6, 1995, pp. 107–125.

Eide, A. and Marek Thee, *The Problems of Contemporary Militarism*, Croom Helm, London, 1980.

Elshtain, Jean Bethke, *Women and War*, Harvester Press, Brighton, 1987.

Enloe, Cynthia, *Bananas Beaches and Bases: Making Feminist Sense of International Politics*, Pandora, London, 1989.

  The Morning After: Sexual Politics at the End of the Cold War, Berkeley CA, 1992.

Erikson, Erik, *Childhood and Society*, Norton, New York, 1963.

Finnemore, Martha, *National Interests in International Society*, Cornell University Press, 1996.

Forsyth, M.G., H.M.A. Keens-Soper and P. Savigear (eds.), *The Theory of International Relations: Selected Texts from Gentili to Treitschke*, Allen and Unwin, London, 1970.

Fox, William T., 'Interwar international relations research: The American experience', *World Politics*, 2, October 1949.

Frank, Andre Gundar, 'Keynesian paradoxes in the Brandt Report', *Third World Quarterly*, 11/4, 1980.

Freedman, Lawrence, *The Evolution of Nuclear Strategy*, Macmillan, London, 1981.

  The Troubled Alliance: Atlantic Relations in the 1980s, Heineman, London, 1983.

Freedman, Laurence and Michael Clarke (eds.), *Britain in the World*, Cambridge University Press, Cambridge, 1990.

Friedan, Betty, *The Feminine Mystique*, Pelican Press, Harmondsworth, 1965.

Fukuyama, Francis, 'Women and the evolution of world politics', *Foreign Affairs*, September/October, 1998, pp. 24–40.

Gaddis, John Lewis, 'International relations theory and the end of the Cold War', *International Security*, 17/3, 1992/1993, pp. 5–58.

  The United States and the End of the Cold War, Oxford University Press, Oxford, 1994.

Galbraith, J.K., *How to Control the Military*, Doubleday, New York, 1969.

Gallie, W.B., 'Essentially contested concepts', Max Black (ed.), *The Importance of Language*, Englewood Cliffs, New Jersey, 1962, pp. 121–146.

Galtung, Johan, *There are Alternatives: Four Roads to Peace and Security*, Spokesman, Nottingham, 1984.

Garcia, Soledad (ed.), *European Identity and the Search for Legitimacy*, London, 1993.

Garfinkel, Harold, 'A conception of, and experiments with, "trust" as a condition of stable concerted action', in O.J. Harvey (ed.), *Motivation and Social Interaction Cognitive Determinants*, Ronald Press, New York, 1963.

Studies in Ethnomethodology, Prentice Hall, New Jersey, 1967.

Garnett, John (ed.), *Theories of Peace and Security: A Reader in Contemporary Strategic Thought*, Macmillan, London, 1970.

Gellner, Ernest, *Nations and Nationalism*, Blackwell, Oxford, 1983.

George, Jim, 'Of incarceration and closure: neo-realism and the new/old world order', *Millenium*, 22/2, 1993, pp. 197–234.

Discourses of Global Politics: A Critical Re(Introduction) to International Relations, Lynne Rienner, Boulder, 1994.

George, Stephen, *An Awkward Partner: Britain in the European Community*, Oxford University Press, Oxford, 1990.

Giddens, Anthony, *New Rules of Sociological Method*, 1st edition, Hutchinson, London, 1976.

'Nine theses on the future of sociology', *Central Problems in Social Theory*, Macmillan, London, 1979.

The Constitution of Society: Outline of the Theory of Structuration, Polity Press, Cambridge, 1984.

Social Theory and Modern Sociology, Polity Press, Cambridge, 1987.

'A reply to my critics', in David Held and John B. Thompson (eds.), *Social Theory of Modern Societies: Anthony Giddens and his Critics*, Cambridge University Press, Cambridge, 1989.

Sociology, Cambridge, 1989.

Modernity and Self-Identity: Self and Society in the Late Modern Age, Polity Press, Cambridge 1991.

New Rules of Sociological Method, 2nd edition, Polity Press, Cambridge, 1993.

A Contemporary Critique of Historical Materialism, 2nd edition, Macmillan, London, 1995.

Gilpin, Robert G., 'The richness of the tradition of political realism', in Robert O. Keohane (ed.), *Neorealism and its Critics*, New York, Columbia University Press, 1986.

Gleditsch, Nils Petter, 'Democracy and peace', *Journal of Peace Research*, 29/4, 1992, 369–376.

Goffman, Erving, *Encounters*, Bobbs-Merrill, Indianapolis, 1961.

Interaction Ritual: Essays on Face-to-Face Behaviour, Anchor Books, 1967.

Goldblat, Jozef, 'Controversies over the planned enlargement of NATO', *Security Dialogue*, 27/3, 1996, pp. 360–363.

Gouldner, Alvin, *The Coming Crisis of Western Sociology*, Heinemann, London, 1971.

Grant, Robert P., 'France's new relationship with NATO', *Survival*, 38/1, 1996, pp. 58–80.

Green, Philip, *Deadly Logic: The Theory of Nuclear Deterrence*, Ohio State University Press, Columbus, 1966.

Groom, A.J.R. and Paul Taylor (eds.), *Frameworks for International Cooperation*, Pinter, London, 1990.

Grosser, Alfred, *The Western Alliance: European–American Relations Since 1945*, Macmillan, London, 1980.

Grunberg, Isabelle, 'Exploring the 'myth' of hegemonic stability', *International Organization*, 44/4, 1990, pp. 431–477.

Guelke, Adrian, 'The United States, Irish Americans and the Northern Ireland peace process', *International Affairs*, 72/3, 1996, pp. 521–536.

Haas, Ernst, *The Uniting of Europe: Political, Social, and Economic Forces*, Stanford University Press, Stanford, 1958.

'International integration: the European and the universal process', *International Organization*, 15, 1961.

'The uniting of Europe and the uniting of Latin America', *Journal of Common Market Studies*, 5/4, 1967.

'The study of regional integration: reflections on the joy and anguish of pretheorizing' in L. Lindberg and S. Scheingold (eds.), *Regional Integration: Theory and Research*, Harvard University Press, Cambridge MA, 1971.

'Turbulent fields and the theory of regional integration', *International Organization*, 30, 1976.

Haftendorn, Helga, 'The security puzzle: theory-building and discipline-building in international security', *International Security Quarterly*, 35/1, 1991.

Haglund, David G., 'France's nuclear posture: adjusting to the post-Cold War era', *Contemporary Security Problems*, 16/2, 1995, pp. 140–162.

Halliday, Fred, *Rethinking International Relations*, Macmillan, London, 1994.

Hanrieder, Wolfram, *Germany, America, Europe: 40 Years of German Foreign Policy*, Yale University Press, Newhaven, 1989.

Harrison, R.J., 'Neo-functionalism' in A.J.R. Groom and Paul Taylor (eds.), *Frameworks for International Cooperation*, Pinter, London, 1990.

Haugaard, Mark, *Structures, Restructuration and Social Power*, Avebury, Aldershot, 1992.

Hayes, Bernadette and Ian McAllister, 'British and Irish public opinion towards the Northern Ireland problem', unpublished paper, IPSA conference, Drogheda, October 1995.

Held, David and John B. Thompson (eds.), *Social Theory of Modern Societies: Anthony Giddens and his Critics*, Cambridge University Press, Cambridge, 1989.

Hellmann, Gunther and Reinhard Wolf, 'Neorealism, neoliberal institutionalism, and the future of NATO', *Security Studies*, 3/1, 1993, pp. 3–43.

Hennessy, Peter, *Never Again: Britain 1945–1951*, Jonathan Cape, London, 1992.

Hermann, Margaret G., 'One field, many perspectives: building the foundations for dialogue', ISA Presidential Address, *International Studies Quarterly*, 42/4, 1998, pp. 605–624.

Herz, John, 'Idealist internationalism and the security dilemma', *World Politics*, 2, January 1950, pp. 157–180.

Herz, John H., *Political Realism and Political Idealism*, University of Chicago Press, Chicago, 1951.

Hickey, John, *Religion and the North of Ireland Problem*, Gill and Macmillan, Dublin, 1984.

Hobsbawm, E.J., *Nations and Nationalism since 1780*, Cambridge University Press, Cambridge, 1993.

Hobsbawm, Eric, 'Identity politics and the Left', *New Left Review*, 1996, pp. 38–47.

Hobsbawm, Eric and Terence Ranger (eds.), *The Invention of Tradition*, Cambridge University Press, 1995.

Hoffman, Stanley, 'The European process at Atlantic crosspurposes', *Journal of Common Market Studies*, 3, 1964/5.

'Obstinate or obsolete? The fate of the nation state and the case of Western Europe', *Daedalus*, 95, 1966, pp. 862–915.

'An American social science: international relations', *Daedalus*, 106/3, 1977, pp. 41–60.

'Back to Euro-pessimism', *Foreign Affairs*, 76/1, 1997, pp. 139–145.

'The European Community and 1992', *Foreign Affairs*, 68, 1989, pp. 27–47.

Hogan, Michael J. (ed.), *The End of the Cold War: Its Meaning and Implications*, Cambridge University Press, Cambridge, 1992.

Holbrooke, Richard, 'America, a European power', *Foreign Affairs*, 74/2, 1995.

Hollis, Martin, *Invitation to Philosophy*, Blackwell, Oxford, 1989.

Hollis, Martin and Steve Smith, *Explaining and Understanding International Relations*, Clarendon Press, Oxford, 1991.

Holsti, Kal J., *The Dividing Discipline: Hegemony and Diversity in International Theory*, Allen and Unwin, London, 1985.

'Mirror, mirror on the wall, which are the fairest theories of all?', *International Studies Quarterly*, 33/3, 1989.

Howe, Paul, 'The utopian realism of EH Carr', *Review of International Studies*, 20/3, 1994, pp. 277–298.

Hurd, Douglas, *The Search for Peace*, Little Brown, Boston, 1997.

Husserl, Edmund, *Phenomenology and the Crisis of Western Philosophy*, Harper and Row, New York, 1965.

Jary, David and Christopher Bryant (eds.), *Anthony Giddens: Critical Assessments*, Routledge, London, 1997, 4 vols.

Jervis, Robert, *Perception and Misperception in International Politics*, Princeton University Press, Princeton, 1976.

'Cooperation under the security dilemma', *World Politics*, 30/2, 1978, pp. 167–214.

'Security regimes', in Stephen Krasner (ed.), *International Regimes*, Cornell University Press, Ithaca, 1983, pp. 173–194.

Jervis, Robert *et al.*, *The Field of National Security Studies: Report to the National Research Council*, National Research Council, Washington, 1986.

Joffe, Joseph, 'Europe's American pacifier', *Survival*, 26/4, 1984.

Johnson, Robert H., 'Periods of peril: the window of vulnerability and other myths', *Foreign Affairs*, 61/4, 1983.

Jones, Adam, 'Does gender make the world go round? Feminist critiques of international relation', *Review of International Studies*, 22, 1996, pp. 405–429.

Kaldor, Mary and A. Eide, *The World Military Order:The Impact of Military Technology on the 3rd World*, Macmillan, London, 1979.

Kaplan, Fred, *The Wizards of Armageddon*, Simon and Schuster, New York, 1983.

Kaplan, Morton A., *System and Process in International Politics*, John Wiley, New York, 1957.

Katzenstein, Peter, *The Culture of National Security: Norms and Identity in World Politics*, Columbia University Press, New York, 1996.

Kegley, Charles W., 'The new containment myth: realism and the anomaly of European integration', *Ethics in International Affairs*, 5, 1991, pp. 99–114.

Kegley, Charles W. Jr, 'The neoidealist moment in international studies? Realist myths and the new international relations', *International Studies Quarterly*, 37, pp. 131–146.

Kennan, George, *Memoirs 1925–1950*, Bantam, New York, 1969.

Keohane, Robert O., *After Hegemony: Cooperation and Discord in the World Political Economy*, Princeton University Press, Princeton, 1984.

'International institutions, two approaches', *International Institutions and State Power: Essays in International Relations Theory*, Westview, Boulder, 1989, p. 161.

Keohane, Robert O. (ed.), *Neorealism and its Critics*, Columbia University Press, New York, 1986.

Keohane, Robert O. and Stanley Hoffman, 'Conclusions: community politics and institutional change', in William Wallace (ed.), *The Dynamics of European Integration*, Pinter, London, 1990.

Keohane Robert O. and Stanley Hoffman (eds.), *The New European Community*, Westview Press, Boulder, 1991.

Keohane, Robert O. and Joseph S. Nye, *Power and Interdependence*, 2nd edition, Little Brown, Glenview, 1989.

Kilminster, Richard, 'Structuration theory as a world-view', in Christopher Bryant and David Jary (eds.), *Giddens' Theory of Structuration: A Critical Appreciation*, Routledge, London, 1991.

Kissinger, Henry, *A World Restored*, Gollancz, London, 1973.

'A plan for Europe', *Newsweek*, 18 June 1990.

'"New" NATO chips at keystone of US policy', *The Daily Telegraph*, 11 April 1997.

Kolodziej, Edward A., 'What is security and security studies', *Arms Control*, 13, 1992, pp. 1–32.

'Renaissance in security studies? Caveat lector!', *International Studies Quarterly*, 36, 1992, pp. 421–438.

Kolodziej, Edward A. and Roger E. Kanet (eds.), *The Cold War as Cooperation*, Johns Hopkins University Press, Baltimore, 1991.

Krasner Stephen (ed.), *International Regimes*, Cornell University Press, Ithaca, 1983.

Krause, Keith and Michael C. Williams (eds.), *Critical Security Studies: Concepts and Cases*, UCL Press, London, 1997.

Krippendorf, E., 'The dominance of American approaches in international relations', *Millenium*, 16/2, 1987, pp. 207–214.

Kupchan Chas A. and Clifford Kupchan, 'Concerts collective security and the security of Europe', *International Security*, 16/1, 1991.

Laclau, Ernesto and Chantal Mouffe, *Hegemony and Socialist Strategy: Towards a Radical Democratic Politics*, London, 1985, p. 108.

Laing, R.D., *The Divided Self*, Penguin, Harmondsworth, 1965.

Lapid, Yosef, 'The third debate: on the prospect of international theory in a post-positivist era', *International Security Quarterly*, 33/3, 1989, pp. 235–254.

Lawler, Peter, *A Question of Values: Johan Galtung's Peace Research*, Lynne Rienner, London, 1995.

Layne, Christopher, 'Kant or Cant: The myth of the democratic peace', *International Security*, 19/2, 1994, pp. 5–49.

Lieven, Anatol, 'A new Iron Curtain', *Atlantic Monthly*, January 1996, pp. 20–25.

Light, Margot and A.J.R. Groom (eds.), *International Relations: A Handbook of Current Theory*, Pinter, London, 1985.

Lindberg L. and S. Scheingold (eds.), *Regional Integration: Theory and Research*, Harvard University Press, Cambridge MA, 1971.

Lindberg, L.N., *The Political Dynamics of European Economic Integration*, Stanford University Press, Stanford, 1963.

Lippmann, Walter, *US Foreign policy: Shield of the Republic*, Pocket Books, New York, 1943.

Lipschutz, Ronnie (ed.), *On Security*, Columbia University Press, New York, 1995.

Little, Richard, 'Ideology and change', in Barry Buzan and R.J. Barry Jones (eds.), *Change and the Study of International Relations*, Pinter, London, 1981, pp. 30–45.

Little, Richard and M. Smith (eds.), *Perspectives on World Politics*, Routledge, London, 1991 pp. 417–418.

Lukes, Steven, *Essays in Social Theory*, Macmillan, London, 1977.

Lynn-Jones, Sean M. and Stephen E. Miller (eds.), *Global Dangers: Changing Dimensions of International Security*, MIT Press, London, 1995.

Macdonald, Sharon (ed.), *Inside European Identities: Ethnography in Western Europe*, 1997.

MacGinty, Roger, 'American influences on the Northern Ireland peace process', *Journal of Conflict Studies*, 17/2, 1997.

Macmillan, Harold, *Tides of Fortune, 1945–1955*, Macmillan, London, 1969.

Mandelbaum, Michael, *The Dawn of Peace in Europe*, 20th Century Fund Press, New York, 1996.

Manor, James and Gerald Segal, 'Taking India seriously', *Survival*, 40/2, 1998.

Martin, Laurence, 'The future of strategic studies', *Journal of Strategic Studies*, 3/3.

Marx, Karl and Friedrich Engels, *The German Ideology*, Lawrence and Wishart, London, 1970.

Mathews, Jessica Tuchman, 'Redefining security', *Foreign Affairs*, 68/2, 1989.

McCalla, Robert B., 'NATO's persistence after the Cold War', *International Organization*, 50/3, 1996, pp. 445–475.

McGwire, Michael, 'The indivisible Continent: Russia, NATO and European security', in Bill McSweeney (ed.), *Moral Issues in International Affairs: Problems in European Integration*, Macmillan, London, 1998.

McSweeney, Bill 'The religious dimension of the troubles in Northern Ireland', in Paul Badham (ed.), *Religion, State and Society in Modern Britain*, Mellen Press, London, 1988.

'Identity and security: Buzan and the Copenhagen School', *Review of International Studies*, 22/1, 1996, pp. 81–93.

'Durkheim and the Copenhagen School: a response to Buzan and Waever', *Review of International Studies*, 24/1, 1998, pp. 137–140.

Mearsheimer, John, 'Back to the future: instability in Europe after the Cold War', *International Security*, 15/1, 1990.

'Why we will soon miss the Cold War', *Atlantic Monthly*, 266/2, August 1990, pp. 35–50.

'A realist reply', *International Security*, 20/1, 1995.

'The false promise of international institutions' *International Security*, 19/3, 1995, pp. 5–49.

Meimeth, Michael, 'France gets closer to NATO', *World Today*, 50/5, 1994, pp. 84–86.

Meja, Volker and Nico Stehr, 'Sociology of knowledge', in William Outhwaite and Tom Bottomore (eds.), *The Blackwell Dictionary of Twentieth-Century Social Thought*, Blackwell, Oxford, 1995.

Menon, Anand, 'From independence to cooperation: France, NATO and European security', *International Affairs*, 71/1, 1995, pp. 19–34.

'Defence policy and integration in Western Europe', *Security Policy*, 17/2, 1996, pp. 264–283.

Merriam, Charles E., *Systematic Politics*, University of Chicago, Chicago, 1945.

Merton, Robert K., *Social Theory and Social Structure*, Free Press, Glencoe, 1957.

Mills, C. Wright, *The Sociological Imagination*, Oxford University Press, Oxford, 1959.

Milward, Alan, *The Reconstruction of Western Europe 1945–1951*, Methuen, London, 1984.

The European Rescue of the Nation-State, Routledge, London, 1992.

Moravcsik, Andrew, 'Negotiating the Single European Act', in Robert O.

Keohane and Stanley Hoffman (eds.), *The New European Community*, Westview Press, Boulder, 1991.

'Preferences and power in the European Community: a liberal intergovernmentalist approach', *Journal of Common Market Studies*, 31/4, 1993.

Morgenthau, Hans, *In Defense of the National Interest: A Critical Examination of American Foreign Policy*, Alfred Knopf, New York, 1951.

'Another "Great Debate": the national interest of the United States', *American Political Science Review*, 46/4, 1952, p. 972.

Politics Among the Nations: The Struggle for Power and Peace, Knopf, New York, 1972.

Muir, Ramsey, *The Interdependent World and its Problems*, London, 1933.

Murray, A.J.H., 'The moral politics of Hans Morgenthau', *Review of Politics*, January 1996, pp. 81–107.

National Conference of Catholic Bishops, *The Challenge of Peace: God's Promise and Our Response*, US Catholic Conference, Washington, 1983.

Neufeld, Mark, 'Reflexivity and international relations theory', in Claire Turenne Sjolander and Wayne S. Cox (eds.), *Beyond Positivism: Critical Reflections on International Relations*, Lynne Rienner, London, 1994, p. 30.

The Restructuring of International Relations Theory, Cambridge University Press, Cambridge, 1995.

Neumann, Iver, 'Russian identity in the European mirror', *European Security*, 3/2, 1996, pp. 281–300.

Russia and the Idea of Europe, Routledge, London, 1996.

Nietzsche, Friedrich, *On the Genealogy of Morals*, Vintage Books, New York, 1969.

'Morgenthau's struggle with power: the theory of power politics and the Cold War', *Review of International Studies*, 21, 1995, pp. 61–85.

Nobel, Jaap, 'Realism versus interdependence: the Paradigm Debate in international relations', *Bulletin of Peace Proposals*, 19/2, 1988, pp. 167–173.

North Atlantic Council, 'Harmel Report on the future tasks of the Alliance', Brussels, December 1967.

'The Alliance's comprehensive concept of arms control and disarmament', Brussels, May 1989.

'London declaration on a transformed Atlantic Alliance', London, July 1990.

'The Alliance's new strategic concept', Rome, November, 1991.

'Rome declaration on peace and cooperation', Rome, November 1991.

'NATO Summit Declaration', and Partnership for Peace 'Invitation' and 'Framework Document', Brussels, January 1994.

Berlin Communique, Berlin, 3 June 1996, *Nato Review*, 44/4, 1996, pp. 30–35.

Nye, Joseph S. Jr, *Nuclear Ethics*, Free Press, New York, 1986.

'The contribution of strategic studies: future challenges', *Adelphi Papers*, 235, International Institute of Strategic Studies, London, 1989.

Nye, Joseph S. Jr and Sean Lynn-Jones, 'International security studies', *International Security*, 12/4, 1988.

Onuf, Nicholas, *World of our Making: Rules and Rule in Social Theory and International Relations*, Columbia, University of South Carolina Press, 1989.

Parkhalina, Tatiana, 'Of myths and illusions: Russian perceptions of NATO enlargement', *Nato Review*, 3, May–June 1997, pp. 11–15.

Peterson, V. Spike (ed.), *Gendered States: Feminist (re)visions of International Relations*, Lynne Rienner, London, 1992.

Pollner, Melvin, 'Sociological and common-sense models of the labelling process', in Ralph Turner (ed.), *Ethnomethodology*, Penguin, Harmondsworth, 1974.

Pourchot, Georgeta V., 'NATO enlargement and democracy in Eastern Europe', *European Security*, 6/4, 1997, pp. 157–174.

Pravda, Alex, 'Russia and European security: the delicate balance', *Nato Review*, 3, May 1995, pp. 19–24.

Psathas, George, 'Ethnomethods and phenomenology', *Social Research*, 35, 1968, pp. 500–520.

Puchala, Donald, 'Domestic politics and regional harmonization in the European Communities', *World Politics*, 1975.

Ramsey, Paul, *War and the Christian Conscience: How Shall Modern War be Conducted Justly?*, Duke University Press, North Carolina, 1961.

Rapoport, Anatol, *Strategy and Conscience*, Harper and Row, New York, 1964.

Raskin, Marcus G., *The Politics of National Security*, Transaction, New Brunswick, 1979.

Report of the Independent Commission on International Development Issues (Brandt Report), *North–South: A Programme for Survival*, Pan Books, London, 1980.

Report of the Independent Commission on Disarmament and Security Issues (Palme Report), *Common Security: A Programme for Disarmament*, Pan Books, London, 1982.

Report of the New Ireland Forum, Government Publications, Dublin, 1984.

Rex John and D. Mason (eds.), *Theories of Race and Ethnic Relations*, Cambridge University Press, Cambridge, 1986.

Richard, Ullman, 'Redefining security', *International Security*, 8/1, 1983.

Risse-Kappen, Thomas, 'Exploring the nature of the beast: IR theory and comparative analysis meets the EU', *Journal of Common Market Studies*, 34/1, 1996, pp. 53–80.

Rosecrance, Richard and Arthur Stein, 'Interdependence: myth or reality', *World Politics*, 1973.

Rosenberg, Justin, 'What's the matter with Realism?', *Review of International Studies*, 16, 1990.

Rothschild, Emma, 'What is security?', *Daedalus*, 124/3, 1995, pp. 53–98.

Rothstein, Robert L., 'On the costs of realism', *Political Science Quarterly*, 87/3, 1972, pp. 347–62.

Rousseau, J. J., *Oeuvres Completes*, Gallimard, Paris, 1964, vol. III.

Ruggie, John Gerard, 'What makes the world hang together? Neo-utilitarianism and the social constructivist challenge', *Constructing the World Polity: Essays on International Institutionalization*, Routledge, 1988, Introduction.

Russett, Bruce, *Grasping the Democratic Peace: Principles for a Post-Cold War World*, Princeton University Press, Princeton, 1993.

Russett, Bruce and Harvey Starr, *World Politics: The Menu for Choice*, Freeman, San Fransisco, 1981.

Ryle, Gilbert, *The Concept of Mind*, Hutchinson, London, 1975.

Sandholtz, Wayne, 'Choosing Union: monetary politics and Maastricht', *International Organization*, 47, 1993, pp. 1–39.

Sandholtz, Wayne and John Zysman, '1992: recasting the European bargain', *World Politics*, 42/1, 1989, pp. 1–30.

Schelling, Thomas, *The Strategy of Conflict*, Harvard University Press, Cambridge MA, 1960.

Schlesinger, Arthur Jr, *The Cycles of American History*, Houghton Mifflin, 1987, chapter 1.

Schmitter, P.C., 'Three neofunctionalist hypotheses about international integration', *International Organization*, 23, 1969.

Schüssel, Wolfgang, Austrian Vice-Chancellor and Foreign Minister, to participants of Shapex 1997, Mons, 24 April 1997.

Schutz, Alfred, *The Phenomenology of the Social World*, London, 1972.

Schwarz, Benjamin, 'Why America thinks it has to run the world', *Atlantic Monthly*, June 1996, pp. 92–102.

Schwarz, Benjamin C., 'Cold War continuities: US economic and security strategy towards Europe', in Ted Galen Carpenter (ed.), *The Future of NATO*, Frank Cass, London, 1995.

Seers, D., 'Muddling morality and mutuality', *Third World Quarterly*, 11/4, 1980.

Shapiro, Michael, *The Politics of Representation: Writing Practices in Biography, and Policy Analysis*, Madison, 1987, p. 93.

Shaw, Martin, 'There is no such thing as society: beyond individualism and statism in international security studies', *Review of International Studies*, 19, 1993, pp. 159–175.

Shultz, Richard, Roy Godson and Ted Greenwood (eds.), *Security Studies for the 1990s*, Brasseys, New York, 1993.

Sjolander, Claire Turenne and Wayne S. Cox (eds.), *Beyond Positivism: Critical Reflections on International Relations*, Lynne Rienner, London, 1994.

Slovo, Gillian, *Every Secret Thing: My Family, My Country*, Little, Brown, 1996.

Small, Melvin and J. David Singer, 'The war proneness of democratic regimes', *The Jerusalem Journal of International Relations*, 1, 1976, pp. 50–69.

Smith, Dan, *Pressure: How America Runs NATO*, Bloomsbury, London, 1989.

Smith, Anthony, 'The ethnic sources of nationalism', *Survival*, 35/1, 1993; *National Identity*, Penguin, London, 1991.
    'A Europe of Nations – Or the Nation of Europe?', *Journal of Peace Research*, 30/2, 1993, pp. 129–135.

Smith, Steve, 'Mature anarchy, Strong States and Security', *Arms Control*, 12/2, September 1991, pp. 325–339.
  'The self-images of a discipline', in Ken Booth and Steve Smith (eds.), *International Relations Theory Today*, Polity Press, Cambridge, 1995.
Smith, Steve, Ken Booth and Marysio Zalewski, *International Theory: Positivism and Beyond*, Cambridge University Press, Cambridge, 1996.
Smoke, Richard, 'National security affairs', in Fred Greenstein and Nelson W. Polsby (eds.), *Handbook of Political Science, vol VIII, International Politics*, Addison-Wesley, Reading MA, 1975, pp. 247–362.
Sorensen, Georg, 'Kant and processes of democratization: consequences for Neorealist Thought', *Journal of Peace Research*, 29/4, 1992, pp. 397–414.
Starr, Harvey, 'Democracy and integration: why democracies don't fight each other', *Journal of Peace Research*, 34/2, 1997, pp. 153–162.
Stein, Arthur A., *Why Nations Cooperate: Circumstance and Choice in International Relations*, Cornell University Press, London, 1990.
Stinchcombe, Arthur L., *Constructing Social Theories*, Harcourt Brace and World, New York, 1968.
Strange, Susan, 'Cave! hic dragones: a critique of regime analysis', in Stephen Krasner (ed.), *International Regimes*, Cornell University Press, Ithaca, 1983, pp. 337–354.
Sylvester, Christine, *Feminist Theory and International Relations in a Postmodern Era*, Cambridge University Press, Cambridge 1994.
Talbott, Strobe, 'Why NATO should grow', *New York Review of Books*, 10 August 1995.
  'The US the EU and our common challenges', remarks at the transatlantic conference 6 May 1997, USIA, London.
Taylor, Charles, *Sources of the Self: The Making of the Modern Identity*, Cambridge University Press, Cambridge, 1989.
Taylor, Paul, 'Supranationalism', in A.J.R. Groom and Paul Taylor (eds.), *Frameworks for International Cooperation*, Pinter, London, 1990.
Tickner, J. Ann, *Gender in International Relations*, Columbia University Press, New York, 1992.
Tombs, Robert (ed.), *Nationhood and Nationalism in France: from Boulangism to the Great War 1889–1918*, Harper Collins, London, 1991.
Touraine, Alain, *The Self Production of Society*, University of Chicago Press, Chicago, 1977.
Turner Ralph (ed.), *Ethnomethodology*, Penguin, Harmondsworth, 1974.
Turner, Jonathan H. *The Structure of Sociological Theory*, 5th edition, Wadsworth, Belmont CA, 1991.
Ullman, Richard, 'Redefining security', *International Security*, 8 January, 1983.
Valki, László, 'Russia and the security of East-Central Europe', *European Security*, 5/3, 1996, pp. 448–469.
Vasquez, John A., 'The post-positivist debate: reconstructing scientific enquiry and international relations theory after enlightenment's fall', in Ken

Booth and Steve Smith (eds.), *International Relations Theory Today*, Polity Press, Cambridge, 1995.

Wade, Peter, ' "Race", Nature and Culture', *Man*, 28, 1996, pp. 17–33.

Waever, Ole, 'Region, subregion and proto-region: security dynamics in Northern Europe in the 1980s and 1990s', Working paper 21, CPCR Copenhagen, 1990.

'Identity integration and security', *Journal of International Affairs*, 48/2, 1995, pp. 389–431.

'Securitization and desecurization', in Ronnie D. Lipschutz (ed.), *On Security*, Columbia University Press, New York, 1995.

'Identity integration and security', *Journal of International Affairs*, 48/2, 1995, pp. 389–431.

'What is security? The securityness of security', in Birthe Hansen (ed.), *European Security 2000*, Copenhagen Political Studies Press, Copenhagen, 1996.

Waever, Ole, Barry Buzan, Morten Kelstrup and Pierre Lemaitre, with David Carlton, *Identity, Migration and the New Security Agenda in Europe*, Pinter, London, 1993.

Waever, Ole, Pierre Lemaitre and Elzbieta Tromer (eds.), *European Polyphony: Perspectives Beyond East West Confrontation*, London: Macmillan, 1990.

Waever, Ole, 'The rise and fall of the inter-paradigm debate', in Steve Smith, Ken Booth and Marysio Zalewski (eds.), *International Theory: Positivism and Beyond*, Cambridge University Press, Cambridge, 1996.

Walker, Brian, *Dancing to History's Tune*, Institute of Irish Studies, Belfast, 1996.

Walker, R.B.J., 'Security, sovereignty, and the challenge of world politics', *Alternatives*, 15/1, 1990, pp. 3–27.

Inside/Outside: International Relations as Political Theory, Cambridge University Press, Cambridge, 1993.

Walker, William, 'International nuclear relations after the Indian and Pakistani test explosions', *International Affairs*, 74/3, 1998.

Wallace, Helen, W. Wallace and C. Webb (eds.), *Policy-making in the European Community*, 2nd edition, Wiley, Chichester, 1983.

Wallace, William, 'Less than a federation, more than a regime: the Community and the nation-state', in H. Wallace, W. Wallace and C. Webb (eds.), *Policy-making in the European Community*, 2nd edition, Wiley, Chichester, 1983.

The Transformation of Western Europe, Pinter, London, 1990.

Wallace, William (ed.), *The Dynamics of European Integration*, Pinter, London, 1990.

Walt, Stephen M., *The Origins of Alliances*, 2nd edition, Cornell University Press, New York, 1990.

'The renaissance of security studies', *International Studies Quarterly*, 35, 1991, pp. 211–239.

'Why alliances endure or collapse', *Survival*, 39/1, 1997, pp. 156–179.

Waltz, Kenneth, *Man, the State, and War: A Theoretical Analysis*, Columbia University Press, London, 1959, p. 211.

Foreign Policy and Democratic Politics: The American and British Experience, Little Brown, Boston, 1967.

'The myth of national interdependence', in Charles Kindleberger (ed.), *The International Corporation*, MIT Press, Cambridge MA, 1970.

Theory of International Politics, Addison-Wesley, Reading MA, 1979.

'Response to my critics' in Robert O. Keohane (ed.), *Neorealism and its Critics*, New York, Columbia University Press, 1986.

'The emerging structure of international politics', *International Security*, 18/2, 1993, pp. 44–79.

Walzer, Michael, *Just and Unjust Wars*, London, 1977.

Watson, J.B., *Psychology from the Standpoint of a Behaviourist*, Pinter, London, 1983.

Webb, Carole, 'Theoretical perspectives and problems' in Helen Wallace, William Wallace and Carole Webb (eds.), *Policy-making in the European Community*, 2nd edition, Wiley, Chichester, 1983.

Weldes, Jutta, 'Constructing national interests', *European Journal of International Relations*, 2/3, 1996, pp. 275–318.

Wendt, Alexander, 'The agent-structure problem in international relations theory', *International Organization*, 41/3, 1987, pp. 335–370.

'Anarchy is what states make of it: the social construction of power politics', *International Organization*, 46/2, 1992, pp. 391–425.

'Collective identity formation and the international state', *American Political Science Review*, 88/2, 1994, pp. 384–396.

'Constructing international politics', *International Security*, 20 January 1995, pp. 71–81.

'On constitution and causation in international relations', *Review of International Studies*, 1998, pp. 101–117.

Social Theory of International Politics, Cambridge University Press, Cambridge, forthcoming 1999.

Wertheim, Margaret, *Pythagoras' Trousers: God, Physics, and the Gender Wars*, Fourth Estate, London, 1997.

Wiberg, Hakan, 'Societal security and the explosion of Yugoslavia', in Ole Waever, *Identity, Migration*, pp. 93–109.

Winch, Peter, *The Idea of a Social Science*, Routledge, London, 1958.

Wittgenstein, Ludwig, *Philosophical Investigations*, Blackwell, Oxford, 1968.

Wolfers, Arnold, 'National security as an ambiguous symbol', *Political Science Quarterly*, 67/4, 1952.

Discord and Collaboration: Essays on International Politics, Johns Hopkins University Press, Baltimore, 1962.

Wolff, Larry, *Inventing Eastern Europe: The Map of Civilization on the Mind of the Enlightenment*, Cambridge University Press, Cambridge, 1996.

Wootton, A. J., *Interaction and the Development of Mind*, Cambridge University Press, Cambridge, 1997.

World Commission on Environment and Development (Brundtland Report), *Our Common Future*, Oxford University Press, Oxford, 1987.

Wörner, Manfred, 'The Atlantic Alliance in a new era', *NATO Review*, 39/1, 1991, pp. 3–10.

Wright, Frank, 'Protestant ideology and politics in Ulster', *European Journal of Sociology*, 14, 1973.

Wright, Quincy, *A Study of War*, 2nd edition, University of Chicago Press, Chicago, 1965.

Yergin, Daniel, *Shattered Peace: The Origins of the Cold War and the National Security State*, Pelican, London, 1977.

Yosef, Lapid, 'The third debate: on the prospect of international theory in a post-positivist era', *International Security Quarterly*, 33/3, 1989, pp. 235–254.

Yosef, Lapid and Friedrich, Kratochwil (eds.), *The Return of Culture and Identity in IR Theory*, Lynne Rienner, London, 1996.

Young, Oran R., *International Cooperation: Building Regimes for Natural Resources and the Environment*, Cornell University Press, Ithaca, 1989.

Index

CAMBRIDGE STUDIES IN INTERNATIONAL RELATIONS